Curriculum and Assessment

Curriculum and Assessment

Edited by David Scott

International Perspectives
on Curriculum Studies,
Volume 1

ABLEX PUBLISHING
Westport, Connecticut • London

Library of Congress Cataloging-in-Publication Data

Curriculum and assessment / edited by David Scott.
    p. cm.—(International Perspectives on Curriculum Studies, ISSN 1530–5465)
    Includes bibliographical references and index.
    ISBN 1–56750–520–1 (cloth)—ISBN 1–56750–521–X (pbk.)
    1. Educational tests and measurements—Cross-cultural studies. 2. Curriculum
planning—Cross-cultural studies. I. Scott, David 1951–
LB3051.C865 2001
375'.001—dc21   00–026073

British Library Cataloguing in Publication Data is available.

Library of Congress Catalog Card Number: 00–026073
ISBN: 1–56750–520–1
      1–56750–521–X (pbk.)
ISSN: 1530–5465

First published in 2001

Ablex Publishing, 88 Post Road West, Westport, CT 06881
An imprint of Greenwood Publishing Group, Inc.
www.ablexbooks.com

Printed in the United States of America

The paper used in this book complies with the
Permanent Paper Standard issued by the National
Information Standards Organization (Z39.48–1984).

10 9 8 7 6 5 4 3 2 1

Contents

Series Foreword

The purpose of the series *International Perspectives on Curriculum Studies* is to provide scholarly and authoritative debate about current curriculum issues. The series includes overviews of research in this area, examination of theoretical models and principles, discussion of the work of key curriculum theorists, and the reporting of new empirical research. Contributors to the various volumes in the series are not asked to provide definitive answers to questions that theorists and practitioners working in this field are asking. What they have been asked to do is to critically assess ways of thinking, influential models and current policy initiatives that relate to the curriculum.

The curriculum is defined in its widest sense, and it refers to programs of teaching and learning which take place in formal settings. Examples of formal settings are schools, colleges and universities. A curriculum may refer to a system, as in a national curriculum, an institution, as in the school curriculum, or even to an individual school, as in the school geography curriculum. The four dimensions of curriculum are: aims and objectives, content or subject matter, methods or procedures, and evaluation or assessment. The first refers to the reasons for including specific items in the curriculum and excluding others. The second refers to the knowledge, skills or dispositions which are implicit in the choice of items, and the way that they are arranged. Objectives may be understood as broad general justifications for including particular items and particular pedagogical processes in the curriculum; or as clearly defined and closely delineated outcomes or behaviors; or as a set of appropriate procedures or experiences. The third dimension is methods or procedures and this refers to pedagogy and is determined by choices made about the first two dimensions. The fourth dimension is assessment or evaluation and this refers to the means for determining whether the curriculum has been successfully implemented. A range of issues have been surfaced and debated in relation to these four dimensions.

The series focuses on these issues and debates. The first volume examines the relationship between curriculum, pedagogy and assessment, and, as with subsequent volumes, adopts a cross-sector and comparative approach. This series is timely as administrators and policy-makers in different parts of the world have taken an increased interest in education, and as moves to centralize curriculum provision have gathered pace. This has in some cases driven a wedge between curriculum theory and curriculum practice, as policymakers have developed and implemented proposals without referring to academic debates about these issues. It therefore seems to be an important task to reassert the need to discuss and debate the curriculum in a critical manner before implementation occurs. This series will attempt this difficult, but much needed, task.

David Scott, Series Editor
The Open University, United Kingdom

1

Introduction
David Scott

This volume examines the relationship between curriculum and assessment, and adopts a comparative and cross-sector approach. Contributors present cases from England (e.g., Black, Elwood, Scott and Lunt, and Wiliam), Scotland (e.g., Harlen, and Simpson), France (e.g., Broadfoot et al.), Hong Kong (e.g., Klenowski), and the United States (e.g., Nitko). They also focus on primary (e.g., Harlen, Simpson, Broadfoot et al., and Black), secondary (e.g., Harlen, Elwood, Black, and Wiliam), post-compulsory (e.g., Harlen), and university (e.g., Scott and Lunt, and Klenowski) sectors of education systems. This is deliberate as the debates about assessment and curriculum rehearsed in this volume refer to education systems round the world and to their various parts.

Some of the debates referred to in this volume are:

- Summative versus formative assessment;
- Differentiation versus inclusion;
- Psychometric frameworks of assessment versus holistic frameworks;
- Decontextualized versus contextualized assessments;
- Symbol-processing approaches to learning versus situated cognitionist approaches to learning;
- Integrated versus connected assessments;
- High stakes assessment versus low stakes assessment.

The contributors come with a wide range of perspectives and from different backgrounds. The rationale for this volume is not to reach an agreement about assessment and curriculum frameworks, but to air the various debates referred to above and develop new frameworks for understanding these important issues.

Paul Black in chapter two examines formative assessment and identifies the consequences of adopting such systems for the development of the curriculum. He uses a wide definition of curriculum, so that it embraces content, learning in schools, and other dimensions of the educational process. Reviewing four significant research projects, he concludes that effective learning includes enhanced feedback to students from their teachers, active involvement by those students in their learning, and adjustments by teachers as a response to formative feedback. He argues that these processes help poor attainers more than the rest and thus reduce the spread of attainment within the institution concerned.

He is pessimistic about the adoption by teachers in the United Kingdom of procedures that are genuinely formative, and suggests that this may be as a result of current models of pedagogy in use. He argues that: "a transmission model does not call for frequent interaction," and frequency of interaction is one marker of adopting formative assessment procedures. In relation to this, Black identifies three approaches to learning theory: the behaviorist, the constructivist, and the situated cognitionist, and discusses these in relation to his central theme. He identifies four examples of the contribution that formative assessment can make to learning: the capacity of the student to work strategically by clarifying aims and present understandings; the development of habits of productive engagement in dialogue; the promotion of task-related feedback; and the enhancement of the confidence of students to tackle tasks that are beyond their present capabilities. His argument is that the development of these capacities cannot take place in learning situations that ignore the contextualized nature of learning.

Mary Simpson in chapter three examines the issue of differentiation and how it relates to the curriculum in Scottish schools. She identifies two models of differentiation: the "measure and match" model and the "pick and mix" model. The first of these is understood as incorporating a number of principles: pupils have fixed general capacities; these general capacities can be measured; a match can be effectively made between pupils' performances and levels of difficulty of curricular material; and this process of matching can be further fine-tuned through summative assessment. On the other hand, the "pick and mix" model is understood as comprising the following principles: the competencies of pupils are influenced by a variety of alterable factors; levels of performance in the classroom will be influenced by these factors; therefore, the teacher is confronted with a range of different pupil needs; and as a result, differentiated materials and support needs to be provided to address these different needs.

In line with Black (see above), she suggests that most of the research conducted in this field would indicate that pupils understand that their achievements are not as good as they could be, and that what is needed is a flow of individually tailored assessment information that provides feedback on their performance. She also suggests that teachers in Scotland are attempting to operate in this way, though there are formidable obstacles to the general application of the principles she advocates.

Patricia Broadfoot, Marilyn Osborn, Keith Sharpe, and Claire Planel in chapter four offer a comparative analysis of assessment practices in English and French primary schools. Their focus is the way that assessment impacts on the learning processes of students and they suggest that there has been a relative dearth of studies about this important aspect of learning. They also suggest that assessment is the most influential of the three message systems in the classroom, the other two being curriculum and pedagogy. Their central thesis is that in order to understand how particular assessment practices impact on learning, they must be studied in the context of the more general cultural setting in which the interaction between teacher and pupil takes place.

Such study, they argue, "must start from a recognition that any assessment act—formal or informal, covert or overt, formative or summative—is a process of interaction, a form of communication typically, but not always, between pupil and teacher, that is vulnerable to misinterpretation as any other type of social intercourse." In particular, they examine in this chapter the linguistic or communicative dimension of assessment, and conclude that assessment practices convey particular cultural messages, as exemplified in their two comparative case studies.

Portfolio assessment forms the major theme of Val Klenowski's chapter and she illustrates her argument with frequent references to its use across a number of countries, but in particular, to teacher training in Hong Kong. She argues that portfolio assessment has been developed and used for a number of different purposes: summative description, certification or selection, support for teaching and learning, appraisal or promotion, and professional development. Furthermore, portfolio assessment incorporates three important learning processes: self-evaluation, substantive conversation, and reflective practice. She therefore, as other authors in this volume have done, ties closely together assessment and learning; indeed, she understands the process of completing a portfolio as central to teaching and learning in a range of different contexts.

However, she identifies a tension between their use as instruments for enhancing learning and their use as summative documents for accountability purposes. In particular, she suggests that portfolio assessment may become detached from learning processes if it is used in contexts that are examination driven and highly regulated. As she argues in relation to the current situation in England with regards to teacher training, the use of portfolios may be counterproductive because systems that are even now being set in place are antithetical to the development of more generative and open methods of assessment that could underpin good teaching.

Jannette Elwood in chapter six analyzes issues of validity and how it effects pupils' performances in examinations. Her chapter in particular makes reference to two important debates. The first of these is the debate between those who favor psychometric and technical frameworks for understanding assessment processes and those who wish to replace such frameworks, because they believe them to be inadequate to new tasks and new assessment arrangements, with more holistic and integrated approaches.

The second debate concerns the issue of contextualization in assessment. For Elwood, all assessments are located in specific and particular contexts; in other words, assessment practices are not and cannot be technical devices that are socially neutral, but are social techniques that have social consequences. In her chapter, she explores the implications of this in relation to three important assessment devices: coursework, differentiated levels of entry into the examination for students, and choice of items in examinations. She concludes that examinations are socially constructed, and that the choices made by examiners can impact negatively on specific sub-groups of examinees and hence place them at a disadvantage. Given the importance attached to examinations in modern societies, this has potentially disastrous consequences, since the point she is making is that it is not the learning experiences of children, which in this case contribute to their disadvantage in later life, but the assessment processes which they undergo.

David Scott and Ingrid Lunt in chapter seven examine the introduction of taught doctorates in the United Kingdom, conscious all the time that the United States and Australia have been at the forefront of this development for some time. Their chapter reprises a theme developed by Broadfoot et al. in this volume, which is that of the three message systems that structure educational activities and systems, assessment is the most influential and the most important. By adopting a framework of weak and strong framing and applying it to the academic/practitioner divide that they understand as the principle tension within taught doctorates, they show how curricula can only be understood by looking at the wider picture, and that power is ever present in assessment and learning settings.

Wynne Harlen in chapter eight describes and analyzes an educational system in its entirety and one that is undergoing substantial changes to the way it is organized. Her example is from Scotland, which has a different system from the other parts of the United Kingdom. She characterizes the system as: nonstatutory and implemented by consent; allowing for a lengthy change process where change is achieved, as far as possible, by consensus; able to cater for a full range of abilities and needs; outcome-based; broad, balanced, coherent, and progressive.

She argues that there is a strong interaction between curriculum and assessment; the main characteristics of the latter being: criterion-referenced; dependence on teacher assessment; comprehensiveness, in that all the intended learning outcomes are assessed; formative and summative with neither dominating the other; and target setted. She concludes by sounding a warning that an over-emphasis on external testing may hinder the development of proper learning, and thus she echoes two of the principal themes of this volume: the tension between external and internal accountability systems and the tension between assessments that are formative, integrated and productive of learning and assessments that are summative, intended to raise standards, and have high stakes attached to them.

In chapter nine, Anthony Nitko takes a broader perspective on issues related to assessment and the curriculum. In particular, he suggests that assessment developers need to be aware of appropriate ways of identifying weaknesses to their assessment frameworks and as a result improving them. He presents a particular model for evaluating these frameworks, the Capacity Maturity Model, and in addition, provides a discussion of what quality assessment means. In it he focuses on the quality of interpretations made by assessors and how that assessment information is used. He further develops a generalizability theory to identify the impact of multiple sources of measurement error. The chapter concludes with a discussion of a developmental framework that examines problem-solving along a dimension of novice to expert.

The final chapter by Dylan Wiliam provides an overview of the relationship between assessment and the curriculum. In particular, Wiliam focuses on one of the tensions identified at the beginning of this introduction: between formative and summative forms of assessment. Referring to assessment systems at the national level, he identifies three possibilities: (1) teachers are not involved in summatively assessing their students; (2) teachers are not involved in formatively assessing their students; and (3) ways of ameliorating the tension between summative and formative functions of assessment are developed. Having rejected the first two of these as unacceptable, he proceeds to sketch out an argument in support of the third. Rejecting the idea that the formative/summative distinction applies to the assessment itself, he argues that it really only applies to the way the information that is collected is used. This allows him to develop his thesis that systems that are designed to be both formative and summative can be internally coherent. Though he accepts that the tension between the two will always be there, he suggests that it can be mitigated to some extent.

These then are short accounts of the contents of each chapter. They provide a flavor of the arguments and debates that are present in the field of curriculum and, in particular, in the field of assessment. What this volume has suggested, both in terms of the way it has been structured and in terms of its contents, is that assessment cannot be separated from teaching and learning, and is an implicit part of the curriculum. There has in recent times been a tendency to treat assessment as a decontextualized and technical issue. The intention of this volume is to show that this approach is misguided in two senses. The first is that choices made by assessors have pedagogic and curriculum consequences. The second is that frameworks for understanding assessment issues are themselves social artifacts and cannot provide neutral descriptions of the processes they refer to. The contributions in this volume are designed to broaden our understanding of these important issues.

2

Formative Assessment and Curriculum Consequences

Paul Black

INTRODUCTION

The purpose of this chapter is to explore links between its two headline topics—formative assessment and curriculum. This Introduction will take the first step in the journey by setting out the perspective on the two topics that is to be adopted here, and will then explain the structure and rationale for what follows. The term formative assessment does not have a tightly defined and widely accepted meaning. In this chapter, I shall adopt the definition formulated by Black and Wiliam (1998). They specified that the term was:

To be interpreted as encompassing all those activities undertaken by teachers, and/or by their students, which provide information to be used as feedback to modify the teaching and learning activities in which they are engaged. (p. 7)

This is a very broad definition, and it may not be consistent with definitions used by other authors. For example, Perrenoud (1991) has a simpler formulation:

Any assessment that helps the pupil to learn and develop is formative. (p. 80)

The difference between these two may appear subtle, but the shift from "all those activities" to "any assessment" may help to unravel the meaning behind a later statement of Perrenoud in the same article, where a discussion of effective classroom interaction ends thus:

This action is formative, but that does not mean that there is "formative assessment."

In the absolute, an ideal teaching approach would do without all formative assessment. In other words, all the feedback necessary for learning would be incorporated in the situation, without it being necessary for a teacher to observe and intervene to bring about learning progress. (p. 84—italics as in the original)

The importance of adopting the broader definition will emerge throughout this chapter. The point is emphasized here because readers who may start with an assumed definition tied narrowly to formal assessments—which I have found to be the case with many teachers when discussing the subject—could misinterpret or be puzzled by some of what follows.

The term "curriculum" must also be understood as broadly defined. Indeed, if it were to be narrowly defined as the list of content topics to be learned, it might be argued that the interaction with formative assessment is so trivial that this chapter is hardly necessary. However, few would adopt such a narrow definition. More commonly, definitions range over the three examples offered below.

The curriculum is a field of enquiry and action on all that bears on schooling, including content, teaching, learning and resources. (OECD 1998, p. 33)

The most useful definition we could adopt . . . was one which is loose enough and broad enough to embrace all the learning that actually goes on in schools and all dimensions of the educational process. (Kelly 1988, p. 24)

A curriculum is an attempt to communicate the essential principles and features of an educational proposal in such a form that it is open to critical scrutiny and capable of effective translation into practice. (Stenhouse 1975, p. 4)

The first is as broad as could be. The second is more circumscribed, but is adequately broad for the purpose here. The third is more narrow—adopted by Stenhouse because he did not wish to focus on the educational purposes that a school should seek to attain. While much of the discussion here will be relevant to this narrower view, it will also deal with issues where the development of formative assessment does depend on priorities of purpose in the curriculum.

The normal distinctions between levels, to be understood, for example, as the intended, experienced and achieved curriculum, make the agenda clearer. It will be argued that formative assessment has a powerful effect on the gap between the intended and the achieved, and will discuss evidence that current practice is weak so that the gap is wider than it should be. A discussion, on theories of learning, begins to call in question the issue of purposes, but will form a basis for consideration of the more complex interplay of intended, experienced and achieved, in relation to the teacher's role and to the student's role. Finally, the relevant points that have emerged so far will be drawn together in a discussion of curriculum implications.

WHY IS FORMATIVE ASSESSMENT IMPORTANT?

This section presents brief accounts of four research publications which, taken together, illustrate some of the main issues involved in research which aims to secure evidence about the effects of formative assessment. The *first* publication is a meta-analysis of 21 different studies of the effects of classroom assessment, with children ranging from preschool to grade 12 (Fuchs and Fuchs 1986). The main focus was on work for children with mild handicaps, and on the use of assessment information by teachers. The studies all involved comparison between experimental and control groups, with assessment activities occurring between 2 and 5 times per week. The mean effect size obtained was 0.70, which is much higher than most innovations achieve. The authors noted that in about half of the studies teachers worked to set rules about reviews of the data and actions to follow, whereas in the others actions were left to teachers' judgments. The former produced a mean effect size of 0.92 compared with 0.42 for the latter. Two additional features of this work are relevant here. The first is that the authors compare the striking success of the formative approach, which is essentially inductive, with the unsatisfactory outcomes of programs that were essentially deductive in that they worked from a priori prescriptions for individualized learning programs for children, based on particular learning theories and diagnostic pretests. The second feature is that where both normal and handicapped children were involved in the same study, the handicapped showed the larger learning gains.

The *second* example is a description of work undertaken with 838 five-year old children in kindergarten (Bergan et al. 1991) drawn mainly from disadvantaged home backgrounds in six different regions in the United States. The underlying motivation was a belief that close attention to the early acquisition of basic skills is essential. The teachers of the experimental group implemented a system that required an initial assessment input to inform teaching at the individual pupil level, consultation on progress after two weeks, new assessments to give a further review and new decisions about students' needs after four weeks, with the whole course lasting eight weeks. There was emphasis on a criterion-referenced model of the development of understanding, and the diagnostic assessments were designed to help locate each child at a point on a scale defined in this model. The results showed that the experimental group achieved significantly higher scores in tests in reading, mathematics, and science than a control group. Furthermore, of the control group, on average 1 child in 3.7 was referred as having particular learning needs and 1 in 5 was placed in special education; the corresponding figures for the experimental group were 1 in 17 and 1 in 71.

The researchers concluded that the capacity of children is underdeveloped in conventional teaching so that many are "put down" unnecessarily and so have their futures prejudiced. One feature of the experiment's success was that teachers had enhanced confidence in their powers to make referral decisions wisely. This example illustrates the embedding of a rigorous formative assessment routine within an innovative program based on a model of the development of performance linked to a criterion based scheme of diagnostic assessment.

In the *third* example, the authors started from the belief that it was the frequent testing that was the main cause of the learning achievements reported for mastery learning experiments (Martinez and Martinez 1992). One hundred and twenty American college students in an introductory algebra course were placed in one of four groups in a 2x2 experimental design for an eighteen week course covering seven chapters of a text. Two groups were given one test per chapter, the other two were given three tests per chapter. Two groups were taught by a very experienced and highly rated teacher, the other two by a relatively inexperienced teacher with average ratings. The results of a posttest showed a significant advantage for those tested more frequently, but the gain was far smaller for the experienced teacher than for the newcomer. The authors concluded that the more frequent testing was indeed effective, but that much of the gain could be secured by an exceptional teacher with less frequent testing.

This study raises the question of whether frequent testing really constitutes formative assessment—a discussion of that question would have to focus on the quality of the teacher student-interaction and on whether test results constituted feedback in the sense of leading to corrective action taken to close any gaps in performance (Sadler 1989). It is possible that the experienced teacher may have been more skilled in providing feedback informally, so preempting the benefits of the tests.

The *fourth* example involved work to develop an inquiry-based middle school science-based curriculum (White and Frederiksen 1998). The teaching course used a practical group-inquiry approach for the study of force and motion, and the work involved twelve classes, of thirty students each, in two schools. In each class, a sequence of conceptually based issues was explored through experiments and computer simulation. The first half of the classes formed a control group who used some periods of time for a general discussion of the module, while the carefully matched second half formed an experimental group who spent the same time on discussion, structured to promote reflective assessment, with both peer assessment of presentations to the class and self-assessment. All students were given the same basic skills test at the outset. One outcome measure was a mean score on projects carried out during the course. On this measure, when the students were divided into three groups according to low, medium or high scores on the initial basic skills test, the low scoring group showed a superiority, over their control group peers, of more than three standard deviations, the medium group just over two, and the high group just over one. A similar pattern, of superiority of the experimental group that was more marked for students with low scores on the basic skills test, was also found for scores on a posttest of concept understanding. Among the students in the experimental group, those who showed the best understanding of the assessment process achieved the highest scores.

This science project again shows a version of formative assessment that is an intrinsic component of a more thoroughgoing innovation to change teaching and learning. While the experimental-control difference here lay only in the development of "reflective assessment" among the students, this work was embedded in an environment where such assessment was an intrinsic component. One other distinctive feature of this study is that the largest gains were among students who would have been labeled "low ability."

The review by Black and Wiliam (1998) shows that, from the literature published since 1986, it is possible to select at least twenty studies similar to the examples above in that the effects of formative assessment have been tested by quantitative experiment-control comparisons. All of these studies show that innovations that include strengthening the practice of formative assessment produce significant, and often substantial, learning gains. These studies range over ages (from five-year olds to university undergraduates), across several school subjects, and over several countries. The typical effect sizes achieved, between 0.4 and 0.7, are larger than most of those found for educational interventions. The fact that such gains have been achieved by a variety of methods that have, as a common feature, enhanced formative assessment indicates that it is this feature that accounts, at least in part, for the successes.

Important features that seem to characterize reports of the success of formative assessment may be summarized as follows:

- All such work involves new ways to enhance feedback from students to their teacher, that require new modes of pedagogy so involving significant changes in classroom practice.
- Underlying the various approaches are assumptions about what makes for effective learning—in particular that pupils have to be actively involved.
- For assessment to function formatively, the results have to be used to adjust teaching and learning.
- Several of these studies show that improved formative assessment helps the (so-called) low attainers more than the rest, and so reduces the spread of attainment while also raising it overall.
- The ways in which assessment can affect the motivation and self-esteem of pupils, and the benefits of engaging pupils in self-assessment, both deserve careful attention (Butler 1987, 1988).

CURRENT PRACTICES

There is a wealth of research evidence that the everyday practice of assessment in classrooms is beset with problems and shortcomings, as the following quotations, all from studies of classroom formative practice, indicate:

Marking is usually conscientious but often fails to offer guidance on how work can be improved. In a significant minority of cases, marking reinforces under-achievement and under-expectation by being too generous or unfocused. Information about pupil performance received by the teacher is insufficiently used to inform subsequent work. (General report on secondary schools, OFSTED 1996, p. 40)

Why is the extent and nature of formative assessment in science so impoverished? (U.K. secondary science teachers, Daws and Singh 1996, p. 99)

The criteria used were "virtually invalid by external standards." (Belgian primary teachers, Grisay 1991, p. 104)

Indeed they pay lip service to it but consider that its practice is unrealistic in the present educational context. (Canadian secondary teachers, Dassa, Vazquez-Abad, and Ajar 1993, p. 116).

The most important difficulties, which are found in the United Kingdom, but also elsewhere, may be briefly summarized in three groups. The first is concerned with *effective learning*:

- Teachers' tests encourage rote and superficial learning, even where teachers say they want to develop understanding.
- The questions and other methods used are not critically reviewed with other teachers.
- Some teachers tend to emphasize quantity and presentation of work and to neglect its quality.

The second group is concerned with *negative impact*:

- The marking or grading functions are overemphasized, while the learning functions are underemphasized.
- Teachers use approaches in which pupils are compared with one another, so creating a climate of competition rather than of personal improvement—in such a climate pupils with low attainments are led to believe that they lack "ability" and are not able to learn.

The third group focuses on the *managerial role* of assessments:

- Teachers' feedback to pupils seems to serve social and managerial functions rather than learning functions.
- Teachers can predict pupils' results on external tests—because their own tests imitate them—yet they know too little about their pupils' learning needs.
- Test results are collected to fill up records rather than to discern learning needs; furthermore, some teachers pay no attention to the assessment records of previous teachers of their pupils.

Of course, not all of these descriptions apply to all classrooms. Nevertheless, these general conclusions have all been drawn by authors in several countries, including the United Kingdom, who have collected evidence by observation, interviews, and questionnaires from many schools.

Any attempt to explain this situation must be speculative. One possibility is that teachers are not aware of the improvements in learning that formative assessment can secure. Related to this might be the models of pedagogy that teachers hold—a transmission model does not call for frequent interaction, although even in this model adjustment of what is transmitted in the light of evidence about reception would seem advisable. A further reason might be a foreseen difficulty of doing anything about the evidence—in the absence of any strategies for differentiation, for example, it will not be possible to deal with the full range of learning needs that good feedback might expose. The following statement by a teacher in France about the expectation that they respond to data derived from nationally set diagnostic tests in mathematics illustrates this problem:

The emphasis on "remediation," following the proposals made at national level, raised expectations that could not be satisfied for lack of means. The transition from the assessment findings to an analysis of wrong answers and the development of remedial techniques—the original goal of the training exercise—seemed impossible to achieve. (Black and Atkin 1996, p. 111)

A curriculum that is overcrowded, in situations where teachers feel compelled to "cover" all topics, is an obvious contributor to such difficulties.

A further cause might lie in the theories of learning on which teachers base their work, an issue to be taken up below. Finally, the influence of summative assessments might be a negative one. Most high-stakes tests provide instruments and models for assessment that are inappropriate for formative work. Furthermore, the pressure on the teacher to produce results on these tests might lead to all tests being treated as ends in themselves rather than as means to the end of good learning, so that all testing and assessment come to be regarded as inimical to effective learning.

THEORIES OF LEARNING

Three approaches to learning theory will be considered here—the behaviorist, the constructivist, and approaches that emphasize situated cognition and social discourse. Each has different implications for pedagogy and for curriculum (for a full discussion see Greeno et al. 1996). Analysis of their implications for formative assessment will link directly to implications for pedagogy and lead to interactions with curriculum.

A behaviorist approach will view teaching and learning in the light of stimulus-response theory. Because the response is the only observable, attention is paid only to the observable aspects of reception; any models of the thinking process of the pupil that might intervene between stimulus and response are too speculative to be useful. It follows that distinctions between rote learning and learning with understanding are not considered—what is needed is to deliver appropriate stimuli, teach by repetition and then reward the appropriate responses. Related assumptions are that a complex skill can be taught by breaking it up and teaching and testing the pieces separately; and that an idea that is common to action in many contexts can be taught most economically by presenting it in abstract isolation so that it can then be deployed in many situations. A test composed of many short, "atomized," out-of-context questions, and "teaching to the test," are both consistent with this approach.

Numerous studies have exposed the shortcomings of rule bound traditional learning. For example, Nuthall and Alton-Lee (1995) showed that long-term retention of taught material, even by the criteria of atomized knowledge tests, depends on the capacity to understand and so reconstruct procedures, and Boaler (1997) showed that only those taught by open methods could see the applications of school mathematics in their daily lives. A consequence for both formative and summative assessment is that the capacity to apply cannot be inferred from tests that call only for recall of the "pure" knowledge and understanding. Another aspect is illustrated by the following quotation:

Even comprehension of simple texts requires a process of inferring and thinking about what the text means. Children who are drilled in number facts, algorithms, decoding skills or vocabulary lists without developing a basic conceptual model or seeing the meaning of what they are doing have a very difficult time retaining information (because all the bits are disconnected) and are unable to apply what they have memorized (because it makes no sense). (Shepard 1992, p. 303)

In rejecting behaviorism, current "constructivist" theories focus attention on the need for models of the mental processes involved when anyone responds to new information or to new problems. The learner is taken to be active in analyzing and transforming any new information or question. We learn by actions, by self-directed problem-solving aimed at trying to control the world, and abstract thought evolves from concrete action. Wood spells out the consequence of this view:

Teaching that teaches children only how to manipulate abstract procedures (e.g., learning how to solve equations) without first establishing the deep connections between such procedures and the activities involved in the solution of practical concrete problems (which the procedures serve to represent at a more abstract level) is bound to fail. (Wood 1998, p. 9)

It is also evident that transformations of incoming ideas can only be achieved in the light of what the learner already knows and understands, so the reception of new knowledge depends on existing knowledge and understanding. It follows that formative assessment must be skillfully directed to reveal important aspects of understanding, and then be developed, within contexts that challenge pupils' ideas, in order to explore response to such challenge (see e.g., Fensham et al. 1994 for implications in the learning of science).

The directions in which children's ideas should be changed are to be chosen in the light of the learning aims of each subject. Thus, both curriculum, pedagogy and assessment have to be fashioned in the light of assumptions, both about how learning is best achieved and about the epistemology of the subject under consideration. Progress in learning physics (say) may be quite different from progress in learning history. The idea of "progress" implies that any teaching plan must be founded on some notion of what constitutes progress toward the learning goals of the subject taught. A model of progress would serve to guide the construction both of formative assessment procedures and of items of helpful diagnostic quality, and could set criteria for grading summative assessments. This idea lay behind the—controversial—level system (originally 10-level, now 8) for the national curriculum in England and Wales (Black 1997).

The role of the teacher as supporter rather than director of learning was given prominence by Vygotsky (1962), who started from a view that learning proceeds by an interaction between the teacher and the learner. This approach was taken further in the concept of "scaffolding" (Wood et al. 1976): the teacher provides the scaffold for the building, but the building itself can only be constructed by the learner. In this supportive role, the teacher has to discern the potential of the learner to advance in understanding, so that new challenges are neither too trivial nor too demanding. Thus, there is an area of appropriate and productive challenge which Vygotsky called the "zone of proximal development." This is the gap between what the learner can do on his own and what he can do with the help of others. One function of assessment would then be to help to identify this zone accurately and to explore progress within it.

Thus the dependence of learning on teacher-pupil interaction is a very specific one, linked to the nature of the teacher's guidance. Brown and Ferrara (1985) highlight one facet of low achievement, by showing that low-achieving students lack self-regulation skills, and that when these are taught to them, they progress rapidly. In such teaching, low-achieving students can be seen to start with a wide zone of proximal development, the gap between their initial achievement and their potential being wide because of the lack of self-regulation.

Such views link naturally with the theories that focus on social discourse as a key element of learning. Most theorists, after Piaget, emphasize, albeit to different extents and within different theoretical frameworks, the importance of language in learning. Interaction takes place through language discourse, which is learned and understood in particular social contexts. Vygotsky's emphasis on interaction arose from his interests in the historical and cultural origins of our thought and action. The terms and conventions of discourse are socially determined, and they only acquire meaning within the conventions and culture of a particular community. It would follow that the nature of our learning depends on the particular "communities of discourse," and its effectiveness on the extent to which its terms and conventions are shared, be it a committee meeting, an academic seminar or a school lesson (Wenger 1999).

Within the classroom community, the meaning of many important terms, and the practices and criteria for thinking and argument, will only be acquired within that community—learning in this view is seen as enculturation. It follows that there are serious dangers of alienation of pupils who cannot share the culture expressed and so cannot share in the discourse. In assessments as in pedagogy, activities that challenge pupils have to be very carefully framed, both in their language and context of presentation, if they are to avoid bias, that is, unfair effects on those from particular gender, social, ethnic or linguistic groups. The importance of the context of any presentation is also a significant issue. Two well researched examples are that tests set about use of mathematics in the street might be failed by a student who can use the same mathematics in a familiar school context, and tests on paper about designing an experiment produce quite different results when the same task is presented with real equipment in a laboratory. The account in this section has been limited to the cognitive aspect of links between assessment and student response. Other important elements will be explored in the course of the next section.

THE TEACHER'S ROLE

In the research studies such as those quoted above, the effective programs of formative assessment involve far more than the addition of a few observations and tests to an existing program. They require careful scrutiny of all of the main components of a teaching plan. As the argument develops it becomes clear that curriculum, instruction, and formative assessment are indivisible.

To begin at the beginning, the choice of tasks for class and homework is important. In content it will be guided by the framework of the curriculum, and in particular by the model(s) of progression in the learning of the subject area that are expressed, albeit implicitly, in that framework. But planning of a classroom task will also be guided by the need to adopt a style of work that supports the broader aims of the curriculum—notably to promote effective learning and success for all. Thus, classroom tasks have to be justified in terms of the learning aims that they serve, and they support effective learning if opportunities for pupils to communicate their evolving understanding are built into the planning.

Discussions, in which pupils are led to talk about their understanding, provide the opportunity for the teacher to respond to and reorient the pupil's thinking. However, teachers often respond, quite unconsciously, in ways that inhibit the learning of a pupil. Recordings commonly show that teachers often look for a particular response and, lacking the flexibility or the confidence to deal with the unexpected, try to direct the pupil toward giving the expected answer (Filer 1995; Pryor and Torrance 1996). Over time the pupils get the message—they are not required to think out their own answers. The object of the exercise is to work out, or guess, what answer the teacher expects to see or hear, and then express it so that the teaching can proceed.

The posing of questions by the teacher is a natural and direct way of checking on learning, but is often unproductive. However, where, as often happens, a teacher answers her or his own question after only two or three seconds, there is no possibility that a pupil can think out what to say. In consequence, pupils don't even try—if you know that the answer, or another question, will come along in a few seconds, there is no point in trying. It is also common that only a few pupils in a class give answers. Then the teacher, by lowering the level of questions, can keep the lesson going but is actually out of touch with the understanding of most of the class—the question-answer dialogue becomes a ritual, one in which all connive and thoughtful involvement suffers.

To break this particular cycle, pupils must have time to respond, perhaps to discuss their thinking in pairs or in small groups before responding. On the constructivist and social discourse views of learning, it is essential that any dialogue should evoke thoughtful reflection in which all pupils can be encouraged to take part, for only then can the formative process be effective.

Class tests, and tests or other exercises set for homework, are also important means to promote feedback. However, the quality of the test items, that is, their relevance to the main learning aims and their clear communication to the pupil, needs scrutiny. Given questions of good quality, it is then essential to ensure the quality of the feedback—here both relevance to the learning aims and sensitivity to the effects on the recipient are important.

Several research studies focusing on feedback in classroom assessment, notably by Butler (1987, 1988), have shown that if pupils are given only marks or grades, they do not benefit from the feedback on their work, whereas, in closely matched situations, those who are given only relevant comments do benefit. One comparison, between four groups given comments only, grades only, praise only, and no feedback respectively, showed that only the comments group showed significant learning gains, while the two given grades or praise showed enhanced "ego-involvement"—that is, an introverted focus on their performance to the detriment of attention to the learning tasks. Thus, feedback should only give specific guidance on strengths and weaknesses, with the means and opportunities to work with the evidence of difficulties—the way in which test results are reported back to pupils so that they can identify their own strengths and weaknesses is a critical feature. The worst scenario is one in which some pupils get low marks this time, they got low marks last time, they expect to get low marks next time, and this is accepted as part of a shared belief between them and their teacher that they are just not clever enough.

A fundamental determinant of teachers' approach to their work will be their beliefs about their pupil's capacity to learn. At one extreme there is the *"fixed IQ"* view: if it were true that each pupil has a fixed, inherited intelligence, then all a teacher can do is to accept that some can learn quickly while others can hardly learn at all. At the other pole is the *"untapped potential"* view, which starts from the view that so-called "abilities" are complexes of skills that can be learned. In this view, all pupils can learn more effectively if one can clear away any obstacles set up by previous difficulties. The evidence shows that formative assessment, which assumes *"untapped potential,"* does help all pupils to learn and can give particular help to those who have previously fallen behind.

Most of the initiatives that have been found helpful take more class time, particularly when a central purpose is to change the outlook on learning and the working methods of pupils. Thus, teachers have to take risks in the belief that such investment of time will yield rewards in the future.

THE STUDENT'S PERSPECTIVE

The ultimate user of formative assessment is the pupil. As has been emphasized above, where the classroom culture focuses on rewards, "gold stars," grades or place-in-the-class ranking, then pupils look for ways to obtain the best marks rather than at the needs of their learning that these marks ought to reflect. One reported consequence is that pupils tend to avoid difficult tasks. They also spend time and energy looking for clues to the "right answer." Many are reluctant to ask questions for fear of failure, particularly if they have been led to believe that they lack "ability."

The positive aspect is that such outcomes are not inevitable. What is needed is a culture of success, backed by a belief that all can achieve. Feedback to any pupil should be about the particular qualities of his or her work, with advice on what he or she can do to improve, and should avoid comparisons with other pupils.

Many of the successful innovations have developed self- and peer-assessment by pupils as ways of enhancing formative assessment, and such work has achieved some success with pupils from age five upward. Indeed, on a constructivist view of learning, self-assessment must be an essential feature. The main problem that those developing self-assessment encounter is not the problem of reliability and trustworthiness: it is that pupils can only assess themselves when they have a sufficiently clear picture of the targets that their learning is meant to attain. This accords with Sadler's (1989) analysis that emphasizes that the action in learning has to be directed to close the gap between the present state of the learner and the goal of the learning, and that this has to be done by learners themselves. Surprisingly, and sadly, many pupils do not have any clear picture of the goals of their learning, and appear to have become accustomed to receiving classroom teaching as an arbitrary sequence of exercises with no overarching rationale. It requires hard and sustained work to overcome this pupils' culture of passive reception (Fairbrother 1995; Parkin and Richards 1995).

Thus, the involvement of pupils in their own assessment changes both the role of the pupil as learner and the nature of the relationship between teacher and pupil, making the latter shoulder more of the responsibility for learning and calling for a radical shift in pupils' own perspectives about learning. A science teacher in Spain reported on the difficulty in achieving this aim:

The idea of self-evaluation is a difficult one, because the students don't fully comprehend the idea and only really think in terms of their exam mark. Generally speaking they don't reflect on their own learning process in an overall fashion. [They think] their assessment has more to do with the effort they made than with what they have actually learnt. (Black and Atkin 1996, p. 99)

This quotation shows that the expectations that pupils have built up from their experiences of assessment in school can constitute an obstacle to their taking a positive role in assessment. This is supported in an account of a study of primary pupils in the Geneva Canton (Perrin 1991). Here, it emerged that the pupils believed that the summative assessments of them were for the school's and their parents' benefit, not for themselves. The weak pupils believed the purpose was to make them work harder. Since the assessment was not used to tell them how to work differently, they saw it as a source of pressure, which made them anxious. As a consequence of such evidence, the Canton decided to reduce its summative tests and to enhance the formative role of assessment.

When innovations in learning practices, including formative assessment, are introduced, many pupils will resist attempts to change accustomed routines, for any such change is threatening, and emphasis on the challenge to think for yourself (and not just work harder) can be disturbing to many. Pupils will find it hard to believe in the value of changes for their learning before they have experienced the benefits of such changes. Where formative assessment has been emphasized, it has been found that pupils bring to the work a fear of assessment from their experience of summative tests, and it takes some time for them to become more positive about formative work. They share with teachers a difficulty in converting from norm-referenced to criterion-referenced ways of thinking.

CURRICULUM IMPLICATIONS

In framing curriculum aims, that is, in the intended curriculum, three particular features bear on the practice of formative assessment. The first of these has to do with those general aims concerned with the habits and capacities for learning that should be developed in the pupil. "Life-long learning," albeit a catch-phrase, focuses on a very important aim. Here there are points of convergence between the principles of formative assessment and the intended curriculum, for as it enhances the learning of pupils, formative assessment should contribute in the long term to their capacity to learn. Specific examples of such contributions are:

- capacity to work strategically by first clarifying the aims of a learning activity and then auditing the present state of one's understanding in relation to these aims;

- developed habits of productive engagement in dialogue, so that one can use discussion to try out and reformulate one's ideas, learning from the reactions of others and deriving benefit from their feedback;
- a realization, learned from experience, that task-related feedback is a help to one's learning and that one should not react to it as if it were an attack on one's ego;
- confidence, arising from experience of success, in one's capacity to learn.

Such aims are ambitious, and they can only be achieved if the formative practices entailed are embedded in the *experienced* curriculum. They cannot be so embedded in any and every possible approach to curriculum design and pedagogy. The model of learning within which any curriculum is framed and any pedagogy implemented has to be one that is based on a recognition that the active involvement of the learner, and dialogue between learners about their learning, are essential elements. Enough has already been said about implications of formative assessment for pedagogy, but implications for curriculum need more discussion.

The second feature relates to curriculum content. The obvious need to define aims in a clear way has rather demanding implications. The planning of progression is an essential part of any teaching plan, and the assessment of one's own progress against aims by a learner, both call for a framework or model of progression in learning relevant to each particular content, conceptual understanding or skill. Such a framework has to be adequately detailed so that the immediate aims for a learner are both achievable in the short term and intelligible. Such aims and framework have to be shared with the learner, a requirement that makes stringent demands on the language in which they are formulated.

The implications here might be quite different between different subject disciplines. Thus, depth of understanding might be the key dimension of progress in a mathematics curriculum, topic coverage with developing conceptual range might be jointly involved for progression in a science curriculum, while personal maturity and insight might feature strongly in progress in expressive writing. Thus, each discipline requires its own specific dimensions of progression, and hence will have its own specific emphases in the productions by pupils that will be the basis for formative feedback.

The third feature relates to the different possible types and styles of learning activity. For example, if the capacity to carry out holistic, authentic, and thereby complex tasks, for example, solve real mathematics problems or carry out realistic science investigations, is an aim of the curriculum, then practice in component knowledge and skills is not enough—learners also have to experience the real complex activity. It follows that both formative and summative assessment have to have such holistic activity as their focus. Just as pedagogy appropriate to such activity will be rather different in character from that called for in training in skills or in developing specific knowledge or conceptual understanding, so will formative assessment have to be different. While tests, perhaps at frequent intervals, with feedback and opportunities to work with difficulties exposed, might be appropriate, even optimum, for the analytic aspects of a curriculum plan, they will have little useful role in holistic work. Such work would rather call for feedback through discussions, between peers, and with a teacher, probably conducted at several stages during the progress of the work, and particularly in the initial stages of formulating a plan of action, and the final stage of evaluating and interpreting the outcomes. The students' productions and directions of thought will be unpredictable so the formative guidance of such work will have to involve flexible response rather than set rules or procedures, so making the teacher's role particularly demanding. If there is to be effective peer-assessment and development of self-assessment in such work, there has to be adequate time for reflection and thoughtful discussion: the work reported by White and Frederiksen (1998) and discussed above is a good example—and one that shows the benefits of such an approach.

What becomes clear across these three features is that there is no single method for formative assessment, but rather a need for varying the styles of both pedagogy and formative assessment to match the different components of a curriculum according to the differing nature of the aims that these components serve. It is also clear that across all of the various possibilities, an overcrowded curriculum, with the oppressive effects of high-stakes summative testing, can debilitate the practice of formative assessment, and so undermine the pursuit of some important curriculum aims.

For the *achieved* curriculum, the main lesson has been spelled out above—that improved formative assessment can raise standards of achievement. There remains the question of what exactly is so achieved. Deeper understanding is achieved if pupils can talk about the meaning of what they have done, but such achievement can only be evaluated by listening to pupils' talk and looking at what they produce, be this in writing or through other artifacts, with holistic styles of summative assessment appropriate to judgment of enriched understanding and development of capacity to learn in complex contexts. For at least some of the experimental studies reviewed by Black and Wiliam (1998), learning gains were achieved even on traditional types of testing to which the formative emphasis was not particularly attuned. There is a limitation here: comparative evaluation ought to use measures of achievement that are matched to the pupils' learning experiences, so different measures ought to be used when approaches to learning are significantly different. Then comparisons become a matter of judging how one values what has been achieved in each alternative rather than a simple and automatic comparison of quantitative measures on identical scales.

Thus, the values of formative assessment are not to be seen as extras to be added to any particular regime of curriculum and pedagogy. It is rather the case that, as with any consideration of curriculum and pedagogy, with the addition of formative assessment as a third element to these two, it is only through appraising the values embodied and so realized in the articulation of all three that any judgment can be made.

REFERENCES

Bergan, J. R., Sladeczek, I. E., Schwarz, R. D., and Smith, A. N. 1991. "Effects of a Measurement and Planning System on Kindergartners' Cognitive Development and Educational Programming." *American Educational Research Journal* 28(3):683–714.

Black, P. J. 1997. "Whatever Happened to TGAT?" In C. Cullingford (Ed.), *Assessment vs. Evaluation.* London: Cassell, pp. 24–50.

Black, P. J., and Atkin, J. M. 1996. *Changing the Subject: Innovations in Science, Mathematics and Technology Education.* London: Routledge for OECD.

Black, P., and Wiliam, D. 1998. "Assessment and Classroom Learning." *Assessment in Education* 5(1):7–74.

Boaler, J. 1997. *Experiencing School Mathematics: Teaching Styles, Sex and Setting.* Buckingham, U.K.: Open University Press.

Brown, A. L., and Ferrara, R. A. 1985. "Diagnosing zones of proximal development." In J. V. Wertsch (Ed.), *Culture, Communication and Cognition: Vygotskian Perspectives.* Cambridge: Cambridge University Press, pp. 273–305.

Butler, R. 1987. "Task-Involving and Ego-Involving Properties of Evaluation: Effects of Different Feedback Conditions on Motivational Perceptions, Interest and Performance." *Journal of Educational Psychology* 79(4): 474–482.

Butler, R. 1988. "Enhancing and Undermining Intrinsic Motivation: The Effects of Task-Involving and Ego-Involving Evaluation on Interest and Performance." *British Journal of Educational Psychology* 58:1–14.

Daws, N., and Singh, B. 1996. "Formative Assessment: To What Extent is its Potential to Enhance Pupils' Science Being Realised?" *School Science Review* 7(281):93–100.

Dassa, C., Vazquez-Abad, J., and Ajar, D. 1993. "Formative Assessment in a Classroom Setting: From Practice to Computer Innovations." *The Alberta Journal of Educational Research* 39(1):111–125.

Fairbrother, R. 1995. "Pupils as Learners." In R. Fairbrother, P. J. Black, and P. Gill (Eds.), *Teachers Assessing Pupils: Lessons from Science Classrooms.* Hatfield U.K.: Association for Science Education, pp. 105–124.

Fensham, P. J., Gunstone, R. F., and White, R. T. 1994. *The Content of Science: A Constructivist Approach to its Teaching and Learning.* London: Falmer.

Filer, A. 1995. "Teacher Assessment: Social Process and Social Product." *Assessment in Education* 2(1):23–38.

Fuchs, L. S., and Fuchs, D. 1986. "Effects of Systematic Formative Evaluation: A Meta-Analysis." *Exceptional Children* 53(3):199–208.

Greeno, J. G., Pearson, P. D., and Schoenfeld, A. H. 1996. "Implications for NAEP of Research on Learning and Cognition." In R. Glaser, R. Linn, and G. Bohrnstdet (Eds.), *Assessment in Transition: Monitoring the Nation's Educational Progress, Background Studies.* Stanford, CA: National Academy of Education, pp. 3–49.

Grisay, A. 1991. "Improving Assessment in Primary Schools: 'APER' Research Reduces Failure Rates." In P. Weston (Ed.), *Assessment of Pupils Achievement: Motivation and School Success.* Amsterdam: Swets and Zeitlinger, pp. 103–118.

Kelly, A. V. 1988. *The Curriculum: Theory and Practice* (3rd. ed.). London: Paul Chapman.

Martinez, J. G. R., and Martinez, N. C. 1992. "Re-examining Repeated Testing and Teacher Effects in a Remedial Mathematics Course." *British Journal of Educational Psychology* 62:356–363.

Nuthall, G., and Alton-Lee, A. 1995. "Assessing Classroom Learning: How Students Use Their Knowledge and Experience to Answer Classroom Achievement Test Questions in Science and Social Studies." *American Educational Research Journal* 32(1):185–223.

OECD. 1998. *Making the Curriculum Work.* Paris: Centre for Educational Research and Innovation, Organisation for Economic Co-operation and Development.

OFSTED. 1996. *Subjects and Standards. Issues for School Development Arising from OFSTED Inspection Findings 1994–5.* London: Her Majesty's Stationery Office.

Parkin, C., and Richards, N. 1995. "Introducing Formative Assessment at KS3: An Attempt Using Pupils' Self-Assessment." In R. Fairbrother, P. J. Black, and P. Gill (Eds.), *Teachers Assessing Pupils: Lessons from Science Classrooms.* Hatfield U.K.: Association for Science Education, pp. 13–28.

Perrenoud, P. 1991. "Towards a Pragmatic Approach to Formative Evaluation." In P. Weston (Ed.), *Assessment of Pupils Achievement: Motivation and School Success.* Amsterdam: Swets and Zeitlinger, pp. 79–101.

Perrin, M. 1991. "Summative Evaluation and Pupil Motivation." In P. Weston (Ed.), *Assessment of Pupils Achievement: Motivation and School Success.* Amsterdam: Swets and Zeitlinger, pp. 169–173.

Pryor, J., and Torrance, H. 1996. "Teacher-Pupil Interaction in Formative Assessment: Assessing the Work or Protecting the Child?" *The Curriculum Journal* 7(2):205–226.

Sadler, R. 1989. "Formative Assessment and the Design of Instructional Systems." *Instructional Science* 18:119–144.

Shepard, L. A. 1992. "Commentary: What Policy Makers Who Mandate Tests Should Know About the New Psychology of Intellectual Ability and Learning." In B. R. Gifford and M. C. O'Connor (Eds.), *Changing Assessments: Alternative Views of Aptitude, Achievement and Instruction.* Boston and Dordrecht: Kluwer. pp. 301–328.

Stenhouse, L. 1975. *An Introduction to Curriculum Research and Development.* London: Heinemann.

Vygotsky, L. S. 1962. *Thought and Language.* New York: Wiley.

Wenger, E. 1999. *Communities of Practice: Learning, Meaning and Identity.* London: Cambridge University Press.

White, B. Y., and Frederiksen, J. R. 1998. "Inquiry, Modeling, and Metacognition: Making Science Accessible to All Students." *Cognition and Instruction* 16(10):3–118.

Wood, D. 1998. *How Children Think and Learn: The Social Contexts of Cognitive Development* (2nd ed.). Oxford : Blackwell.

Wood, D., Bruner, J. S., and Ross, G. 1976. "The Role of Tutoring in Problem Solving." *Journal of Child Psychology and Psychiatry* 17:89–100.

3

Differentiation and Assessment
Mary Simpson

INTRODUCTION

The curriculum has to satisfy two seemingly contradictory requirements. On the one hand it has to reflect the broad aims of education which hold good for all children, whatever their abilities and whatever the schools they attend. On the other hand it has to allow for differences in the abilities and other characteristics of children, even of the same age. (HMI 1980)

The requirement for schools to take account of the variety of the characteristics of pupils is not a new one, but professional views on how to deal appropriately with individual differences have changed considerably—and are changing still. Near the beginning of the last century, a new teacher described her perception of the role ahead:

Drudging unwillingly at the graceless task of compelling many children into one disciplined, mechanical set, reducing the whole set to an automatic state of obedience and attention, and then commanding their acceptance of various pieces of knowledge. The first great task was to reduce sixty children to one state of mind, or being. (Lawrence 1915)

The changes that have resulted in the very different educational practices prevalent in classrooms in the United Kingdom at the end of the last century have been driven as much by social, political, and economic considerations as by educational ones. Society is now striving toward equity and equality in social provision—recognizing that while individual children are different, they must be seen as equally valuable. Employers are urging schools to develop the general skills of their students as much as their specific knowledge, and to infuse the workforce of the future with flexibility, independence and a predilection for life-long learning. Traditional teaching practices have been challenged by theories of the social, constructed and contextual nature of knowledge and by research evidence on the variety of factors, for example, prerequisite concepts, misconceptions, learning styles, self-esteem, expectancies, gender, race and social class that influence the effectiveness of learning in any given context. And to the once universal, norm-referenced systems of assessment, designed merely to rank pupils by attainment, have been added the complexities of criterion referencing, grade related criteria, and formative and diagnostic assessment.

Far from clarifying the role of teachers and assisting them to find direction and coherence in generating solutions to their practical difficulties in dealing with the *"seemingly contradictory requirements"* set upon them, the accumulating information and pressures from theory, research, professional concerns, and social expectations have served to create a confused and increasingly complex situation. Within this complexity, governments demand rising standards of attainment, teachers strive to find manageable, yet defensible, working practices within the constrained organization of the school and the complexities of the classroom (Bearne 1996; Hart 1996), and researchers are challenged to demonstrate or "prove" what works best (e.g., Harlen and Malcolm 1997; Sukhnandan and Lee 1998).

Although these features are evident in the educational systems of other countries, particular priority has been given in Scotland to research and development with respect to differentiation. In reviewing some of the key factors that have determined current practices in the management of differences between pupils and reflecting on the changing role of assessment in contributing to its realization within the classroom, I shall draw on exemplification primarily from the Scottish context.

PEDAGOGICAL PRACTICES, POST SELECTION: LET 1,000 FLOWERS BLOOM

It has been suggested that the policies that prevailed prior to the introduction of comprehensive schools in the 1960s and 1970s, and which promoted the selective school system based on the predictive power of the 11+ examination, were "cloaked in spurious educational thinking about children's minds, backed by supposedly scientific methods of measuring intelligence" (Benn and Chitty 1996, p. 6).

These thoughts and methods that informed the use of the selection mechanisms were nonetheless the legitimate outcomes of the typical educational research of the period and had at least the merit of offering schools and practitioners a clear theoretical base and practical framework for the organizational and pedagogical practices of the selective school system. The changes initiated to remove selection from state education were driven primarily by social and political considerations (Benn and Chitty 1996; McPherson and Raab 1988) toward goals that were *"conflicting, vague, and contested"* (McPherson and Wilms 1987). Undoubtedly there was debate in some educational circles concerning the pedagogy of mixed ability and the possible characteristics of a common core curriculum. For most classroom teachers the effect of comprehensivization was to find themselves confronted with severe practical difficulties in relation both to offering a curriculum structure and to devising methods of classroom management that took into account the differences in attainment of pupils. They found little guidance from either established educational theory or from current research on the efficacy of alternative classroom practices. Thus, while giving universal access to academic schooling may have served to resolve some political and societal concerns, it generated a multitude of practical and philosophical educational problems for the teaching profession.

From his detailed study of the introduction of comprehensive schools in the West of Scotland, Watt (1991) reported that there was little evidence of the development of radically new approaches to the curriculum or of any serious thought being given to the curricular implications of the end of selection. As a result: "Curriculum development muddled on, targeted principally at the provision of instant assistance for hard pressed teachers rather than deriving from an underlying philosophy based on new objectives" (p. 35). In the midst of "a veritable avalanche of worksheets" teachers conducted "a series of cautious experiments" which, by the 1980s, had resulted in the establishment of a wide range of practices in schools across the United Kingdom, particularly in the early years of secondary schooling and in primary classrooms where there was now no pressure to prepare pupils for the high-stakes testing of the selection process.

Within some secondary schools, covert and overt forms of streaming were retained. The most common of these forms were "broad-banding," dividing pupils on much the same criteria as for streaming, but into classes with wider ranges of test scores, setting by subject attainment, resulting in the allocation of individuals to the same or very similar pupil groups across many subjects. However, in most schools in Scotland the decision was taken to have mixed ability classrooms. Many teachers in these schools saw the abandonment of streaming as a pragmatic response to an acknowledged problem—that of managing pupils in the lower streams who had been demotivated by failure in the 11+ examination and were consequently disaffected. In some of these schools, differentiation took a variety of forms, for example, all pupils working through the same, or different, curricular material, but at their own pace (as in resource based learning or individualized learning schemes); ability grouping based on informal teacher assessment (as in many primary classrooms), or whole class teaching of a common curriculum, but with different kinds and degrees of individual pupil or group support being given and widely different levels of expected outcomes. However, in most Scottish secondary schools, a "fresh start" policy was adopted in which, for the first two years, all pupils were taught the same curriculum at the same pace in mixed ability classes. This policy allowed pupils an extended period in which they were expected to settle into the new environment and to sort themselves out, before being selected by tests compiled by subject teachers to enter different levels of the certification courses. Teachers' responses to the different attainment levels and learning characteristics of pupils during this period of their schooling were absent, idiosyncratic, or unsystematic. Such schools had clearly not addressed the central problem of dealing with differences between pupils, but had merely deferred it; this policy was only recently challenged by the introduction in the 1990s of the 5–14 national curriculum.

It is not surprising then, that there is currently little consensus within the profession as to the meaning of the term "differentiation" and, as recent studies suggest, even apparent agreements sometimes hide very different concepts (Weston et al. 1998). Indeed, we should not have expected that the teachers' "cautious experiments" were entirely free from theory or that the concepts that had informed the selection system should be readily abandoned.

TWO CURRENT MODELS OF DIFFERENTIATION

From our study of different approaches to pupil differences in primary and early secondary schools (Simpson and Ure 1993; SOED 1994), we defined the opposing ends of a continuum of practice, "measure and match" and "pick and mix," which are informed by different theories of learning and attainment and that entail critically different forms of assessment.

The *Measure and Match Model* assumes:

- that a stable, underlying characteristic of pupils is a key determinant of pupils' general or specific competencies (intelligence, mathematical ability, etc.);
- that this key feature can be reliably measured by summative assessment at a point in time (e.g., 11+; Kent mathematics tests);
- that a match can then be made between the performance of the pupil and the appropriate level of difficulty of curricular material or course;
- and that matching can subsequently be fine-tuned by further summative assessment.

Although legislation gradually abolished selective schooling in most authorities in England, and universally in Scotland during the 1960s and 1970s, the thinking that had informed its processes and the central role played by varieties of summative assessment have clearly persisted. Underlying the "measure and match" strategy of differentiation is the conviction that the level of attainment, as summatively assessed at a point in time, defines the pupil's learning characteristics sufficiently to determine the next learning task. If more accurate matching is required, it is to be sought in more accurate forms of assessment and in finer gradations of levels of demand in the curriculum. Proponents of this strategy believe that if the spread of attainment is reduced in the class, that group may be taught as if it were relatively homogeneous with respect to learning needs and in consequence levels of attainment may be expected to rise.

Many secondary school staff worked innovatively to find accommodation between this conviction and the requirements for nonselection at school entry.

Broad-banding, and the setting of pupils in specific subjects use summative assessment as the basis for class formation. Within mixed ability classes, a common procedure in many secondary subjects was the development by teachers of worksheets covering topics at three different levels of difficulty and, within mathematics, the use of commercially produced individualized learning schemes. With both these procedures, the summative outcomes of small units of work are used to determine the route of individuals through small preprepared sequential sections of the curriculum. When this latter system was perceived by some teachers to be ineffective, there was a tendency for "more accurate" assessments of attainment to be called for and finer gradations of levels within the curriculum to be devised (Simpson and Ure 1993).

Not only has there been considerable investigation of the efficacy of setting, streaming (or tracking) and ability grouping, but the research has also been subject to regular, rigorous and comprehensive review. Slavin's "best-evidence synthesis" methodology (Slavin 1987, 1990) offered a paradigm for those undertaken more recently in the United Kingdom. These reviews were commissioned by or directed toward policymakers responsible for offering advice to schools following the introduction of the national curricula in Scotland (Harlen and Malcolm 1997) and in England and Wales (Sukhnandan and Lee 1998). The impetus for these reviews was the realization that in response to the national requirements an increasing number of schools had reinstated, or were seeking support for the reinstatement of, a policy on the formal grouping of pupils by ability.

With respect to the positive effects of these organizational approaches to differentiation, the conclusion of these careful and extensive reviews could best be described by the Scottish legal verdict of "not proven." Within both primary and secondary sectors: "There is no consistent and reliable evidence of positive effects of setting and streaming in any subjects or for students of particular ability levels" (Harlen and Malcolm 1997, p. 40). In a recent study of differentiation in secondary schools, the views of pupils were solicited on the extent to which they found that the work they were given in different subject areas was too difficult or too easy (Simpson and Ure 1993). It was found that the pupils' perceived match of their capabilities to the demands of the work they were given to do was markedly poorer in mathematics and science than in English and modern languages. In the former two subjects, differentiation was vested in individualized learning schemes and resource-based learning (measure and match). However, in the latter two subjects, mixed ability teaching within a common curriculum was the norm, and differentiation was vested in the teachers' continuous, verbal, formative interaction with pupils (pick and mix). Paradoxically, the individualized learning and resource-based learning schemes were commonly regarded by secondary school management as paradigms of effective differentiation.

Recent research undertaken in the United Kingdom confirms earlier findings that the setting procedures disadvantage some working-class pupils and lead staff to believe that homogeneity has been achieved in their sets. As a result, teaching is more narrowly focused than is warranted, creating in consequence disaffection among pupils at all levels for whom the pace of their set is inappropriate—including girls in the top set, and demotivating those whose attainments are curtailed by the limits of their set (Boaler 1997).

Thus, research consistently fails to provide secure evidence in support of the overwhelming conviction, apparently held by many professionals and nonprofessionals alike, that some form of setting, streaming, grouping by ability, or the use of multileveled learning schemes will inevitably improve learning outcomes.

The *Pick and Mix Model* assumes:

- that competencies of pupils are determined by a complex and varying, but substantially alterable, range of factors (motivation, classroom relationships, past learning experiences, misconceptions, particular learning difficulties, etc.);
- that levels of performance in classroom work will continue to be influenced by such factors and that formal measures of attainment at any one point in time are useful, but not critical;
- that a range of different pupil needs has to be taken account of in allocating work or responding to learning outcomes;
- that differentiated materials and support should be responsive to a range of different needs and be accessed as and when appropriate for individuals or groups.

In applying this model as a response to differences between pupils in order to promote better learning, practitioners recognize that merely securing physical access to a common curriculum for all pupils or allocating individuals to particular levels of curricular materials is insufficient—active professional intervention is needed to make that curriculum accessible.

I feel I should be the differentiator. I access the material to the children. I make sure that they can all understand what they can. I can talk to them and give them a feel for the material. I can help them with the material and the tasks. For an experienced teacher, this is what it is all about. In my opinion, it's a worse stigma to be deemed incapable of trying something, than to be given the chance and the appropriate support. (Secondary school teacher of English, SCCC 1995)

The mechanism for the determination of the intervention is the application of the knowledge and skills of the teacher through the informal assessment of the immediate need of individuals. One secondary teacher itemized the following as important:

There is their lack of confidence, need for attention, need to be encouraged or chivvied, degree of basic competence, ability, ability to attend, high or low motivation, ability to work independently. You can't be infinitely flexible, but I do try to optimise the situation to take account of these. (Simpson and Ure 1993, p. 38)

The full application of this model would be represented by mixed ability teaching of the purest form. But whatever the strategy for its management, it clearly makes significant demands upon the teacher; are the benefits to learners commensurate with these demands? The positive outcomes most consistently documented by research are those that are socially desirable—greater equality of opportunity, a degree of social integration, and the avoidance of the negative motivational effects upon low attaining pupils caused by setting. However, the hope that the teachers' recognition and response to a wider range of needs, and a more informed matching of work to individual pupils would result in enhanced learning seems not to be realized (Sukhnandan and Lee 1998).

Researchers examining nonset teaching contexts merely find a different, but equally variable set of patterns of inequity or mismatch in the experiences of different groups of pupils as are found by those examining setting and streaming. For example, two studies in particular looked in detail at the experiences of individual pupils within primary classrooms in which teachers had been identified as being better than average or as being good differentiators by their local authority (Bennett et al. 1984; Simpson 1997). They showed that, contrary to the teachers' stated intentions, the pupils were frequently assigned classroom activities that were inappropriate to their abilities and attainments. Able pupils were frequently occupied in practicing skills in which they were already able to demonstrate competence in more complex tasks, and lower-attaining pupils were often allocated work in areas where they were not able to show understanding or competence in simpler or prerequisite skills.

The two paradigms of differentiation, "measure and match" and "pick and mix" have different merits and demerits. The former has the advantage of being congruent with the beliefs of many within education, and a considerable proportion of parents, but is associated with social and motivational disadvantage for many learners; the latter directly addresses a range of differences between pupils but at the cost of an excessive level of demand on all but the most skilled of teachers. That research has failed to confirm the superiority of one over the other, however they are exemplified, suggests one of two possibilities. Either that the gains and losses in attainment associated with the merits and demerits of the two paradigms are fortuitously balanced, or, more probably, that there are some features of the teaching practices common to both that set limits to pupil attainment. Desforges (1985) has argued that "the classroom as presently conceived has reached levels of productivity . . . consistent with its design limitations. Improvements might require radical reconceptions of the teaching and learning situations." Intrinsic to those reconceptions must be the development of strategies, practices, and concepts of relationships that will allow pupils' needs as learners to be more readily recognized and responded to.

IDENTIFYING AND RESPONDING TO THE NEEDS OF LEARNERS

The development of today's teaching practices has been informed by the education profession's ideas of what pupils need if they are to learn effectively. It is only comparatively recently that researchers have directly sought the opinions of pupils on their perceptions of their experiences as learners—what has helped and what has hindered them (see, e.g., Cooper and McIntyre 1992; Simpson and Ure 1993; Boaler 1997).

The needs identified by pupils appear unexceptional, but are clearly not met in many U.K. classrooms. Pupils express a need to know what they should be learning; however, a mere list of intended learning outcomes is not sufficient to let them see the relationship between what they are doing in class and what they are supposed to be learning from it. They want reassurance that they are progressing in their development of skills and knowledge—particularly important if they are slow learners. Only rarely do pupils in the top sets regard reminders of the high standards expected of them to be motivating. Indeed, the element of competition engendered within the setting context appeared to be counterproductive to positive engagement with learning. It seems that pupils are calling for a self-referenced system of tracking their attainment. But they seek more than records of achievement—they want constructive feedback on their attempts at learning, which will point the way toward action. Although teachers readily apply the rule that praise is motivating, pupils signal that having their weaknesses identified, and being given practical advice on how to deal with them, are as important. They want flexibility in the pace of the requirements and the ability to engage with different learning styles appropriate to them or to the task in hand. There are areas over which they feel it appropriate and possible to have control, and autonomy and control over aspects of their learning appear to be key factors in determining the level of their engagement with many of the requirements of their classroom work.

They express a need for a teacher who adopts the role of helpful monitor and mentor beside them. The relationship with the teacher sets the social context within which pupils seek to have a productive interaction with a knowledgeable adult. The sharing of information, agreements about mutual and different responsibilities, shared pleasure in successful outcomes, identification of and planning to overcome learning difficulties, and blocks to progress—all of these are key components of sharing the management of learning in a meaningful way.

ASSESSMENT THAT INFORMS LEARNING AND TEACHING

The findings from the studies noted above indicate that the pupils perceive their own attainments to be far from optimal and suggest that a central requirement in meeting the conditions for improvement is a flow of individually tailored assessment information that gives them informed feedback on their performance, but which is intimately linked to remedial guidance and future direction.

Teachers in the Scottish studies of differentiation had similarly identified the requirement for a continual flow of assessment information as a necessary component for the improvement of their management of differentiation. However, in order to be an effective tool for the enhancement of learning, the information on an individual child's attainments has to take the form of a history of that individual's achievements interpreted within a curricular framework. While the guidelines of the national curricula provided such a framework, teachers soon recognized that the volume and detail of information covering aspects of learning in all areas of the curriculum, which could be identified as a prerequisite of effective differentiation, was potentially overwhelming.

Clearly, when the role of assessment in differentiation moves from being that of the instrument used to sort pupils toward that of informing the teaching and learning processes of individuals, teachers appear to be faced with another *"seemingly contradictory requirement"*—the need to generate and have immediate access to the extensive and detailed information on each pupil that is necessary if assessment is to have value as an instrument to inform teaching and learning, and the need to avoid information overload on the teacher. However, as understanding of the potential for assessment to contribute to the learning process develops (Gifford and O'Connor 1992), it has become increasingly clear that the use of assessment in a formative way requires more than simply the development of practical solutions to the management of accumulating information.

It requires nothing less than a reconceptualization of assessment as a process designed to serve the teaching and learning interaction rather than as a procedure at the end of instruction directed judgmentally toward the pupil. Some of the components of that reconception are as follows. There must be changes in the teachers' concepts of the limiting factors to pupils' attainment, leading to the adoption of the view that all pupils can learn more effectively given the appropriate context, knowledge, and support. Within the accepted curriculum, there must be a clear articulation and sharing of the learning goals considered appropriate for individuals when engaging in particular classroom activities. Finally, there must be a change from pupils being passive recipients of educational instruction, to being knowledgeable with respect to information hitherto held only by teachers, and to being proactive in the search for successful learning strategies. Clearly, the introduction of formative assessment requires significant changes to take place in the thinking and practices of many teachers, and a redefining of their roles and of the relationships between them and their pupils.

To incorporate formative assessment into their teaching would involve teachers in far more than acquisition of the necessary skills. Their view of the aims of the teaching of their own subject might have to change if they are to be close to their students in guiding them. The changes in classroom practice might also involve profound changes of role, even for teachers regarded by themselves and others as already successful. (Black 1993)

Having reviewed the research evidence, Black and Wiliam (1998, p. 19) are confident that "We know of no other way of raising standards for which such a strong prima facie case can be made on the evidence of such large learning gains." This is a view in considerable contrast to that of the educators who see the route to more successful learning and differentiation to lie primarily in the reduction in class size or the attainment range of classes of pupils.

PARTNERSHIP IN ASSESSMENT AND LEARNING

If teachers are going to engage in the demands and difficulties of developing innovative assessment systems, then certain conditions need to be met. Teachers need to have the new strategies explained in professional language that they understand and trust—they abhor "technical jargon." They need to be clear about the aims of the new strategies and they have to perceive the changes as having the potential to solve current problems and deal with present professional concerns rather than as creating difficulties that are just as formidable as the existing ones. They need to have models of what the new strategies might actually comprise in practice, together with examples developed by other teachers and already in use in classrooms. And finally, they need to have enough of a grasp of the underlying principles involved to customize, with confidence, the strategies already available in order to make them manageable and effective within their own context. The necessary context for these requirements includes a wide professional base of adequately developed understanding of the underpinning theoretical rationale, and the support and commitment of policymakers. Within Scotland, the precursors for providing these key conditions had been developing in the two decades prior to the introduction of the national curriculum, the 5–14 Development Programme, in the early 1990s (Simpson and Hayward 1998).

The SOED *Guidelines on Assessment 5–14* (SOED 1991) were developed independently from the guidelines on national testing and they promoted many of the characteristics of formative assessment outlined above and presented the ideas in the context of language and processes familiar to teachers—planning, teaching, evaluating, recording, and reporting. But despite these guidelines, there is evidence that many teachers, both in primary and secondary schools, continue to respond as if their assessment has only a summative purpose, concerned with the establishment of a detailed record of achievement for each pupil. Such teachers perceive assessment to inform teaching as an additional burden on them, describing the requirement as "horrendous." They see no compensating benefit to them in their classroom teaching, and regarded a detailed record of pupil attainments of little use. "Who," asked some primary teachers dismissively, "would read it?" (Harlen et al. 1995). Clearly, compiling such assessments would tend to reduce the quality of differentiation since they fail to provide accessible information to the classroom teacher at the point of use and reduce the amount of time available for formative verbal interaction between pupil and teacher.

Other teachers have responded differently. They recognize that if they are to be more effective in monitoring pupil progress, in identifying difficulties, in expecting particular qualities of pupil response and in matching pupils more accurately to work, which would promote progression, they have to abandon the concept of assessment as an episodic process concerned with the formation of a historic record of pupils' attainments. They have to move to the concept in which assessment is seen as continuous, concerned with the creation of a flow of contemporary information on pupil progress that will genuinely inform the teaching and learning processes. Many were already developing classroom systems that matched this new concept and saw in the assessment guidelines a validation of their beliefs and developing practices. But they also recognized that the burden of keeping track of pupils' achievements would be intolerable if they were to attempt to bear it alone. Assessment information had to be shared with the pupils. And for such teachers, the answer to the question: "Who would read it?" had to be "the pupils."

Another "series of cautious experiments" has been contributing to the reconceptualization of pupil/teacher relationships mentioned above. Improvement of learning is their focus; pupils are given a central role in the management of their own learning, but are also given the knowledge and skills to discharge their responsibilities—there is, therefore, a sharing of professional knowledge and vocabulary with pupils and the joint planning of action to surmount difficulties and advance learning. Additionally, the developments would be initiated or carried forward by the teachers themselves. Like their pupils, they would be active participants in the processes of development, not passive recipients of directives. A variety of innovations in assessment exemplify these characteristics in very different ways. One secondary school example is linked to the requirements of the 5–14 Programme and was developed as an extension of a profiling initiative that a group of secondary teachers developed "with a strong formative element" within mixed ability classes in their first and second year courses (Simpson, Goulder, and Tuson 1995).

We have the assessment criteria set out down one side of the profile, with self-assessment built in, and we are trying to say, "This is what we expect out of this piece of work, this is what you need to do for a good piece of work," in that type of writing, say personal writing, and get them to evaluate their own writing against those criteria and say, "OK, I'm weak at this" and build in support with worksheets etc., and there's space on the profile for targeting, "What I need to do next to improve my writing." So, we're not saying, "You might be a level B"; there's a lot more to it than that.

Formative comments from the teacher were written on small yellow "post-its" that were stuck on the appropriate part of the profile and this information was carried forward into their next assignment. These teachers had the professional confidence to adapt the learning objectives set out in the national guidelines to meet what they perceived to be the requirements of their pupils. They indicated that: "It's been very much trial and error trying to identify the needs of the pupils rather than the requirements of the curriculum guidelines. We've gone for something more pupil than guideline based." One teacher had sought the pupils' views on this system and described their reactions as enthusiastic, particularly with respect to the element of informed responsibility which it afforded them.

In the primary sector, a "partnership model" of assessment, generated by a small group of teachers working with low attaining pupils, deployed a strategy that added a further element to the sharing of knowledge (Simpson 1997). Similar to the practice of compiling a folder of best work, they introduced a "best bag" of work that allowed children with poor writing skills to include in their collection photographs, tapes, or models. However, the pupils were required to indicate why they wanted to select the work to keep in the bag and why they thought it good. The teacher too selected work when appropriate, and shared her criteria in a context of nonjudgmental communication. The outcome was that low attaining pupils generated, learned, and applied standards of "goodness" to their work and began in a genuine collaboration with their teachers to plan ways in which they themselves, as well as their teachers, wished to see it improved. By comparing their new work with that previously selected, they were able to provide evidence of learning success to parents, peers, and teachers and, perhaps more importantly, to see for themselves that they were indeed improving and progressing in their skills—an experience seldom vouchsafed to slow learners. This strategy, designated *"Partnership in Assessment"* has been widely disseminated through in-service.

In the final example, a teacher gives an account of wrestling with the shortcomings of his normal assessment procedures in a third year secondary science certification course (age 15/16 yrs):

What do you say to a pupil who achieves 40% on a problem solving test? Typically I was saying "must work harder at problem solving." I was saying the same thing to a lot of pupils and found that in terms of reporting it was very dissatisfying and rather stereotypic. In addition, the comments did nothing to help the pupils with the problems they had. In fact the problems were not identified as such, all that existed was a percentage and a grade. The likelihood was though that these problems would therefore persist. Exactly the same could be said for knowledge and understanding.

He and his colleagues embarked on a series of explorations on how to improve these practices. They found the key in releasing to the pupils the codings for each test item. The codings identified the component skill of problem-solving at which the item tested and that had been attached to the test items to allow the test setters to compile a balanced paper. Normally these were removed on the final test paper. However, armed with these, and introduced to strategies for marking and monitoring their progress in the different skill areas using a simple grid, pupils were able to identify their areas of strength and weakness, to select further material and work appropriate to the areas in which they had weaknesses and to solicit help from their teacher only if these self-support strategies failed to assist. The feedback and response were thus individualized without the teachers being overstretched, and the pupils' responsibilities for managing their own learning were set within assessment and recording procedures that were sufficiently clear and economical that they could be operated by the pupils themselves (Simpson and Ure 1993). Sharing the examination board item codes with pupils may seem a very small step indeed in terms of changes in practice, but for some teachers it is nevertheless a momentous one. Moreover, the types of changes in practice outlined above are likely to be lasting, since they were initiated by teachers in response to problems identified for themselves and that are located in areas of practice central to the traditional role of secondary teachers as assessors and testers of pupils.

CONCLUDING REMARKS

As the examples above illustrate, groups of teachers in Scotland have found ways of enabling them to identify and respond to the needs of their pupils through the generation of a variety of innovative strategies for assessment that circumvent the difficulties of manageability through sharing professional information and its use with pupils. Not surprisingly, given the fairly radical nature of the requirements of such formative assessment procedures, the rhetoric somewhat exceeds the reality of their general application in Scottish classrooms (Simpson and Goulder 1998), and it is too early yet for the classroom initiatives to show real returns in terms of widespread improvements in pupil attainment. However, key aspects of those developments that have already taken place give rise to considerable optimism for the health of the concept in the future. The assessment strategies illustrated above were initiated by teachers as a means of enhancing their own teaching, but they are clearly informed by ideas about learning and teaching cognate with those in the research literature and are in harmony with, and supported by, policy documents on assessment. Whetton (1997) notes that in England too, although the notion of teacher assessment integrated into the curriculum for teaching purposes has become widespread, teachers' understanding of and ability to manage the process is considerably underdeveloped. However, in contrast, there has been much more of a critical mass of professionals in all areas of the Scottish educational system—teachers, teacher educators, researchers, local authority staff, school inspectors, and civil servants—who believed in its potential to improve learning and who were committed to promote and protect it against the domination and encroachment of summative assessment for monitoring and accountability which has been given priority in England and Wales (Simpson and Hayward 1998).

Additionally, in the present period of rapid technological change, it is clear that school leavers need to have more than just high standards of attainment in subject areas, it is also essential that they gain the capacity to learn throughout life and to adapt to new environments. They need, therefore, to be motivated and committed to continued learning, to be self-determined, to feel they have the power to promote their own development, and to have confidence that they can succeed and continue to progress. This requires the learner to develop attributes of self-motivation, self-monitoring, self-reflection and self-reliance. Teachers involved in the development of these innovative assessment procedures report that the discrepancies between what pupils are capable of and the demands of the tasks they have been set, have started to reduce and that motivation and attainment have risen as pupils have begun to take on a meaningful and responsible role in monitoring their own learning and in determining the next targets to be aimed for. For example, during the early stages of the development of the Partnership Model with low attaining pupils in primary schools (Smithers and Brodie 1992), the teachers noted a change in the responses of pupils. Whereas formerly pupils would say, "This is my best work" when selecting items for their file, later they were heard to say, "This is *going to be* my best work" when starting a task. This change might appear slight, but it represents a significant achievement in terms of the development of that elusive character—the motivated, informed and independent learner.

In planning for this outcome, as in planning for improvements in learning, the limiting factor common to both the "measure and match" and the "pick and mix" models is that they do not lead to any change in the traditional role of the teacher: as the skilled professional who has sole possession of the specialist knowledge, who alone defines the pupils' learning needs, and who alone determines and controls the pace and nature of transactions in the classroom. Indeed it seems that whichever of these models is used, the search for the matching of instruction to pupil learning needs is as elusive as happiness. Both of these desirable states are subject to the shared paradox that the more single-mindedly they are pursued as goals, the less likely they are to be achieved. They are not goals to be directly aimed at, but are by-products of a different search. In the context of schools, that search is for models of partnership between teacher and pupil in which learning goals are discussed and jointly agreed, assessment of progress jointly monitored, difficulties and their resolution jointly addressed, next steps jointly planned and achievement jointly celebrated.

REFERENCES

Bearne, E. 1996. *Differentiation and Diversity in the Primary School.* London: Routledge.
Benn, C., and Chitty, C. 1996. *Thirty Years On: Is Comprehensive Education Alive and Well or Struggling to Survive?* London: Fulton.
Bennett, N., Desforges, C., Cockburn, A., and Wilkinson, B. 1984. *The Quality of Pupils' Learning Experiences.* London: Lawrence Erlbaum Associates.
Black, P., and Wiliam, D. 1998. *Inside the Black Box: Raising Standards Through Assessment.* London: King's College.
Black, P. J. 1993. "Formative and Summative Assessment by Teachers." *Studies in Science Education* 21:49–97.

Boaler, J. 1997. "Setting, Social Class and Survival of the Quickest." *British Educational Research Journal* 23(5):575–595

Cooper, P., and McIntyre, D. 1992. *Teachers' and Pupils' Perceptions of Effective Classroom Learning: Conflicts and Commonalities.* Paper presented at the Annual Conference of the British Educational Research Association, Stirling University.

Desforges, C. 1985. "Matching Tasks to Children." In N. Bennett and C. Desforges (Eds.), *Recent Advances in Classroom Research.* Edinburgh: Scottish Academic Press.

Gifford, B. R., and O'Connor, M. C. 1992. *Changing Assessments: Alternative Views of Aptitude, Achievement and Instruction.* Boston: Kluwer Academic Publishers.

Harlen, W., and Malcolm, H. 1997. *Setting and Streaming: A Research Review.* Edinburgh: Scottish Council for Educational Research.

Harlen, W., Malcolm, H. C., and Byrne, M. 1995. *Evaluation of the Implementation of the 5–14 Development Programme: The Primary Project. Assessment and National Testing in Primary Schools.* Edinburgh: Scottish Council for Research in Education.

Hart, S. 1996. *Differentiation and the Secondary Curriculum: Debates and Dilemmas.* London: Routledge

Her Majesty's Inspectors. 1980. *A View of the Curriculum.* London: HMSO.

Lawrence, D. H. 1915. *The Rainbow.* London: Secker.

McPherson, A., and Raab, C. 1988. *Governing Education: A Sociology of Policy since 1945.* Edinburgh: Edinburgh University Press.

McPherson, A., and Wilms, J. 1987. "Equalisation and Improvement: Some Effects of Comprehensive Reorganisation in Scotland." *Sociology* 21(4):509–539.

Scottish Consultative Council on the Curriculum. 1995. *Reflections on Learning and Teaching: Making Sense of Differentiation.* A CDi and resource pack for staff development. Dundee: SCCC.

Scottish Office Education Department. 1991. *Guidelines on Assessment 5–14.* Edinburgh: SOED.

Scottish Office Education Department. 1994. *Studies of Differentiation in Primary and Secondary Schools.* Interchange No 30. Edinburgh: SOED. (Available via World Wide Server, via Internet and JANET: http://www.ed.ac.uk/riu)

Simpson, M. 1997. "Developing Differentiation Practices: Meeting the Needs of Teachers and Pupils." *The Curriculum Journal* 8(1):85–104.

Simpson, M., and Goulder, J. 1998. "Promoting Continuity and Progression: Implementing the 5–14 Development Programme in Secondary School Mathematics and English Language Departments." *Scottish Educational Review* 30(1):15–28.

Simpson M., Goulder J., and Tuson J. 1995. *Evaluation of the Implementation of the 5–14 Programme in Secondary Schools: The Professional Journey.* Aberdeen: Northern College.

Simpson M., and Hayward L. 1998. "Policy, Research and Classroom Based Development: Changing the Assessment Culture in Scottish Schools." *European Journal of Education.* 33(4):445–458

Simpson, M., and Ure, J. 1993. *What's the Difference? A Study of Differentiation in Scottish Secondary Schools.* Aberdeen: Northern College.

Slavin, R. E. 1987. Ability grouping and student achievement in elementary schools: a best-evidence synthesis. *Review of Educational Research* 57(3):293–336.

Slavin, R. E. 1990. "Student Achievement Effects of Ability Grouping in Secondary Schools: A Best-Evidence Synthesis." *Review of Educational Research* 60(3):471–499.

Smithers, I., and Brodie, L. 1992. *Teachers and Children—Partners in Assessment.* Inservice Support Reader. Aberdeen: Northern College.

Sukhnandan, L., and Lee, B. 1998. *Streaming, Setting and Grouping by Ability: A Review of the Literature.* Slough: National Foundation for Educational Research.

Watt, J. 1991. "Going Comprehensive in the West of Scotland: Natural Progression or Cultural Shock?" *Scottish Educational Review* 23(1):32–42.

Weston, P., Taylor, M., Lewis, G., and MacDonald, A. 1998. *Learning from Differentiation: A Review of Practice in Primary and Secondary Schools.* Slough: National Foundation for Educational Research.

Whetton, C. 1997. "The Psychometric Enterprise—Or the Assessment Aspiration." In S. Hegarty (Ed.), *The Role of Research in Mature Educational Systems.* Slough: National Foundation for Educational Research.

4

Pupil Assessment and Classroom Culture: A Comparative Study of the Language of Assessment in England and France

Patricia Broadfoot, Marilyn Osborn, Keith Sharpe, and Claire Planel

INTRODUCTION

Assessment is a pervasive phenomenon. It is a defining feature of social life and a fundamental tool for human beings to use to make sense of both the natural and the social world. It is a necessary element in the reasoning process that must be gone through in order to map out a trajectory of action to achieve a desired goal. In the context of the particular social world of education, the goals are more specific but the same logic still applies. Helping pupils to learn and thus, knowing what steps need to be taken to help them individually to achieve a given learning goal requires the same kind of assessment process to be undertaken. Teachers and students, separately or together, must work out what they need to do if they desire to achieve a given learning outcome. Whether this goal is an externally imposed one—as in, for example national curriculum targets, or whether it is a more personal aspiration—as in conceptions of lifelong learning—it will be necessary to take a series of steps to achieve it.

However, until recently, the nature of these steps has rarely been studied explicitly. More typically, steps have been decided upon in the form of syllabuses and schemes of work and the assumption made that the exposure of the student to the teaching of appropriate content will result in the desired goals being achieved by most students. This view remains very prevalent today and is well represented in the current English "Literacy Hour" and "Numeracy Hour" initiatives that are firmly focused on shaping *teaching* strategies.

The relative neglect of the way in which assessment actually impacts on the learning processes of students is all the more surprising given its overwhelmingly dominant role in the classroom, for assessment is an even more pervasive feature of classroom life than it is of social life in general. Tests and exercises, marks and grades, questions and answers, observation and appraisal are some of the most characteristic and defining elements of the teacher-pupil relationship. Yet until recently, this key element of professional practice has been largely unexamined both by teachers themselves and by educational researchers. Assessment remains one of the weakest aspects of teachers' classroom practice—at least in England— as judged through school inspections (OFSTED, 1998). Although teacher education programs are now required to include training in assessment, very little teacher training in any country has arguably been concerned to equip teachers with an understanding of the relationship between classroom assessment practices and student learning. This makes it difficult for teachers to judge effectively between the merits of different techniques to achieve a given learning outcome (Mavrommatis 1995; Bachor and Anderson 1994). In the past, many teachers learned to assess by imitating their colleagues and hence helped to reproduce already well-established assumptions and practices. In adopting particular approaches they were likely to be influenced as much by issues of practicability, such as whether the test would effectively occupy most pupils for the time available and whether it would be easy to mark, as they were by more fundamental concerns as to the utility of the assessment device chosen for helping or hindering the learning of individual students (Scarth 1984).

The relative neglect of classroom assessment as a field of study is all the more surprising given—as is now increasingly being recognized—its central role in shaping the learning environment experienced by each individual pupil (Broadfoot 1996a). While, as Bernstein (1977) argued, there are three message systems in the classroom—curriculum, pedagogy, and assessment—it is arguably assessment that provides the vital bridge between what is offered by the teacher and the reaction to it by the pupil; that carries both the cognitive and the affective charge that will determine whether a given pupil is "switched on" and "energized" to learn, or not.

While assessment may often appear to be a one-way form of communication centered on the transmission of praise or blame, affirmation or correction by the teacher, the assumption that pupils will react to assessment messages in some way is the basic premise on which such activity is founded. Like electricity, it is necessarily a circuit that links teacher, pupil, and peers in a learning "field of resistance." Yet the rationale for assessment remains an activity that teachers find difficult to articulate at a level of detail much beyond the familiar "carrot and stick," correction and feedback set of explanations. While the language of curriculum is now familiar to most teachers, the language of assessment, if it is familiar at all, is the summative language of measurement rather than the more formative language aimed at promoting learning.

Yet, it is through the discourse of assessment in its various forms, oral, written, and nonverbal, and its various modes—that include cognitive feedback, behavior management, and encouragement—that individual pupils build up a sense of their identity as learners. It leads ultimately to that range of conditioned responses that is manifest in typical types of motivation, meta-cognition and hence, achievement, for any given learner. Just how important assessment is in influencing a student's approach to learning is convincingly demonstrated by recent comprehensive reviews of relevant psychological research (see e.g., Crooks 1988; Black and Wiliam 1998), both of which document the definitive effect of assessment in determining students' attitudes to learning and their learning strategies in the short, medium, and long term.

Recently, however, this relative lack of interest in the conduct and effects of classroom assessment has given way to an increasingly intense concern on the part of policymakers, researchers, and practitioners to redress the balance. Why this should be the case at the present time is beyond the scope of this chapter. However, it does seem likely that the commitment currently being made by many governments in the developed world to raising the overall level of student achievement—in response to the employment needs of a postindustrial economy and increasingly cut-throat international competition—is giving a new significance to questions concerning how both the desire, and the ability to learn of the majority of students, can be increased. Moreover, these same pressures are bringing about changes in curriculum emphasis in which traditional concerns with the inculcation of knowledge are being replaced by a much greater emphasis on the development of the skills that will be called for in an age dominated by the ready availability of information-retrieval devices and lifelong learning.

Thus, in addition to the introduction of national assessment systems designed to monitor, and in many cases improve, national standards—which is another reflection both of the growth in international competition and of the growing realization on the part of governments of how powerful assessment can be as a policy tool—recent years have seen a significant number of policy initiatives designed to make the use of classroom assessment more effective in promoting learning. Such assessment practices have become dignified by the term "formative assessment," which includes the range of diagnostic tools and strategies for evaluative communication that are designed to guide both teacher and student toward the appropriate next steps.

One of the manifestations of this trend is the fact that many countries—including England, Scotland, Australia, New Zealand, Canada, and the United States, and even less developed countries such as Hong Kong and Mauritius (Broadfoot 1996a)—have introduced curriculum and assessment frameworks in which a series of explicitly defined learning targets are linked to provision for regular assessment. Thus, teachers can both identify student progress against standardized yardsticks and have the information they need to engage in the necessary remediation. Linked to such policy-initiatives in many cases, has been the growing recognition that improved student learning requires more individualized and effective intervention on the part of teachers. Moreover, the ever-widening range of competencies and skills, which now feature in the curriculum, have helped to underpin the international trend toward recognizing the necessity of ceding a measure of responsibility to teachers for summative assessment since this is the only way many learning goals can be validly assessed. The result has been a growing commitment on the part of policymakers to improving teachers' class-room assessment skills (Gipps 1995).

The increasingly intense international spotlight being turned on classroom assessment practices seems likely to be both a cause and an effect of the significant developments in technique that have taken place in recent years (Broadfoot et al. 1996). The use of, for example, records of achievements and portfolios, pupil self-assessment and observation check-lists, profiles and performance-based assessments, reflects a very widespread interest in developing approaches to assessment that can document this broader range of achievements.

Yet despite the very significant growth of interest among both policymakers and practitioners in the development of new approaches to assessment, we arguably still know relatively little about whether such new developments are likely to enhance learning and even less about why. Attempts to link the results of psychologists' well-established, but rather specialist, research into the relationship between instruction, assessment and learning with teachers' day-to-day classroom practice remain few and far between. Moreover, the long-standing division between sociological and psychological theories has, arguably, led to a tendency to divorce considerations regarding the interpersonal factors affecting learning from those that reside in the social context. Thus, although there is an extensive psychological literature that explores the way in which children approach different learning tasks, and their implications for which learning styles and teaching strategies are most likely to lead to enduring and successful learning, there appears to have been little attempt to apply such insights as part of routine classroom teaching and learning arrangements.

Even less explored, however, is the significance of different educational cultures in this respect. How a learner engages with a particular learning opportunity is likely to be influenced by their own social background that will reflect the influence of variables such as their gender and the particular ethnic, social class, and geographic background from which they come. It will be influenced by characteristics of the school, by the particular classroom culture and the behavior and attitude of the teacher. Such local sociocultural dimensions are complemented by national cultural traditions. What is normal and expected behavior on the part of teachers or pupils in one educational culture may be very different in its implications in another. For assessment practice, as for any other aspect of education, conventions, and expectations dictate the meaning and the significance of any given action. Thus a whole variety of social influences come together to exert a major force on a learner's approach to, and success in, learning. These influences are realized through social interaction that produces the meanings that are socially patterned and sustained through cultures—in this case educational cultures.

In this chapter we argue that any attempt to understand the way in which a particular assessment practice is likely to help or hinder learning must study it in the context of the more general cultural setting in which the interaction between teacher and pupil is taking place. It must start from a recognition that any assessment act—formal or informal, covert or overt, formative or summative—is a process of interaction, a form of communication typically, but not always, between pupil and teacher, that is as vulnerable to misinterpretation as any other kind of social intercourse. The teacher (or in some cases other pupils or even, in the case of self-assessment, learners themselves) is using assessment as a particular language, a mechanism of communication in which they are seeking to identify both achievements and needs and the learner is interpreting the teacher's signals in order to make the appropriate response.

Whatever this latter response is, it is certainly not a mechanistic one, nor is it totally predictable. It is determined by the learner's perceived "interests at hand" and the complex mixture of long- and short-term influences that are relevant to that particular judgement. As Charlot et al. (1992, p. 19–20) argue:

The subject creates his own environment, in so far as he selects possibilities from it and works in it according to particular logics to make sense—his own sense—out of it in so far as he constructs it for himself as a world. But there is also an argument that even if the environment does not produce the subject, it does constitute the universe of meaning from which the subject must construct his world.

Thus, when teachers make calculations concerning how they may most effectively intervene to facilitate a pupil's learning, they are making predictions based on assessments of an extraordinarily complex kind (Torrance and Pryor 1998). By the same token, when they mobilize the assessment language itself for this purpose, they are using a tool that is a delicate and far from perfect form of communication.

In his study of teachers' classroom assessment practices in Greek primary schools, Mavrommatis (1995) identified four different purposes that inform teachers use of classroom assessment: the *intellectual,* which is concerned with identifying understanding and providing feedback; the *psychological,* in which teachers use encouragement and other affectively-intentioned strategies to encourage pupils; the *managerial,* which is concerned with assessing pupils and concentration; and the *social,* when the assessment is directed toward monitoring and achieving the desired learning environment for the whole class. Each "assessment episode"—consisting of the four stages of pupil behavior, teacher interpretation, teacher response, and pupil response—can, he suggests, be identified as fulfilling one of these four purposes. Thus, in terms of the dimension of purpose alone, the decision-making process that informs an "assessment episode" is both complex and relatively unpredictable.

Nevertheless, for learners to be able to function effectively in a given classroom, they need to develop the ability to interpret the purpose behind teachers' various evaluative responses and thus respond in the manner that is expected. Individual teachers are likely to vary in the way in which they interact with pupils to achieve these various assessment purposes and, as with every other aspect of classroom interaction, pupils need to develop quite rapidly the ability to "suss" or decode the system of expectations and intentions informing a particular teacher's assessment language. In short, the meaning of a particular assessment utterance or behavior, either as initiated by the teacher or as perceived by the pupil, needs to be seen as a function of the particular cultural context that defines its meaning and hence, its significance. Thus, efforts to understand the way the assessment language works to promote or inhibit learning and more generally, the part it plays in classroom interaction, need to encompass this important variable.

In what follows, we seek to illustrate the salience of this argument through an examination of both teachers' and pupils' perspectives in primary schools in two different national settings—France and England. These are countries in which, as our research has revealed (Broadfoot et al. 1996), there have been marked differences in both teachers' perspectives and practices concerning assessment. Predictably, parallel research on pupils' perspectives of schooling in the same two countries has also revealed significant differences in attitude and expectations, both of the teacher and of themselves as learners (Broadfoot et al. 1996). The two countries thus provide a fertile setting for examining culturally-derived differences in how assessment is perceived by teachers and pupils, and hence of the specificity of the way in which the assessment language might operate in the classroom to bring about a particular effect. How far are such differences material to the learning process? In particular, what lessons can they teach us about the increasingly universalistic use of assessment as a policy tool to raise standards?

As suggested above, this chapter is based on insights gathered over the course of a series of research projects that have been conducted in both France and England since the early 1980s and that are still on-going. These include the "Bristaix" project that ran from 1993–1997; the PACE project that ran from 1989–1997; the STEP project that ran from 1992–1993; the QUEST project that ran from 1996–1998, and the ENCOMPASS project that ran from 1998–1999. These various studies have embraced both teachers' and pupils' perspectives, policy-making, and classroom practice in England and France. They have been linked by the common rationale of using a comparative approach to illuminate key features of the teaching and learning process. A particular focus has been the impact of the recent major policy changes in the two countries and the challenge they represented for teachers to change in more or less fundamental ways their professional perspectives and traditional ways of working. In this chapter, we draw on these data to illuminate cultural influences on the meaning and practice of assessment as perceived by both the teachers and the pupils in the study. Our intention is that by so doing we can demonstrate the central importance of understanding the *relativity* of this aspect of classroom interaction.

All the studies except the most recent have focused on primary schooling. They have combined both quantitative and qualitative data-collection techniques and have included the use of questionnaires, interview, and classroom observation. They have sought to map developments in these two traditionally very different education systems both of which are currently in the throes of quite significant change in response to the international pressures referred to above. Both systems have thus been the subject of a series of major policy-initiatives with the broadly similar goal of both raising standards of achievement and of encouraging the acquisition of nontraditional skills and competencies. Given their very different starting points however, the nature of the steps taken to achieve these objectives has been starkly contrastive in the two countries.

Thus, policy-making in French education in recent years has been informed by the desire to make the famously centralized system more responsive to local needs; to provide for more leadership and autonomy at the institutional level and to encourage teachers to adopt a more individualized pedagogy that addresses the strengths and weaknesses of each pupil. The 1989 Jospin Reform in particular was a watershed in seeking to encourage French teachers to review their typically didactic pedagogic approach and to consider more individualized approaches to teaching. Associated with this goal, the Jospin Reform called for more emphasis on diagnostic assessment, on collaboration between teachers and school-specific policies. In England and Wales, by contrast, the spate of policy-initiatives that were initiated by the 1988 Education Reform Act have been informed by a commitment on the part of government to increasing the degree of central control within the system on the one hand, and to making schools and teachers more accountable by exposing them to market forces on the other. Again, assessment has been a central focus but this time the pressure has been toward greater "performativity" in the introduction of a system of overt, formal judgments of pupil achievements in relation to a hierarchical series of explicit targets and levels.

The changes that are currently taking place in each system—some as a direct response to government directives, some provoked in opposition to government policy, and still others initiated by teachers as a professional response to perceived need—provide an ideal opportunity to study both the different characteristics of the assessment culture in the two systems as well as their common features. Not only do assessment issues, predictably, have a high profile in each of the reforms, the process of change itself exposes many taken-for-granted elements of the existing culture. Thus, an analysis of these taken-for-granted elements makes it possible to achieve both a greater understanding of any differences in the way in which the assessment language operates in these traditionally contrasting educational settings and hence the possibility of generating more general insights into the role that assessment plays in learning.

PRIMARY TEACHERS IN ENGLAND AND FRANCE

Perspectives

Our broadly representative sample of English and French teachers was asked to consider twenty educational objectives and to rate the "degree of importance" of each of them on a five-point scale. Their responses suggested that objectives relating to academic work were of equal importance to French and English teachers. However, compared to the "Bristaix" findings, many French teachers in the mid-1990s had widened their view of the nature of children's learning to include the importance of motivating and encouraging children academically and making them autonomous learners. By contrast, English teachers were placing greater emphasis on academic goals than in the past but they had not relinquished their emphasis on children's personal and social development.

Table 4.1 shows how teachers *felt* they had changed in their practice since the reforms.

Table 4.1
The Importance of Different Aspects of Pedagogy: The Percentage of French and English Teachers Stating That They Gave the Following Aspects More Importance Since the Reforms

	England	France
	%	%
Assessment skills	83.7	69.1
Subject knowledge	72.8	7.7
Clear aims	67.4	37.7
Classroom organization	44.6	43.0
Teaching skills	37.0	23.2
Knowledge of children	16.3	33.3
Maintaining order	15.2	13.5
Relations with children	10.9	29.5

Source: PACE Project: 92 teacher interviews; STEP Project: 203 teacher questionnaires

As can be seen in Table 4.1, both French and English teachers reported that the aspect of their pedagogy that had changed most since the reforms related to assessment. In France, the particular emphasis of the Jospin Reform appeared to have had an impact in that nearly half of the teachers in the sample felt they were now thinking more seriously about classroom organization and nearly one-third attributed greater importance to knowledge of, and relationships with, children. In England, likewise, the introduction of the National Curriculum appeared to have had the desired effect in that primary school teachers were much more aware of the importance of subject knowledge and of having clear aims. English teachers also saw classroom organization as a more important concern than previously and over one-third also reported focusing on teaching skills. Knowledge of, and relationships with, children were seen as being of "more importance" by relatively few teachers in England, reflecting the traditionally high priority of these goals for English primary teachers.

Overall, the study indicated that one-quarter of the French teachers thought their approach to teaching had changed "substantially," with a further one-fifth reporting that it had changed "a little." But almost one-third felt that they had not changed at all. These perceptions are borne out by the observations we conducted at that time and are reported in the next section. Given that the French context is likely to be less familiar to the readership of this book, the following account also provides some descriptive details.

Practices

As explained above, a basic intention of the French Jospin Reform was the development of forms of teaching that would be more responsive to children. The particular points of emphasis were that teaching was to become more "individualisée" and "active." However, systematic observation data of teachers documented continuing significant differences in the proportions of whole class instruction and individual work in the two countries, as Table 4.2 shows.

Table 4.2
Main Teaching Context of Teacher Observations (Percentages of Observed Time)

Teaching Context	French Teachers of 7/8/9 year olds	English Teachers of 7/8/9 year olds
Whole class context	44.4	29.8
Individual context	33.3	44.8
Group context	11.1	8.9
Other contexts	2.6	2.1
No main teaching context	8.6	14.4
	100	100

Source: PACE Project: 92 teacher interviews; STEP Project: 203 teacher questionnaires

Table 4.2 shows the dominance of whole class contexts in the observed behavior of French teachers, and is significantly higher than for English teachers. However, at 44% it is not as high as the "Bristaix" study found ten years earlier. Similarly, the French figure of 33% of teacher time on individual work is particularly interesting in respect of the style of whole class pedagogy that has traditionally dominated in France. However, fieldnotes suggest that this balance between whole class teaching and individualized work in France may be explained by the form of control that the teachers exercised over their children and by developments within the underlying pattern or structure of a "leçon."

A "leçon" has traditionally been, and remains, the key instructional episode used by French primary school teachers. As observed in our study, it commonly followed a six stage pattern:

1. The teacher led the children through an explanation of an aspect of knowledge, skill, or understanding. To accomplish this first stage, the topic was broken down into a sequence, each with its own problem to be solved and usually involving a revision of steps that had already been studied. The teacher achieved class involvement by selecting children who gave either a verbal or graphic explanation of each step. This first stage was thus carried out collectively, was usually visibly demonstrated on the blackboard, and was achieved by the teacher leading the children.

2. The second stage, which was sometimes omitted, was for the teacher to take the class through an exercise based on the "leçon." This was also done usually collectively, often using the blackboard, and with the teacher leading and individual children contributing.

3. In the third stage, the children carried out a similar exercise but this time in almost complete silence and individually.

4. In the fourth stage, the work was sometimes marked as a class exercise. The process was similar to that of the first stage.

5. The fifth stage (which was not observed as it often involved homework), was for the children to carry out another similar exercise or commit the "leçon" to memory.

6. Finally, the children were required to show their understanding in an assessment test or "contrôle" at a later date.

Thus, in 1994, whole class instruction and the use of the blackboard was still the dominant method of instruction in the French schools studied as it had been in the Bristaix classrooms ten years before. However, in 1994 teachers were observed to focus on individual children in stages 1, 2, and 4 and were often seen to concentrate on those who were having difficulty. In addition, the teachers were seen to spend a great deal of time working with individual children on a private basis during the third stage. The teachers either moved among the children monitoring their work and offering assistance to those who needed it, responded to requests for help, or they positioned themselves at their desks and again either selected children or were sought after by them. However, they did not appear to base their expectations on assessments of individual pupil's levels of prior attainment, nor did they build into their teaching the possibility of children working at different levels. Only occasionally were children divided into groups or sets for additional, targeted help. While, pupil participation was one of the basic characteristics of the whole class teaching observed, there was a great deal of variation in the extent to which teachers encouraged or followed individual children's interests.

The seating arrangements observed in the Bristaix classrooms had involved most children sitting in rows facing the front. Ten years later there were significant variations in this respect. Some teachers now favored a classroom arrangement based on small groups with individual children not necessarily facing the front. There also appeared to have been some development in classroom displays which, though the teacher dominated, included more pupil work.

"Autonomie" is a term that was frequently used by the French teachers and was regarded by them as one of their aims—helping the child to learn to organize him/herself and his/her methods of working so that he/she could learn to work more independently—a clear element of "la pédagogie individualisée." It seemed to form part of the main goal of concentrating on the individual. However, there appeared to be significant differences between the French concept of "individualized" and the English view of "autonomy" as a form of independent learning. To most French teachers, autonomy seemed to mean teaching children a method of analysis, particularly through each "leçon" in Maths and French, so that once acquired, the approach could be used independently. This was observed within direct instruction, as in the "leçon," in encouraging children to find answers for themselves when doing exercises and in the assessment process of correcting schoolwork. Regarding the latter, teachers were seen to use three different approaches: child self-correction, correction as a whole-class activity and teacher marking with an individual child. However, children carried out almost all such tasks on their own and, in some cases, were seen to hide their work from their neighbors to avoid being copied from. In short, despite a greater element of individual focus, French classrooms were still "catechistic" (Sharpe 1992) in the sense of using tried and tested methods to inculcate a given body of received wisdom in the form of knowledge and skills to the next generation.

As well as a greater element of individualization, it was clear that there had been changes in teaching style, even in the main subjects of French and Maths, with some teachers being more flexible and active in their approach. Children in the French classrooms of 1994 had more freedom of movement, choice of activity, and resources available to them. In various classrooms they were observed to move around the classroom selecting a book to read, using wall displays, playing with Lego-type bricks, and drawing pictures following the completion of set tasks. The degree of freedom allowed depended on the teacher. The existence of book corners and the children's access to them was a clear difference from ten years before. Reading seemed to be more accepted as an enjoyable pastime.

In terms of curriculum focus, the Jospin Reform had given teachers more flexibility in the hours per week suggested for subjects, which were given simply in terms of maximum and minimum time. However, most teachers tended to follow previously established practices. Table 4.3 shows the percentages of time for "main" curriculum contexts that were observed in England and France as being spent on what, in England, are known as "core," and "foundation," and "other foundation" subjects.

Table 4.3
Main Curriculum Contexts of Teacher Observations (Percentages of Observed Time)

	France (Classes of 7/8/9 year olds)	England (Classes of 7/8/9 year olds)
French or English	55.6	27.3
Maths	30.8	20.3
Science	0	6.5
Other foundation subjects (incl. RE and Pers/Social Ed)	6.8	22.2
No main curriculum context	6.8	23.7
	100	100

Source: Spring 1994 STEP Project; 1993 and 1994 PACE Project

Table 4.3 shows how the curriculum in the sample of French classrooms was dominated by the teaching of French and mathematics, with no science teaching being recorded. Other subjects and cross-curricular activities took just 7% of observed time each. In England, PACE data show that the curriculum for children of the same age was significantly more wide-ranging and varied in subject coverage. Almost one-quarter of curriculum time in the English classrooms was used in cross-subject activities at this time although this may well have changed following the introduction of the national Literacy and Numeracy Hour initiatives. In terms of the range of different activities being undertaken by teachers, as Table 4.4 shows, the activity of French teachers was coded as being "instructional" for over one-half of the observed time, a significantly greater proportion than that recorded in English classrooms.

Table 4.4
Observed Teacher Activity (Percentages of Observed Time)

	French Teachers of 7/8/9 year olds	English Teachers of 7/8/9 year olds
Assessment	10.2	5.8
Control	6.1	6.1
Direction	22.1	33.6
Encouragement	0.1	4.0
Instruction	50.7	41.1

Negative	1.9	0.8
Hearing reading	1.1	4.1
Other activity	4.5	3.7
Not recorded	3.3	0.8
	100	100

Source: Spring 1994 STEP Project; 1993 and 1994 PACE Project

It is noteworthy that higher levels of formal assessment activity were recorded in France, but lower amounts of child management "direction." This may be attributable to the use of simpler forms of classroom organization and task management.

Since the tasks in which the French children were engaged tended to be of a whole class and sedentary type, this facilitated the teacher's control. Sanctions against individual children were seen to take the form of: public reprimand; removal of a "bon point," changing a child's seating place; writing a child's name on the board; speaking to parents after school; physical punishment and taking a child to the headteacher. As Table 4.4 also shows, the French teachers used negative sanctions slightly more and encouragement slightly less than their English counterparts.

The French teachers varied in their teaching style with the children, but all made their position of authority very clear: it was they who controlled not only the content and timing of the tasks, but the exercise book to be used, the color of the pen, page layout, and so on. Some teachers began lessons with no settling in period nor explanation of what was to come. However, others started the day by asking the children to talk about any interesting experiences they had had the evening before and some teachers talked about the program for the day and wrote it on the board. Another way in which teachers were able to reinforce their authority was in the assessment feedback that they gave to the children that constituted 10% of teacher activity. In form, it was also much more public and categoric than the forms of ongoing teacher assessment used in England. Indeed, teachers often allowed peers to express negative reactions toward individual children who made mistakes in whole class lessons.

Together, these data suggest evidence that in French classrooms, there was a movement toward a more active type of learning. Some French primary teachers were trying to involve the children's interests and experience and to use different approaches that might appeal to children. There was also some evidence of children being encouraged to work together. But, despite some significant changes in pedagogic practices in French primary school classrooms, in terms of emphasis on the provision of support for individuals—particularly children with difficulties—a more flexible environment, more diverse resources, some encouragement of pupil choice, and a continued emphasis on pupil "autonomie," a relatively narrow curriculum remained, as did strong teacher control. Assessment practices—and the assumptions underpinning them—continued to both reflect and reinforce the deeply-rooted culture of French primary education in which the teacher is expected to be the instrument of delivering an explicitly defined and long-established body of knowledge and skills to the next generation. Central to this process is the exercise of assessments that categorize mastery or nonmastery, publicly and explicitly.

In English classrooms, by comparison, there was some indication of a very different trend toward more formal, whole class teaching and overt assessment. Like their French counterparts, English primary teachers have been faced with implementing changes in every aspect of their professional lives during the last decade. Evidence from the PACE study (Osborn et al. 2000) suggests that most have embraced these changes in a positive way. They have moved from being "intuitive practitioners" to a more collaborative, planned, systematic, and universalistic approach to teaching, designed to enable as many pupils as possible to reach externally defined curriculum goals. At the same time, they feel that this has been achieved at a price—a loss of spontaneity in the curriculum, diminishing time for personal and social development, a sense of jumping through externally imposed hoops.

PRIMARY PUPILS IN ENGLAND AND FRANCE

This account of some of the changing characteristics of French and English primary classrooms underlines the dynamic nature of teachers' practice as it responds to both policy initiatives and their changing perceptions of pupils' needs. However, it also underlines the enduring perspectives, beliefs, and traditions that are rooted in the culture of a particular education system and, arguably, are much more important in defining the process of teaching and learning. Recent developments are only scratches on the surface of the enduring and very different educational cultures of the two education systems. It is these different cultures that continue to shape the perspectives, experiences, and learning outcomes of pupils in the two systems. In this second section of the chapter we briefly describe some of these differences as they have been documented in the recently completed QUEST project (Broadfoot et al. 1996). We use these data to argue that, despite the significant changes that have characterized teachers' practice in the two countries in recent years, and hence, the growing similarity in this respect between them, significant differences in pupils' perspectives reflect important and enduring characteristics of the two systems that have a profound impact. In particular, they inform the *assessment language* of the two systems as it shapes pupils' sense of learning goals, and of themselves as learners.

Our overall findings suggested that children in both countries shared many perceptions in common as a result of their shared structural position as pupils. However, there were, nevertheless, some highly significant differences in French and English children's views of schooling. On the whole, children in both countries felt positively about their schools and their teachers but it was striking that French children were more strongly positive about school, more enthusiastic about teachers, and more likely to see teaching as helpful and useful to them. French children also presented themselves as more highly educationally motivated and keen to do well in class.

French children were more strongly positive about school and about their teacher. They saw school as both useful and enjoyable as well as encouraging independence. For example, 64% of French children strongly agreed with the statement "I like my teacher," compared with 30% of English children; 86% strongly agreed that they wanted to do well at school, compared with 66% of English children; 43% felt strongly that they really enjoyed most lessons, compared with 20% of English children. English children were more likely to find their school work difficult and to see it as taking a long time to complete. French children saw their work as relatively more interesting and more fun than English children did, though English children more often saw work as a collaborative effort, sometimes done with others and when talking with friends.

However, English children were more likely to see the social uses of school. For example, 76% compared with 58% of French children felt that school helped them to get on with people. As we suggested earlier, English teachers felt responsible for children's social and personal development as well as academic objectives and these wider goals of schooling were reflected in the children's responses. Like their teachers, English children had an "extended" conception of the function of schooling, while French children had a more "restricted" and more focused conception of what school is for.

French children emphasized usefulness and the important role played by marks and formal assessment slightly more strongly. As reported above, in our observations in French classrooms, we had noticed that French teachers were far more likely to criticize children's work in an overt way in front of the class. However, this was reflected only partially in what the children themselves said. While to the eyes of English researchers, the French primary teachers were often surprisingly harsh with the children (it was not at all uncommon for a teacher to shout at a child and to threaten him—it was more often him—with "redoublement"—repeating the year), the children themselves were only slightly more likely to say that "it quite often happens that the teacher says somebody's work is bad or wrong in front of the class."

Although French children did perceive their teachers to be critical on some occasions, they were also far more likely to agree that their teacher often praised children for good work. In other words, assessment was perceived as more overt and public in French classrooms. It was also perceived as a normal part of classroom life that had continued in the same way since children entered the "maternelle" at age 4 or 5 and was, therefore, not necessarily damaging to self-esteem in the way an English observer might assume. Other research in the early secondary years suggests that French pupils' self-esteem is, on the whole, higher than that of comparable English pupils despite an apparently harsher and more critical approach by the teacher (Robinson et al. 1990; Robinson 1992). This may well be a result of the "distancing of the self" in French education and the separation of the personal and the cognitive. When the teacher criticizes, it is only the child's academic performance that is being referred to, not other aspects of personality, and this is clearly understood by all pupils (Dubet et al. 1996).

The children were asked to choose from a set of possible reasons for wanting to do well and to complete the sentence "When I want to do good work it's because . . ." French children were more likely to fear being shouted at if they did not do their best work, but they were also far more strongly motivated by a desire for praise from the teacher (46% compared with 18%), by the urge to be the best in the class (46% compared with 19% were in strong agreement with this), and to get a good mark (71% compared with 32%). Overall, they appeared to feel much more strongly than English children about the importance of doing good work. Eighty-six percent of the French sample compared with 60% of the English sample emphasized this. From the children's other comments it was clear that this lower motivation was a result of peer group pressure in the class. The English children in our study similarly disliked the idea of being a "goodie."

As Table 4.5 shows, all the children attributed success to hard work and effort, although this was a more important factor for English children than for French. English children appeared to believe more strongly in innate ability, saying that success was due to being clever or to having better brains. However, it appeared from other responses that French children saw cleverness or intelligence as something you could get better at in time rather than as a fixed quality.

Table 4.5
The Three Most Important Reasons Given by Pupils for Educational Success

I think some children do better at school than others because

England

1. they work harder 77.1%

2. they listen to the teacher more 59.4%

3. they don't mess about so much 58.2%

France

1. they listen to the teacher more 68.5%

2. they work harder 55.2%

3. they're clever 45.9%

Source: Spring 1994 STEP project; 1993 and 1994 PACE project.

The data in Table 4.5 suggest that the importance of hard work and the work ethic is more firmly entrenched in French schools and accepted as necessary by children. This was confirmed when the children were asked to write in an open-ended way about their teacher. French children consistently wrote that they wanted teachers who made them work hard while English children wanted teachers who did not give too much work and consistently mentioned a concern with fairness. English children also emphasized the teacher's strong concerns with responding to individual differences while French children's responses demonstrated the shared nature of both pupils' and teachers' objectives, in particular, completing the syllabus and moving up to the next class.

TWO SYSTEMS, TWO GOALS

These data paint a picture of children with different, culturally-shaped, perceptions of education and of their role within it. Together with the documented differences concerning teachers' perspectives and practices in England and France, they lead us to characterize the French education system as being essentially focused on the achievement of defined goals whereas the English education system is more concerned with social integration. For the French system this description is embodied in its more utilitarian conception of school; its orientation to future occupational success; and the acceptance that learning will be business-like rather than enjoyable, intrinsically interesting, or fun. This is, in turn, associated with the expectation that teachers will exert authority and teach what it is necessary to learn. By the same token, teachers do not expect to undertake a pastoral or social role, nor are they expected to do so by French society. Above all, however, these profoundly different cultural characterizations of education are reflected in the role played by assessment.

As we have described, the work-centered, formal French classroom is one in which expectations and performance are both explicit. Children know precisely how they are doing on the basis of the regular, public allocation of marks. If they cannot perform in class when required they may be subject to public disapproval and humiliation by the teacher. It is not surprising that pupils' satisfaction is often, in consequence, linked to overt evidence of academic achievement and that fear of failure motivates pupils of all kinds to try harder. As in many other countries, however, this apparently punitive regime is moderated in its effects on the pupils' psyche by the attribution of success and failure to effort, rather than to innate ability. As Charlot et al. (1992) argue, "the well-defined levels of achievement coupled with the tradition of 'redoublement' (repeating the year) when that standard has not been reached and the emphasis on cognition in the curriculum facilitates a general understanding of what failure means and acceptance by pupils, teachers and parents of a certain brutal logic. Hence in part at least, the readiness of pupils to discuss their progress or lack of it, their articulacy in doing so and their awareness of a variety of reasons for it" (Beattie 1994, p. 190).

In contrast, English primary education is informed by a concern for the whole child, for the school as a community, and for each individual within it. The characteristic pedagogic emphasis on trying to make learning fun and on a broadly-based curriculum, follow from this basic stance. But once again it is in the assessment language that the most salient differences between England and France, in terms of learning, can be traced. Because of the focus on the whole person in English education, there is a tendency both for teachers to judge pupils in terms of their personal and social characteristics and for pupils themselves to develop their identity as learners in these terms (Pollard and Filer 1996). Differences in "ability" are used as the explanation of differential achievement. Despite English primary teachers' sustained efforts to be pupil-centered, positive, and individual in their evaluations of pupils' performance, and their best efforts to minimize what they perceive to be the unhelpful effects of overt, "categoric" assessment, many English pupils are much less motivated and happy in the school environment than their French counterparts.

CONCLUSION

In this chapter, we have highlighted some of the differences that distinguish English and French primary teachers' professional priorities and practices. We have linked these to enduring differences between the two countries in their educational cultures. We have shown some examples of how responsive such conceptions and practices are to externally-imposed policy changes designed to introduce new priorities and pedagogic approaches. Last but not least, we have highlighted the significance of the different classroom realities so created for the pupils who experience them in terms of the latter's expectations of both their teachers' and themselves as learners. Running through all these perceptions, practices, and experiences is the constant theme of assessment—the evaluative discourse that expresses teachers' priorities and dictates those of pupils. As we have seen in French classrooms, it is assessment that is the visible manifestation of the teacher's power to define the received wisdom and underpins the way in which the pupil's role is defined and constructed as the largely undifferentiated debutant of the national culture. Equally, in England, it is teachers' traditional assessment practice, in its highly individualized and covert form, that communicates their very different definitions of learning and encapsulates their much more comprehensive learning objectives. As in France, it is assessment that conveys these cultural messages to pupils and dictates English pupils' very different expectations and aspirations of the learning process.

In the introduction to this chapter we argued that assessment is one of the most powerful forces shaping pupils' learning. We made the point that until recently, surprisingly little attention has been given to either understanding how it affects the day-to-day learning of pupils or in training teachers in the classroom to capitalize on its powerful effects. This picture is now beginning to change with the growing scholarly interest in assessment as "social practice and social product" (Filer 1999) and in assessment and learning (Broadfoot 1996a). As yet, however, the role of assessment as a "cultural tool" (Wertsch 1991) remains a neglected area in that very little research attention has been devoted to studying the different ways in which assessment messages are likely to affect learning in *different* educational cultures.

Instead we have seen quite the opposite development take place in recent years namely, an exponential growth in the international borrowing of both assessment policies and practices as part of the recent surge of interest in this aspect of educational activity regardless of the potential impact of contextual factors. Most prominent in this respect—and therefore most seductive and dangerous—has been the trend toward the ubiquitous use of assessment to monitor and compare educational standards. Closely related to such "fact-finding" initiatives has been the growth in the punitive use of "high-stakes" testing to drive the curriculum and to raise educational standards through competition and tightly-drawn accountability measures. The result is rather like a sucker on a rose tree—a rapidly-growing shoot that is produced directly by the wild root stock of the original parent plant but one which, because it lacks the refined genetic control of the more developed cultured rose that has been grafted on to it, will, if left unchecked, overcome the whole plant. It will cause the plant to lose all its breeding, especially its flowers, which is the reason for growing the rose in the first place. Knowledgeable rose growers are quick to remove such shoots, using their knowledge of the different genetic potential involved to maximum effect.

For better or worse, assessment is an inevitable part of both classroom life and, increasingly, of institutions and educational systems as a whole; it is not a constant but a social, culturally-embedded, process. Its operation in practice is, therefore, subject to potentially as much variety as there are cultures and the range of educational goals and traditions, understandings and ideologies that they produce. As we have sought to show in this chapter in comparing two such cultures, the effective harnessing of assessment to promote learning depends on the quality of our collective efforts to understand the way in which assessment conveys these cultural messages. If we do not do so, the current rapid growth of assessment activity may well reveal itself as a sucker, spreading out of control to such an extent that it eventually overwhelms the quality of the whole and results in a fruitless and unwelcome intrusion into the carefully-tended garden of teaching and learning.

REFERENCES

Bachor, D., and Anderson, J. O. 1994. "Elementary Teachers' Assessment Practices as Observed in the Province of British Columbia, Canada." *Assessment in Education* 1(1):63–93.

Beattie, N. 1994. "Review of 'Ecole et Savoir dans les Banlieues . . . et Ailleurs' by B. Charlot et al." *Compare* 24(2):190–191.

Bernstein, B. 1977. *Class, Codes and Control,* Vol. 3. London: Routledge and Kegan Paul.

Black, P., and Wiliam, D. 1998. "Assessment and Classroom Learning." *Assessment in Education* 5(1):7–74.

Broadfoot, P. M. 1996a. *Education, Assessment and Society.* Buckingham: Open University Press.

Broadfoot, P. M. 1996b. "Assessment for Learning: A Teacher-Student Partnership." In H. Goldstein and T. Lewis (Eds.), *Assessment: Problems, Developments and Statistical Issues.* Chichester: Wiley and Sons.

Broadfoot, P., Osborn, M., Planel, C., and Pollard, A. 1996. "Assessment in French Primary Schools." *The Curriculum Journal.* 7(2):227–246.

Charlot, B., Bautier, E., and Rochex, J-Y. 1992. *Ecole et Savoir dans les Banlieues . . . et Ailleurs.* Paris: Armand Colin.

Crooks, T. J. 1988. "The Impact of Classroom Evaluation Practice on Students." *Review of Educational Research.* 58(4):438–481.

Dubet, F., Cousin, O., and Guillemet, J-P. 1996. "A Sociology of the Lycee Student." In A. Corbett and R. Moon (Eds.), *Education in France: Continuity and Change in the Mitterand years, 1981–1995.* London: Routledge.

Feiler, A., and Webster, A. 1999. "Teacher Predictions of Young Children's Literacy Success or Failure." *Assessment in Education,* 6(3).

Filer, A. (Ed.). 1999. *Assessment: Social Practice and Social Product.* Lewes: Falmer Press.

Gipps, C. 1995. "Reliability, Validity and Manageability in Large-Scale Performance Assessment." In H. Torrance (Ed.), *Evaluating Authentic Assessment: Problems and Possibilities in New Approaches to Assessment.* Buckingham: Open University Press.

Koretz, D., Broadfoot, P., and Wolf, A. 1998. "Special Issue: Portfolio and Records of Achievement." *Assessment in Education.* 5(3):301–480.

Mavrommatis, I. 1995. *Classroom Assessment in Greek Primary Schools.* Doctoral Thesis, School of Education, Faculty of Social Sciences, University of Bristol, Bristol.

OFSTED. 1998. *The Annual Report of Her Majesty's Chief Inspector of Schools in England: Standards and Quality in Education 1996–1997.* London: The Stationary Office.

Osborn, M., Pollard, A., Abbott, D., Broadfoot, P., and Croll, P. 1994. "Anxiety and Paradox: Teachers' Initial Responses to Change Under the National Curriculum." In H. Torrance (Ed.), *Researching the National Curriculum.* Dialogues Series. London: BERA.

Osborn, M., McNess, E., Broadfoot, P., Pollard, A., and Triggs, P. 2000. *Policy, Practice and Teacher Experience: Changing English Primary Schools.* London: Cassell.

Pollard, A., and Filer, A. 1996. *The Social World of Children's Learning.* London: Cassell.

Robinson, P. 1990. "Academic Achievement and Self Esteem in Secondary School: Muddle, Myths and Reality." *Education Research and Perspectives.* 17:3–21.

Robinson, P. 1992. "Redoublement in Relation to Self Perception and Self Evaluation: France." *Research in Education.* 47:64–75.

Robinson, P., and Taylor, C. 1990. "School Attainment, Self Esteem and Identity: France and England." *European Journal of Social Psychology.* 20:387–403.

Scarth, J. 1984. "Teachers' Attitudes to Examining: A Case Study." In P. Broadfoot (Ed.), *Selection, Certification and Control: Social Issues in Educational Assessment.* London: Falmer Press.

Sharpe, K. 1992. "Catechistic Teaching Style in French Primary Education: Analysis of a Grammar Lesson with Seven-Year-Olds." *Comparative Education.* 28(3):249–268.

Torrance, H. (Ed.). 1995. *Evaluating Authentic Assessment: Problems and Possibilities in New Approaches to Assessment.* Buckingham: Open University Press.

Torrance, H., and Pryor, J. 1998. *Investigating Formative Assessment: Teaching, Learning and Assessment in the Classroom.* Buckingham: Open University Press.

Wertsch, J. V. 1991. *Voices of the Mind: A Socio-Cultural Approach to Mediated Action.* Cambridge, MA: Harvard University Press.

Wertsch, J. V., and Smolka, A. L. 1993. "Continuing the Dialogue: Vygotsky, Bakhtin and Lotman." In H. Daniels (Ed.), *Charting the Agenda: Educational Activity after Vygotsky.* London: Routledge.

5

Portfolio Assessment in Teacher Education

Val Klenowski

INTRODUCTION

This chapter seeks to describe and analyze the use of portfolios for learning and assessment purposes in the context of teacher education, development, and professionalism. The associated process issues and related implications for curriculum and pedagogy are also discussed. Examples are drawn from international contexts where the creative space and research opportunities exist to explore alternative and authentic approaches to assessment and learning.

PORTFOLIOS: ASSESSMENT PURPOSES

Portfolios are used for learning, assessment, appraisal, and promotional purposes in the field of education. Internationally, the contexts and purposes for portfolio use in education are developing and expanding. In teacher education, portfolios are used for assessing the achievement of preservice teachers and serving teachers. Lecturers in higher education and serving teachers are expected to present portfolios for promotion and appraisal. Students in primary and secondary schools develop portfolios of work for learning, assessment, and exhibition purposes. In the vocational education field, portfolios are used extensively for the assessment of competencies. This chapter will focus on portfolio use in the context of teacher education and will consider some associated process issues.

Assessment fulfils a range of purposes that includes summative assessment, certification, and support for the teaching and learning process. The fundamental issues in assessment design are "fit for purpose" and for the mode of assessment to impact positively on teaching and learning (Gipps 1994). When using portfolios for assessment purposes, these principles of design apply. Forster and

Masters (1996, p. 1) state "[d]ifferent kinds of portfolios result from, and are appropriate for, different educational contexts and purposes. A portfolio that serves the assessment needs of a classroom teacher, for example, may not be the most appropriate form of portfolio for use in a state assessment program. There is no one 'portfolio;' there are many portfolios."

The essential consideration in the assessment design of the portfolio is the evidence selected for inclusion. As Forster and Masters (1996, p. 2) indicate, all portfolios are "sources of evidence for judgements of achievement in a range of contexts, from classroom monitoring of student performance to high-stakes summative assessment. All contain 'pieces of evidence.' The more relevant the evidence, the more useful it is for inferring a student's level of achievement in a learning area."

In the context of teacher education, the portfolio of work can fulfill assessment purposes that include summative assessment, certification, promotion, appraisal or support for the teaching and learning process. Each particular purpose requires varying processes for the collection and selection of evidence, such as critical self-evaluation and reflection. A description of these purposes and processes follow. For summative or certification purposes, the portfolio is usually considered along with other evidence. In situations requiring high-stakes decisions the portfolio is embedded within a more comprehensive learning and assessment system.

PORTFOLIO USE FOR SUMMATIVE PURPOSES

Assessment for summative purposes is designed to provide quality information about a student's performance without impacting negatively on good teaching and learning practice. For administrative reasons, such assessment is usually time efficient, manageable and inexpensive. An adequate level of reliability is needed for comparability purposes. A consistent approach and consistent grading must be implemented to ensure equity and fairness. Moreover, consistency of standards ensures quality in the overall assessment process and outcomes (Gipps 1994). Using portfolios for summative purposes requires the specification of standards and contents by an external agency, local authority, academic department or teacher for formal assessment and monitoring.

To illustrate, at the Hong Kong Institute of Education (HKIEd), in the Curriculum and Instruction (C&I) Department, preservice teachers studying for the Certificate in Education course complete two modules in their first year with this department. These modules are titled: *Classroom Teaching Skills* and *Instructional Design and Strategies for Effective Teaching* and are studied in semester one and two respectively. The lecturers responsible for teaching these modules agreed to use portfolios for summative assessment of preservice teacher attainment of the learning outcomes specified in each module. A clear framework and a set of guidelines for portfolio use were produced and refined after a two-year research project that studied the teaching and learning outcomes of portfolio use in this department (Klenowski 1998; Klenowski 1999).

The guidelines (Klenowski, Ledesma, Blachford, Bryant, and Timmins 1997) provide lecturers and preservice teachers with:

- suggestions for introduction and implementation of the portfolio process;
- a framework for the portfolio;
- the learning outcomes and suggestions of evidence suitable to address these outcomes;
- advice regarding self-evaluations and reflective statements;
- criteria to be used in the assessment of the portfolio;
- grade descriptors; and
- exemplars that illustrate standards.

Preservice teachers were made aware of the requirements for developing a portfolio of work for each module. For example, for *Instructional Design and Strategies for Effective Teaching,* preservice teachers are required to demonstrate attainment of ten competencies, two of which relate to self, six to task, and two to impact. These are presented in the guidelines with suggestions of the type of evidence that can be selected for inclusion in the portfolio to demonstrate attainment. A reflective statement accompanies each piece of evidence selected for inclusion. For example, one of the competencies is that the preservice teacher can provide a statement of personal philosophy, goals, and core values. To demonstrate that the preservice teacher has attained this competency, the reflective statement could include a discussion of the preservice teacher's central values as a teacher. These values could be developed from their reading about teaching and learning styles, from their own experiences of teaching and learning and/or from their cultural backgrounds. Preservice teachers are recommended to discuss their opinions about teaching and learning styles and theories, teacher-student relationships, and values they believe underpin their personal beliefs as a teacher. An example of such a statement is included in the guidelines for preservice teacher reference.

The preservice teacher must also provide one piece of evidence to support the claims made in the reflective statement. Suggestions of the types of evidence preservice teachers can choose to include in support of their claims about attaining the competencies are given. For example, to support the claim in the reflective statement for the above competency, preservice teachers can choose to include one of the following:

- a concept map that outlines their central beliefs;
- a video clip that demonstrates the values as shown in the teaching and learning strategies used;
- a research paper that describes clearly the preservice teacher's central beliefs as a teacher;
- an annotated photographic display of teaching and/or learning practices that reflects a preservice teacher's goals as a teacher;
- a piece of evidence of their own choosing.

An exemplar of a reflective statement and a piece of accompanying evidence for this competency are given in the guidelines. The following grade descriptors are used for summative assessment of the portfolio of work. These are shared with the preservice teachers at the outset and discussed throughout the course. The criteria embedded in the descriptors are used for formative feedback purposes throughout the semester.

GRADE DESCRIPTORS USED TO GRADE THE PORTFOLIO OF WORK

Grade Descriptors

Grade A: Distinction

- The evidence selected for the portfolio is of outstanding and exceptional quality in all respects and surpasses the objectives for the module.
- The reflective statements demonstrate deep and original thinking, interpretation, critical thinking, and synthesis. Cogent arguments are used and supported by well-selected references.
- The work is well structured, is expressed with flair and there is little or no redundancy.
- The grade is an expression of the confidence in the ability of the student to progress as an independent learner.

Grade B: Credit

- The evidence selected for the portfolio surpasses the objectives for the module and demonstrates a sound understanding of content.
- Arguments are used in the reflective statements to support the student's point of view and references are used appropriately.
- The work is well structured, well organized, written fluently, and correctly documented.
- The grade is an expression of confidence in the ability of the student to progress with some supervision and guidance.

Grade C: Pass

- The evidence selected for the portfolio achieves the objectives for the module, and demonstrates an adequate grasp of the content, but is confined to the minimum requirement.
- There is little evidence of independent reflection in the reflective statements and research is superficial with a minimum attempt at analysis and/or synthesis.
- The work is lacking in organization and the language is reasonably fluent but has some lapses in grammar and syntax.
- The grade is an expression of confidence in the ability of the student to go further with normal supervision and guidance.

Grade D: Fail

- The evidence selected for the portfolio does not adequately meet the objectives for the module.
- The reflective statement is a simple recall of facts with little or no evidence of research or documentation. There is no effort to supplement evidence with own critical reflections.
- The work is poorly structured, poorly organized, and lacks consistency.
- The grade is an expression that student may resubmit but will find higher level work very difficult. (Students granted a supplementary assessment can qualify for no more than a Pass Grade of C).

Grade E: Clear Fail

- The evidence selected does not achieve the objectives for the module and demonstrates little understanding of the content of the module.
- The reflective statements make assertions without supportive evidence and arguments.
- The work does not meet the minimum levels of presentation for this module: there are major, frequent mistakes in written expression.
- The work does not address the stated requirements and is not organized in an obvious manner.

In this example of the use of portfolios for summative purposes the emphasis is on manageability and reliability of evidence. Consistency of approach is intended by the provision of guidance to preservice teachers and lecturers. The consistency of standards is attended to by the provision of exemplars, grade descriptors, grading instructions, and commentary for exemplars to indicate the rationale for the grade assigned.

PORTFOLIO USE FOR CERTIFICATION AND SELECTION PURPOSES

The certification and selection function of assessment provides the student with a statement of achievement for entry to a profession or for entry to higher education. It is detailed to provide comprehensive coverage of attainment and is reasonably reliable to ensure confidence in the results and comparability across institutions. The focus is on the technical aspects of assessment for credential and selection purposes. The use of portfolios for these purposes requires the contents, or types of evidence for inclusion, to be specified by an awarding body or education authority. It is in the context of teacher education where it is most prevalent for portfolios to be used for the assessment purpose of certification and selection.

In the United States, the use of portfolios in teacher education has accelerated at both the local and national levels. For example, at the local professional level portfolios are used in teacher education programs in the education of new teachers. At the national level, the National Board for Professional Teaching Standards (NBPTS) has incorporated the use of portfolios for Board certification of experienced teachers (Lyons 1998a).

Internationally, the establishment of standards for high levels of competence in the teaching profession has highlighted the importance of:

- Professionalism[1];
- Teachers' lifelong learning;
- Teachers' knowledge[2];
- Ethical and moral stance;
- Knowledge of students and their learning difficulties;
- Teaching theories and strategies;
- Knowledge of teaching resources; and
- Subject-specific teaching knowledge.

These standards embody a complex and demanding vision of a teacher. This is why educators, like Shulman (1998), have developed assessments that are reflective of the complexity of teaching and the performance of effective teachers. Standards and performance assessments that focus purely on outcomes, without clarifying the conception of teaching, and learning they incorporate, are unhelpful (Lyons 1998b).

The portfolio, for certification or selection purposes, is usually developed from an externally defined set of standards. It generally consists of a collection of work that is representative of the individual's strengths and portrays the preservice teacher in the most favorable light. From the outset it is important to consider the warning from Snyder, Lippincott, and Bower (1998, p. 123–124). They advise that to prove one's competence on state-defined teaching standards can supersede portfolio use as an opportunity for a teacher to record growth through critical reflection on the struggles and inevitable failures common to the learning process. They rightly question whether the use of a portfolio for summative evaluation overrides its use as a strategy and process to make visible one's own practice for the purposes of reflection and inquiry.

In teacher education, for high stakes purposes such as certification or selection, the use of a portfolio is usually considered with other evidence such as classroom observations and assessments of collaborating teachers. Shulman, quoted in Lyons (1998b, p. 15) asserts "that the process-product, input-output model of teaching that dominated assessment failed to capture the complex, messy, multiple dimensions of teaching and of teacher learning." The need for the assessment of teachers to include "both content and process" is stressed.

The Extended Teacher Education Program (ETEP) at the University of Southern Maine is a fifth year innovative, professional development school model teacher education program, designed for liberal arts graduates that leads to teacher certification after a one year placement. At the outset of the program preservice teachers are informed of a set of goals or standards that are used for certification. They are also informed of the ETEP outcomes that are described under the following eleven areas:

- Knowledge of child/adolescent development and principles of learning;
- Knowledge of subject matter and inquiry;
- Instructional planning;
- Instructional strategies and technology;
- Assessment;
- Diversity;
- Beliefs about teaching and learning;
- Citizenship;
- Collaboration and professionalism;
- Professional development; and
- Classroom management.

Construction of a portfolio is a requirement. It consists of evidence indicative of competence, such as, a statement of one's teaching philosophy, classroom lessons, students' work (in written and video formats). Critical conversations interrogating one's practice, and carried on with mentors and peers over the course of the program is expected in the development of a portfolio. Such conversations inspire further reflection on the contents of the portfolio. These thoughts are documented and relate to why particular entries are selected for inclusion, the entries themselves, what the preservice teacher has learned from the experience of teaching and learning, why this is important, and the meaning of their own learning. A portfolio presentation to university and classroom faculty and peers then takes place. Finally, a decision about certification is made on the basis of the portfolio and other work of the preservice teacher (Lyons 1998b; Davis and Honan 1998).

PORTFOLIO USE TO SUPPORT THE TEACHING AND LEARNING PROCESS

Assessment, to support the teaching and learning process, aims to help preservice teachers develop and further their learning. Such assessment is enabling rather than limiting and, in this context, the role of assessment is diagnostic. The focus is on the preservice teacher's learning needs, and the development of his or her motivation and confidence. Portfolios used for this purpose include content selected by the preservice teacher, collaboration of preservice teacher and lecturer, collaboration with peers, or collaboration between mentor and preservice teacher.

Through such collaboration, that is integral to this teaching and learning approach, there exists the opportunity for important feedback to the lecturer about the curriculum and their own pedagogical practice. Lecturers can use such feedback to make adjustments or additions to the curriculum and to the teaching and learning strategies they employ.

Formative assessment is dominant and requires a high level of validity in content, construct, and consequential aspects while reliability is not as important for this purpose of assessment. Formative assessment is concerned with gathering data to determine the extent to which preservice teachers have mastered specific aspects of learning with the aim of improving subsequent performance. This form of assessment occurs during the process of completing work for inclusion in the portfolio not when the process of portfolio development is completed. Formative assessment is developmental and aims to identify areas for remediation so that subsequent instruction, study, and development can be improved.

Formative assessment has an important role in relation to learning with understanding or deep learning (Crooks, 1988). When deep learning takes place the learner is actively engaged and integrates learning. The learner understands in relation to his or her own experience and is not just accepting passively ideas or memorizing a collection of isolated facts. The learner has a central role in formative assessment. This is because in order for assessment to function formatively, results have to be used to adjust teaching and learning. That is, feedback that preservice teachers receive from their lecturers or peers on their achievements, strengths or areas for improvement must have a transformative function. Sadler (1989, p. 119), in discussing learning and formative assessment, states:

For students to be able to improve, they must develop the capacity to monitor the quality of their own work during actual production. This in turn requires that students possess an appreciation of what high quality work is, that they have the evaluative skill necessary for them to compare with some objectivity the quality of what they are producing in relation to the higher standard, and that they develop a store of tactics or moves which can be drawn upon to modify their work.

The implication is that it is just as important for the preservice teacher to monitor his or her own process of learning as it is for the lecturer. The use of a portfolio assists in this learning process. It involves formative assessment that supports learning, and involves lecturer-preservice teacher interaction as part of the assessment process itself.

Generally preservice teachers work closely with their lecturers on each of their chosen portfolio items. These are revised until the preservice teacher judges that the work meets the specified standards. Preservice teachers appear to learn a lot from writing, critiquing, and revising their work during this process of preparation of portfolio items. The lecturer or supervisor gives some indication of when the appropriate standard has been reached. Preservice teachers also know the grading criteria so self-evaluation is an integral part of the process. This is a learning process in itself as through substantive conversations with their lecturers, preservice teachers are provided with specific concrete feedback that they can use to improve their performance.

PORTFOLIO USE FOR APPRAISAL OR PROMOTIONAL PURPOSES

Portfolios used for appraisal or promotional purposes include evidence to support the professional development or promotional aspirations of the individual. The employer provides explicit criteria for selection or appraisal and the individual is responsible for selecting portfolio evidence that demonstrates his or her competence in relation to the criteria.

The nature and focus of the structure of the portfolio vary. The focus of the portfolio is selective, and in a teaching context, highlights the core professional and pedagogical knowledge or competencies of the individual teacher. The evidence is collected over time and is representative of both student and teacher work. Some reflective commentary or evaluative statement is included to explain the selected evidence to others.

The Education Department of Western Australia has produced guidance for teachers aspiring to the position of Advanced Skills Teacher (AST). The guide lists the competencies that need to be addressed and the types of evidence that could be used to illustrate competence. The following illustrates one of the competencies and indicators of attainment.

LEVEL 3 CLASSROOM TEACHER COMPETENCIES AND INDICATORS OF ATTAINMENT (EDUCATION DEPARTMENT OF WESTERN AUSTRALIA 1997, P. 7)

Competency 1

Utilize innovative and/or exemplary teaching strategies and techniques in order to more effectively meet the learning needs of individual students, groups and/or classes of students.

Indicators of Attainment

- A rationale for the introduction or use of a particular innovative strategy/technique is developed.
- Innovative/exemplary teaching strategies/techniques are developed to more effectively meet the learning needs of individual students, groups and/or classes of students.
- Innovative/exemplary teaching strategies/techniques utilized assist students to "learn how to learn."
- Innovative/exemplary teaching strategies/techniques are implemented within a supportive learning environment: an environment in which there is recognition and respect

for difference and diversity; and sensitivity to matters of gender, cultural difference, social class, disability, family circumstance, and individual difference.

- Teaching strategies/techniques are developed and implemented in response to school and system level initiatives.

Further guidance on how to compile a teaching portfolio has been published by various professional organizations and committees. For example, the Federation of Australian University Staff Associations (FAUSA) has produced a guide. It describes the portfolio as a summary of an academic's major accomplishments and strengths in the area of teaching. It provides a list of what an academic might select to include. The stress is on choosing evidence to illustrate teaching competence and to give a favorable impression. Four categories of material for inclusion are given. The first category is factual information or hard data, such as courses or numbers of students. The second category is selected factual material to portray the image of a good teacher. The third category is uncorroborated claims, such as descriptions of teaching innovations or reading journals. The final category relates to the opinions of others, such as student feedback or letters of praise. Information detailing how the teaching portfolio should be structured is given. Teachers are advised to select from a given list of items that might be relevant to the teaching accomplishments of an Australian academic. The list comprises items organized into the following areas:

- Introduction;
- Information about courses and supervision;
- Description of current teaching practices;
- Student achievement;
- Scholarship in teaching (i.e., evidence of interest in and of steps taken to evaluate and improve it);
- Evidence of student reactions to teaching; and
- Other evidence of reputation as a teacher (Roe 1987).

It is stressed that this is only a suggested list and that additional items can be included to reflect the individual's unique approach to teaching.

PROFESSIONAL DEVELOPMENT PURPOSES

In the portfolio, used for professional development purposes, are collected materials and samples of work that provide evidence for critical examination of teaching and learning practices. Teachers reflect on and evaluate their own teaching practices, they also engage in dialogue with others that helps to highlight the complexity and diversity of teaching and learning practices. Shulman (1998) suggests that portfolios may be important as a professional development activity through peer review. He was the first to suggest the value of a teaching portfolio in providing an opportunity to discuss one's teaching (Shulman 1992). Others have since recognized the importance of sustained conversations about teaching and learning with colleagues in refining the portfolio. It is for this reason that Davis and Honan (1998) use teams to support the portfolio development process because mentors and peers provide support, give feedback, listen actively, ask questions, and offer different perspectives thereby strengthening the portfolio development process. They conclude that the structure and associated portfolio-based conversations help foster reflection about teaching and enable preservice teachers to better articulate their beliefs about teaching and learning.

The development of the portfolio is a collaborative process. This involves mentored or coached teaching practice and substantive conversations about the teaching and learning. Grant and Huebner (1998, p. 159) indicate that the portfolio should include "a reflective commentary, the result of deliberation and conversation with colleagues, which allows others to examine the thinking and pedagogical decisions behind the documented teaching." They refer to the work of Shulman (1998) and acknowledge "that teacher constructed portfolios make teaching public, including making explicit tacit knowledge, in order to increase professional autonomy, and making public the standards and good work as a source of future wise action." Shulman (1998, p. 34) maintains that research becomes part of the educational community's discourse, however, teaching has remained a private act. His argument for peer review and portfolios in teaching is that "they contribute to making teaching community property in colleges and universities and, therefore, put teaching and research into the same orbit."

Grant and Huebner (1998, p. 152) recommend that portfolios for teachers should be:

- Designed to promote reflective practice;
- Shared with colleagues;
- Encouraged for cooperating and student teachers;
- A bottom-up voluntary process that is owned by teachers and not used for evaluation purposes; and
- Be supported by enabling conditions.

They stress that "key benefits are lost if the reflective culture of professional development is replaced by a culture of compliance where teachers go through the motions of assembling materials according to a predated checklist." Grant and Huebner (1998, p. 152) emphasize two key purposes of portfolio development: first, to develop the habit of mind that views teaching as inquiry, and second, to strengthen the habit of mind that views collaborative learning as the way to come to know teaching.

Cuban (1998) describes a posttenure review portfolio experience as a collaborative venture and indicates that what was so different with the portfolio experience from the usual tenure review was the clear focus on improving, rather than judging, and concentrating on issues raised by himself and others as they met.

The shortcomings of the process related to the lack of structure to the discussions and the uncertainty he faced about what a portfolio, which was focusing on a review of teaching and research, should contain. Portfolios for professional development allow teachers to consider the complex, multifaceted nature of teaching by providing the opportunity to critically reflect on their practice, to engage in professional dialogue with colleagues and to collaborate and develop understanding and ideas on teaching and learning.

PORTFOLIO ASSESSMENT PROCESSES

Whether the portfolio is developed for the purposes of:

- summative assessment;
- certification or selection;
- support of teaching and learning;
- appraisal or promotion; or
- professional development,

there will be key processes required in developing the portfolio. These processes include:

- self-evaluation;
- substantive conversation; and
- reflective practice.

It is somewhat unrealistic to describe these processes in such a decontextualized and unintegrated manner. However, for purposes of clarity and analysis this approach has been used to emphasize the importance of processes in this approach to assessment and learning. As Shulman (1992) has indicated, it is difficult to separate the process from the content when using portfolios for assessment purposes. In the context of teacher education, one of the fundamental intended learning outcomes is for teachers to have developed competence in critical reflection. This is why in the following analyses of processes, related to portfolio use in teacher education, reflective thinking and practice is explored more comprehensively.

SELF-EVALUATION

The development of a portfolio requires one to select from a collection of work to demonstrate competence achieved to a particular standard. Selecting work to demonstrate achievement requires preservice teachers to think critically about their learning and teaching, to understand the standards of performance that drive their work, and to critique their own work in relation to these standards.

The selection of work requires the individual to self-evaluate, which is a learning process in itself. This is because when one evaluates, or judges "the worth" of one's performance, strengths and weaknesses are identified for the purpose of improving one's learning outcomes. The self-evaluator needs to identify explicitly what it is that he or she finds meritorious and the criteria that are used. In a developmental context the other important factor is for the self-evaluator to identify the implications for future action. In this way the preservice teacher monitors and judges aspects of his or her own learning and teaching.

Self-evaluation is described in terms of developing preservice teachers' ability to make judgments about the quality of material. When they identify areas for improvement in their learning, they need to think about what action, in terms of information or research, that they need to find or complete. Improved learning in this context is linked to an understanding of criteria and what constitutes quality in a given context.

The term self-evaluation is used in a broader sense than self-assessment because it refers to ascribing value to the learning and teaching experience, first in the identification and understanding of the criteria or standards used, second by judging what is considered meritorious, and third by synthesizing the implications for future action. In a context of learning and teaching, this is a developmental process that is supported and managed together with the lecturer and the preservice teacher's peers. This self-evaluative process is also broader than self-assessment as preservice teachers are engaged in more than just ascribing grades. They evaluate their performance and measure progress against criteria or standards that emerge from the performance, which have been given, are self-selected, or negotiated with the lecturer or peers. The term self-evaluation emphasizes that it is the preservice teachers themselves who are conducting the evaluation. This concept parallels the notion of improving teaching and learning practices through teacher reflection on classroom practice (Stenhouse 1975).

Definitions of evaluation (Stake 1979; Simons 1987) emphasize the notion of "ascribing value." Wiggins (1989, p. 708) indicates that evaluation is most accurate and equitable when it entails human judgment and dialogue. He states that "[w]e rely on human judges in law and in athletics because complex judgements cannot be reduced to rules if they are to be truly equitable." The implication here is that self-evaluations provide insights into preservice teacher's thoughts, understandings, and explanations. Through the process of self-evaluation it is possible to better understand an individual's progress by checking out if selected evidence, and the given rationale for selection, meet the identified standard. This suggests that in order to explore a portfolio of work, dialogue is needed, to ensure that the individual is fully examined.

IMPORTANCE OF SUBSTANTIVE CONVERSATIONS

The acts of constructing, presenting, and reflecting on the contents or evidence of a portfolio are powerful portfolio processes for teachers and students at all stages of their teaching and learning. Teachers collect work, make a selection, and reflect on that selected piece of work that relates to their teaching experience. They may consider evidence, such as lessons taught, evaluate samples of student work, analyze teaching experiences that have been successful and those that have not been so successful, and explain why these are important to their philosophy and practice. Lyons (1998a, p. 5) indicates that "validation and understanding emerge through portfolio conversations with peers, mentors, the presentation of portfolio evidence, and recognition of the new knowledge of practice generated through this process."

The importance of dialogue, interview or "learning conversation" in the assessment process has been recognized (Broadfoot 1986; Munby with Philips and Collinson 1989; Francis 1994; Smith 1994). Owens and Soule (1971, p. 60) believe that "involving pupils in an assessment dialogue is a simple means of providing a wealth of insight into the impact of teaching, how an individual pupil is coping with that teaching and its effects upon him [or her]. In particular, it can elicit information which must other wise remain the exclusive property of the pupil, but which may be of vital importance to the teacher in relating to that pupil." Such information is very relevant for the teacher when one considers Gipps' (1994, p. 4) contention that "different forms of assessment encourage, via their effect on teaching, different styles of learning."

REFLECTIVE THINKING AND PRACTICE

Stenhouse (1975, p. 89) has defined reflective thought by reference to Metcalf's (1963) definition. That is, the "active, careful and persistent examination of any belief or purported form of knowledge, in the light of the grounds that support it and the further conclusions toward which it ends." Such thinking is necessary in the development of a portfolio of work and requires a pedagogical approach not unlike that outlined by Stenhouse (1975, p. 92). In describing a process curriculum to develop reflective capacity in a specific curriculum project, Stenhouse makes reference to the following pedagogical aims or principles of procedure. These are:

- to initiate and develop a process of question-posing (inquiry method);
- to teach research methodology where students look for information to answer questions that they have raised and use frameworks developed in the course to apply to new areas;
- to help students develop the ability to use a variety of first hand sources as evidence from which to develop hypotheses and draw conclusions;
- to conduct discussions in which students learn to listen to others as well as express their own views;
- to legitimize the search, that is, give sanction and support to open-ended discussions where definitive answers to many questions are not found;

- to encourage students to reflect on their own experiences; and
- to create a new role for the teacher as a resource not an authority.

The development of critical, creative, reflective thinkers requires a similar pedagogical approach or set of principles of procedure. The use of portfolios requires changes that align with some of the pedagogical aims summarized above. For example, in a study of the impact of portfolio use on teaching and learning (Klenowski 1999), the following changes were identified:

- greater lecturer facilitation of learning and less use of didactic and exam-oriented teaching;
- active preservice teacher engagement in learning;
- consistent and formative feedback on learning;
- use of group and team work as a learning strategy;
- flexible teaching and learning approaches;
- opportunities for the development of skills in context; and
- use of self and peer evaluation strategies.

In defining reflection Lyons (1998c, p. 106) refers to the work of Dewey (1910). Reflective thinking for Dewey involves: "first, a state of doubt, hesitation, perplexity, mental difficulty, in which thinking originates and second, an act of searching, hunting, inquiring, to find material that will resolve the doubt, settle and dispose of the perplexity." Lyons suggests that reflective thinking for Dewey is "deliberation."

Zeichner and Liston (1996, p. 7) describe the key features of a reflective teacher as follows:

- examines, frames and attempts to solve the dilemmas of classroom practice;
- aware of and questions the assumptions and values he or she brings to teaching;
- attends to the institutional and cultural contexts in which he or she teaches;
- takes part in curriculum development and is involved in school change efforts; and
- takes responsibility for his or her own professional development.

In discussions of reflective teaching, reference is often made to the work of Schon (1983, 1991). Reflection-on-action occurs before the lesson when teachers think about the lesson and after teaching the lesson when they consider what has occurred. Reflection-in-action occurs when teachers are engaged in teaching and they attempt to frame and think about problems related to the particular situation of practice. Schon's ideas of reflection-in-action and reflection-on-action, Dewey's idea of "deliberation," Stenhouse's concept of reflective thought and process curriculum, and Zeichner and Liston's key features of a reflective teacher are all critical conceptual components for thinking about the education of teachers and the knowledge of reflection.

Reflexiveness or the capacity to review critically and reflectively one's own processes and practices is fundamental to the portfolio process. Portfolios constitute reflections. For example, Wolf (1991, p. 130) agrees with Shulman's observation that portfolios "retain almost uniquely the potential for documenting the unfolding of both teaching and learning over time and combining that documentation with opportunities for teachers to engage in the analysis of what they and their students have done." The careful self-evaluation and monitoring of teaching and learning strategies by teachers provides quality information that can be used to examine growth and progress. Richert (1990, p. 524), in a study on the effect of particular aids to reflection, found that teachers indicated that "the reflection that they felt was most significant was that which occurred during the time they were creating their portfolios. In selecting materials for inclusion they thought about what they did in their teaching and how well they did it, as well as what their materials were like, and how effective the materials were for their intended goals."

Vavrus and Collins (1991, p. 24) found that teachers engaging in the process of portfolio development appeared to become more reflective about their teaching practices "particularly in terms of critiquing the effectiveness of instructional methods in addressing individual student's needs." They found that when the contents of the portfolio were accompanied by reflective explanations, the complexity of teaching appeared to be captured. They also claimed that combinations of different types of documents, such as examples of student work, videotapes of teaching practice, lesson plans and teaching aids, helped to trace the development of teaching from planning through to practice and evaluation.

Lyons (1998b, p. 12) sees the portfolio as a "powerful reflective tool of professional and personal teacher growth and development." She also sees the significance of the portfolio as a "scaffolding for reflective teacher learning" (Lyons 1998a, p. 5). She illustrates how the preservice teacher "finds in conversation an opportunity to look at and reflect on her experiences, to go beyond the entries of her portfolio, to see and make connections about her teaching, her students' learning, and the growth and development as a reflective practitioner" (Lyons, 1998c, p. 104).

In using portfolio interviews to scaffold teacher reflection Lyons required teachers to construct the portfolio, to select entries, and present the portfolio evidence for discussion by interview. This was tape-recorded. After reading the transcripts, or listening to the tape, the teacher was involved in a second follow-up interview that required reflection on the portfolio process and an indication of the meaning given to the experiences of learning to teach. This process facilitated the organization of the reflection.

Lyons (1998c, p. 113) concludes that reflective thinking is more like "a weaving, a threading together of experience, of making connections. This construction of meaning is in part directly in the service of making conscious a teacher's knowledge of practice—a teaching philosophy, the sociopolitical or cultural contexts that influence the understanding of teaching or learning, and the understanding that the ethical may be a daily aspect of teaching. This takes place over time." A more adequate definition of teacher reflection needs to include these dimensions.

Snyder, Lippincott, and Bower (1998) indicate that reflection is made possible in the portfolio process because there is a requirement to document thought and practice as they coevolve. Students collect, select, and reflect upon concrete evidence of their thinking and experiences at various points throughout their professional preparation year. This is how they can make their own growth visible to themselves.

CONCLUSIONS

At this point it would be apparent to readers that a fundamental underlying tension in the use of portfolios, for assessment and learning purposes, exists in contexts that are examination driven and are highly regulated. Snyder, Lippincott, and Bower (1998) warn that in demonstrating competence on standards identified by external agencies the use of the portfolio for developmental purposes can be overlooked. Important processes vital to learning can be trivialized and mindless standardization can follow. Such tensions result in problems that have been identified and discussed by educators such as Broadfoot (1988) and Wolf (1998).

To illustrate, Wolf (1998) describes how the use of portfolios in the context of the General National Vocational Qualification (GNVQ) in England involved detailed specification of evidence requirements. In this context students resorted to "coping strategies," they became "hunters and gatherers of information" and their main objective was to obtain the qualification to the neglect of deep learning. Important process issues were trivialized and much creative copying took place.

It will also be apparent to readers that this chapter has included few examples for the use of portfolios for teacher education purposes from England. This is because the current context in England is antithetical to the development of more generative and open methods of assessment that could underpin good teaching. For example, there exist pressures for simple indicators of educational output, reductionist, and technical approaches to teacher development are advocated by the Teacher Training Agency (TTA) and the Chief Inspector of Schools does not believe that preservice teachers need to develop reflective practice in their initial years of teacher education. To illustrate, Whitty (1994, p. 14) states "the notion in the government's competences list that critical reflection on one's practice has to wait until one has been socialized into existing work practices is both intellectually unconvincing and belied by evidence of best practice within teacher education at the present time." Creative, more flexible forms of assessment that help support good teaching and that empower learners are needed and are being developed internationally. However, while the use of portfolios in teacher education is in its infancy, it is helpful to be reminded of the danger of promising more than can be delivered. Using portfolios for teacher development needs to be contextualized and the technical, practical and political constraints understood.

NOTES

1. Professionalism is used in this context to include theoretical knowledge, practical competence and commitment, see Pring (1998).

2. Teachers' knowledge is detailed, contextually bound and extensive and these qualities need to be acknowledged.

REFERENCES

Broadfoot, P. 1986. "Profiling and the Affective Curriculum." *Journal of Curriculum Studies* 19(1):25–34.

Broadfoot, P. 1988. "Records of Achievement and the Learning Society: A Tale of Two Discourses." *Assessment in Education: Principles, Policy and Practice* 5:447–477.

Crooks, T. J. 1988. "The Impact of Classroom Evaluation Practices on Pupils." *Review of Educational Research* 58:438–81.

Cuban, L. 1998. "A Post-Tenure Review Portfolio: A Collaborative Venture." In N. Lyons (Ed.), *With Portfolio in Hand: Validating the New Teacher Professionalism.* New York: Teachers College Press.

Davis, C. L., and Honan, E. 1998. "Reflections on the Use of Teams to Support the Portfolio Process." In N. Lyons (Ed.), *With Portfolio in Hand: Validating the New Teacher Professionalism.* New York: Teachers College Press.

Dewey, J. 1910. *How We Think.* Boston: Heath.

Education Department of Western Australia. 1997. *Application for Promotion to Level 3 Classroom Teacher (Stage 1) Preparing a Teaching Portfolio, Guidelines for Applicants.* Western Australia: Education Department of Western Australia.

Forster, M., and Masters, G. 1996. *Portfolios,* Victoria: Australian Council for Educational Research.

Francis, H. 1994. *Teachers Listening to Learners' Voices.* London: The British Psychological Society.

Gipps, C. 1994. *Beyond Testing: Towards a Theory of Educational Assessment.* London: Falmer Press.

Grant, G. E., and Huebner, T. A. 1998. "The Portfolio Question: The Power of Self-Directed Inquiry." In N. Lyons (Ed.), *With Portfolio in Hand: Validating the New Teacher Professionalism.* New York: Teachers College Press.

Klenowski, V. 1998. "The Use of Portfolios for Assessment in Teacher Education: A Perspective from Hong Kong." *Asia Pacific Journal of Education* 18:74–86.

Klenowski, V. 1999. "Enriching Preservice Teacher Knowledge of Assessment." *Curriculum Perspectives* 19:33–42.

Klenowski, V., Ledesma, J., Blachford, K., Bryant, S., and Timmins, A. 1997. *Portfolio Use in Initial Teacher Education: A Student Guide.* Hong Kong: Hong Kong Institute of Education.

Lyons, N. (Ed.). 1998a. *With Portfolio in Hand: Validating the New Teacher Professionalism.* New York: Teachers College Press.

Lyons, N. 1998b. "Portfolio Possibilities: Validating a New Teacher Professionalism." In N. Lyons (Ed.), *With Portfolio in Hand: Validating the New Teacher Professionalism*. New York: Teachers College Press.

Lyons, N. 1998c. "Constructing Narratives for Understanding: Using Portfolio Interviews to Scaffold Teacher Reflection." In N. Lyons (Ed.), *With Portfolio in Hand: Validating the New Teacher Professionalism*. New York: Teachers College Press.

Metcalf, L. 1963. "Research on Teaching the Social Studies." In N. Gage (Ed.), *Handbook of Research on Teaching*. Chicago: Rand McNally.

Munby, S., with Philips, P., and Collinson, R. 1989. *Assessing and Recording Achievement*. Oxford: Blackwell Education.

Owens, G., and Soule, L. 1971. "The Individual Profile." *Forum* 13 (Spring).

Pring, R. 1998. *"Universities and Teacher Education."* Paper Presented at the Annual Conference of the Standing Conference on Studies in Education, London.

Richert, A. E. 1990. "Teaching Teachers to Reflect: A Consideration of Programme Structure." *Journal of Curriculum Studies* 22(6):509–527.

Roe, E. 1987. *How to Compile a Teaching Portfolio: A FAUSA Guide*. Melbourne: FAUSA.

Sadler, R. 1989. "Formative Assessment and the Design of Instructional Systems." *Instructional Science* 18:119–44.

Schon, D. A. 1983. *The Reflective Practitioner: How Professionals Think in Action*. New York: Basic Books.

Schon, D. A. (Ed.). 1991. *The Reflective Turn: Case Studies in and on Educational Practice*. New York: Teachers College Press.

Shulman, L. 1992. *"Portfolios for Teacher Education: A Component of Reflective Teacher Education."* Paper presented at the annual meeting of the American Educational Research Association, San Francisco.

Shulman, L. 1998. "Teacher Portfolios: A Theoretical Activity." In N. Lyons (Ed.), *With Portfolio in Hand: Validating the New Teacher Professionalism*. New York: Teachers College Press.

Simons, H. 1987. *Getting to Know Schools in a Democracy: The Politics and Process of Evaluation*. London: Falmer Press.

Smith, K. 1994. *"Evaluation-Assessment-Testing What? How? Who?"* Paper presented at the 28th International IATEFL Conference, Brighton.

Snyder, J., Lippincott, A., and Bower, D. 1998. "Portfolios in Teacher Education: Technical or Transformational?" In N. Lyons (Ed.), *With Portfolio in Hand: Validating the New Teacher Professionalism*. New York: Teachers College Press.

Stake, R. 1979. "Counterpoint: Should Educational Evaluation be More Objective or More Subjective?" *Educational Evaluation and Policy Analysis* 1(1):46–47.

Stenhouse, L. 1975. *An Introduction to Curriculum Research and Development*. London: Heinemann.

Vavrus, L. G., and Collins, A. 1991. "Portfolio Documentation and Assessment Centre Exercises: A Marriage Made for Teacher Assessment." *Teacher Education Quarterly* 18:13–29.

Whitty, G. 1994. "Deprofessionalising Teaching? Recent Developments in Teacher Education in England." *Occasional Paper No 22*. Deakin, ACT: The Australian College of Education.

Wiggins, G. 1989. "A True Test: Toward More Authentic and Equitable Assessment." *Phi Delta Kappan* 70(9):703–713.

Wolf, K. 1991. "The School Teacher's Portfolio: Issues in Design, Implementation and Evaluation." *Phi Delta Kappan* 73(2):129–136.

Wolf, A. 1998. "Portfolio Assessment as National Policy: The National Council for Vocational Qualifications and its Quest for a Pedagogical Revolution." *Assessment in Education: Principles, Policy and Practice* 5:414–442.

Zeichner, K. M., and Liston, D. P. 1996. *Reflective Technology: An Introduction.* New Jersey: Lawrence Erlbaum Associates.

6

Examination Techniques: Issues of Validity and Effects on Pupils' Performance

Jannette Elwood

INTRODUCTION

The United Kingdom has a long established history of examination systems in secondary education (Broadfoot 1996; Sutherland 1996). From the formal qualifying examinations for the professions, which began in the early nineteenth century, to the present day qualifications—such as the General Certificate of Secondary Education (GCSE), General Certificate of Education (GCE) A level, and General National Vocational Qualification (GNVQ)—formal examinations have been used (and continue to be used) to certify students at the end of a particular course of study and to select students for entrance into institutes of higher education and the workplace. Broadfoot (1996) argues that as far as formal examination systems are concerned, the enduring purposes of such systems are "to promote and credit competence, which in turn serves to influence the content of education; to manage the inevitable competition for limited rewards; and to control the priorities and operation of . . . the education system as a whole" (p. 26). In recent times, however, certification and selection are only two of the purposes to which examination performance data is put. Examination data are also being used to evaluate the quality of teachers and schools and for other accountability measures. Using educational assessment outcomes for such a range of purposes invariably leads to conflict between the users of such assessment data and to a distortion of the assessment system itself.

As a consequence of their certification, selection, and evaluation purposes, the public examinations that dominate secondary education in the United Kingdom, operate as high stakes, high status examinations (Airasian 1988); the consequences associated with the examinations are important and the standard for passing the examination is high (Gipps 1994). This high stakes, high status position has tended to have powerful effects on the way that teachers construe their task and the type of impact that such examinations have on teaching, learning, and the curriculum. Madaus (1988) suggests "the more a quantitative social indicator is used for social decision making, the more likely it will be to distort and corrupt the social processes it is intended to monitor" (p. 89). Thus, the power of testing and assessment to influence what is taught, how it is taught, what is learned, and how it is learned is significant and can be both beneficial and detrimental to students and the curriculum alike.

Much of the research into examinations has tended to ignore their social role and impact. Research in testing and examinations has predominantly been concerned with the development and refinement of different approaches to educational measurement and critiques from a technical perspective of the assessment techniques used to assess students (Broadfoot 1996). Such a focus has tended to divert research related to examinations away from the effects of the assessment procedures used on the performance of pupils and the social impact on learning and teaching that assessment techniques generate.

However, in observing a shift in the models that underpin assessment and examination systems (Gipps 1994), and a wider debate about how best to assess students to fully understand their learning, educational assessors now consciously accept that assessment practices are not technical devices, which are socially neutral; they are social techniques that have social consequences (Connell, Johnston, and White 1992). How we choose to assess students and the choice of assessment techniques with which to do this are factors that are not value free nor value neutral. The choices of what to assess, how to assess it, and how it is evaluated all involve subjective judgments about the choice of language used, the contexts deemed appropriate, the selection of items for examination components, and ultimately the standards by which all pupils are assessed (Cresswell 1996; Hildebrand 1996).

The social consequences of assessment also impact on the validity of assessments. Messick (1993) argues that the social consequence of test use and the value implications of test interpretation are all integral aspects of validity—the consequential validity of tests. Including aspects of the social consequences of assessment in considerations of validity has been a major shift in how the concept is defined and used. Gipps (1994) suggests that the shift has been so great in thinking about the social consequences of test validation that is has "taken some time for practitioners to take on board [such] new frameworks" (p. 63). Gipps and Murphy (1994) further add that the social consequences of assessment give rise to not only consequential validity factors but also to issues of differential validity; the inference from a test score being biased when it is not equally valid for different subgroups of test takers.

The consequential and differential validity of examinations and testing, are as important, if not more so, for the interpretation of examination outcomes than traditional conceptualizations of validity (Wiliam 1995). Choosing what to assess and how to assess it ultimately impacts on student performance and how pupils achieve.

The assessment techniques chosen within examination syllabuses become linked to the validity of the examination, not only in whether they are the best ways in which to assess the subject content, but also because assessment techniques themselves have social consequences. These consequences manifest themselves in the form of differential performance between different subgroups and differential impact on how teachers perceive pupils' performances on various assessment techniques.

Many assessment techniques are seen as good assessment activities, they are valid, reliable, and provide a sound instrument from which to gauge students' attainments. However, in reality, the choice of essay papers, multiple-choice papers, coursework components, orals, and/or practical experiments impacts differentially on student performance and ultimately how teachers and students perceive their attainments. Thus, the choice of assessment technique in examination systems is not without consequence. It is the aim of this chapter to illustrate the impact of such choices on the validity of examinations in particular.

This chapter focuses on three specific assessment techniques commonly used in examinations and testing situations in the United Kingdom: coursework, tiered levels of entry, and setting examinations items in everyday contexts. The chapter illustrates how these techniques, all valid ways of assessing subject content and operationalizing large examination systems, operate in practice, and how they interact with the performance of particular subgroups, thus affecting the validity of the examinations in which they are used. The research used to illustrate the arguments in the chapter is predominantly from work that has looked at male and female subgroups, their differences in performance and the role of assessment techniques in creating these differences.

Most of the work in relation to differential performance of subgroups in examinations has been in the field of gender and assessment. Such a focus may well be a consequence of gender being easier to classify, quantify, and analyze (the gender of candidates being automatically recorded on entry for examinations) rather than differences between male and female subgroups being larger, or indeed of more interest, than those of either within same sex groupings or between different classifications of subgroups, such as ethnicity or social class. However, where such research has looked at the effect of assessment techniques or procedures on differences in performance among other subgroups of students I have included it where possible. The limited amount of research that one can draw upon in this area to illustrate the arguments under discussion is proof enough that more research is needed.

COURSEWORK

With the introduction, in 1988, of the GCSE in England, Wales, and Northern Ireland, we have acquired more evidence of the effect of changes in teaching and assessing on the relative performance of pupils. Central to this is the role that coursework has played since it became a common component in mainstream examinations. The introduction of coursework into the GCSE came about mainly through a shift in the model underpinning assessment and examinations

(Gipps 1994; Wood 1990), but also through an acceptance and promotion of a broader view of achievement that requires evaluation of pupils' performance across a range of assessment models (Murphy and Elwood 1998). However, coursework components in GCSE have had a chequered history (Tattersall 1994). Even among those who design and develop examinations there has not always been an agreed perception of what constitutes coursework (Kingdon and Stobart 1988; Macintosh 1986). The "official" view of what constitutes coursework is that offered by the Schools Curriculum and Assessment Authority (SCAA 1995):

Coursework consists of in-course tasks set and undertaken according to conditions pre-scribed by an awarding body. Coursework activities are integral to, rather than incidental to, the course of study. Coursework is normally marked by a candidate's own teacher according to criteria provided and exemplified by the awarding body, taking national requirements into account. It is moderated by the awarding body. (SCAA 1995, p. 13)

In the 1994 examination session, the GCSE was used to test the end of Key Stage 4 (KS4) of the national curriculum in England and Wales. To fit this role some major changes were made to the GCSE in relation to coursework: a maximum 20% coursework in most syllabuses; a return to the option of 100% examination syllabuses in mathematics; and a reduction from 100% to 40% coursework in English (with 20% of this 40% being associated with the oral component). This diminution of the proportion of coursework in GCSE syllabuses gave out a firm message of how such examination components were perceived by the govern-ment of the time. Macintosh (1986) also suggests that coursework, due to long standing attitudes, has fallen foul of the "British obsession for preferring to do worse on those examinations which carry greater prestige rather than to do bet-ter on those that are more useful" (p. 22).

Coursework, however, has generally been welcomed as an effective motivator of pupils that has enhanced overall GCSE performance (HMI 1988). Before 1994, the possibility of following 100% coursework syllabuses in English proved very attractive to teachers, with two-thirds of GCSE English entries being for such syllabuses (Stobart, White, Elwood, Hayden, and Mason 1992b). Even in mathematics, a subject that delayed the introduction of compulsory coursework until 1991, the largest entry group continues to be in those syllabuses with at least 20% coursework (Goulding 1995).

There is also a widespread perception in the United Kingdom that coursework differentially benefits various subgroups (e.g., girls, middle-class pupils) more than others. Stobart, Elwood, and Quinlan (1992a) showed some empirical sup-port for this in relation to gender illustrating a direct relationship between the improvement in girls' examination grades between 1985 and 1988 and the type and weighting of coursework in GCSE syllabuses (Quinlan 1990). However, fur-ther investigations suggested that such a relationship was an oversimplification. In subjects with substantial written coursework (e.g., English, history), gender-related differences in performance in the GCSE were greater than in previous examination systems. However, it was noted that in certain subjects (e.g., French), which had no compulsory coursework, girls also performed better than boys. Such patterns of performance were suggested to be the result of the radical change in the nature and style of the tasks between different examination systems and that girls had made the transition to these types of tasks more successfully than boys (Stobart et al. 1992a).

Cresswell (1990) investigated center effects in the GCSE and how they interacted with gender effects in accounting for differences in performance. He analyzed entry and result patterns in English, mathematics, and integrated science from mixed-sex schools. His analyses showed that there was considerable variation between the coursework component and the written examinations, particularly in maths. When the average gender effects were looked at after controlling for center effects, a clear pattern emerged that showed that girls' average coursework marks were higher than boys' in every case and also girls' coursework marks were more "bunched" (in terms of the variance) than those of the boys.

These differences in the mark distributions between coursework and written examinations were suggested to come about for two reasons (Cresswell 1990). First, examiners are less likely to use the full mark range when marking coursework than when marking examination papers thus, restricting the range of marks awarded on the coursework component and the discrimination between candidates.[1] This smaller range (or spread) of marks then effects the contribution that coursework components make to the overall grades. Second, there is a large variation in the type of work set to candidates by centers under the heading of "coursework" with a sizeable minority of centers setting work that does not allow candidates to fully demonstrate their attainment against all the specified assessment objectives.

Stobart et al. (1992b) investigated the effect of coursework on differential performance of boys and girls in examinations. Evidence from the study suggested that even when the proportion of coursework within the syllabus was substantial (e.g., 50%), it played only a minimal role in explaining patterns of gender-related performance. Through an analysis of the "achieved weighting" of components (Adams and Murphy 1982), Stobart et al. showed that coursework does not contribute disproportionately to the final grade. This was illustrated through coursework marks being more bunched than those on the examination papers. In such a situation it is the examination papers, on which pupils' performance differs considerably, that is likely to play the main role in determining pupils' rank order and hence contribute most to the overall grade distribution.

Furthermore, Stobart et al. (1992b) discovered that coursework marks were more influential on the grade distributions of boys than on those of girls. For boys, coursework offered slightly more discrimination than the examination component. For girls, both the coursework and examination component made much the same contribution to the final grade. Thus, an interesting paradox arises in that coursework begins to play a more significant role for boys at the subject level, than for girls.

"WEIGHTS" OF EXAMINATION COMPONENTS

The Stobart et al. (1992b) study discussed above relied on the concepts of "intended" and "achieved" weights of examination components. The *intended* weights are the weightings that have been built into components through the allocation of specified numbers of marks whereas the *achieved* weights are the extent to which the component actually influences the final result in practice (Adams and Murphy 1982; Cresswell 1987). In order to arrive at the aggregated total on which examination grade boundaries are fixed, marks from the various examination components are added together according to the specified "weighting" of each component, that is, ". . . the percentage of marks allocated to it as an indication of the relative importance in the overall framework of knowledge and skills being assessed" (Hayden, Richards, and Thompson 1992, p. 3).

Hayden (1991) and Hayden et al. (1992) review the research that has investigated the influence of different examination components on the final rank order of candidates. Hayden et al. (1992) suggest that the extent of the influence of one component on an aggregated total is determined ". . . by the spread of marks of that component with respect to others contributing to the same total, as well as the intercorrelation between various component distributions" (Hayden et al. 1992, p. 3). Hayden (1991) suggests that "weightings apparently built into the components of an examination by the allocation to them of specified numbers of marks, will not necessarily be reflected in the extent to which each component affects the overall result" (Hayden 1991, p. 126).

One of the concerns of this chapter is that the implication of components not operating as intended in the actual examination and not reflecting their intended weight, is that the validity of the examination is reduced; that is, the intended (and published) weightings of the various components do not operate as specified in the syllabuses. Thus, the social or consequential impact of examination components operating differently than intended is that results from examination components become misleading for teachers and students who are guided by the intended weightings of components in their preparations for examinations. A further concern is that not only will the validity of examinations be affected by components operating differently between intention and practice, but that this effect is different for different subgroups of candidates: that is, the components are differentially valid for different subgroups. The various components of the examination may differentially influence the performance of different subgroups of pupils and thus affect their final rank order. It is in this respect that different components contribute to differential performance and the consequential validity of this is negative backwash for different groups of students and their teachers in perceptions of performance and in actual achievements.

CONSEQUENTIAL AND DIFFERENTIAL VALIDITY OF EXAMINATION COMPONENTS: AN EXAMPLE

Elwood (1999) analyzed the comparison between intended and achieved weights of the 1997 GCSE examination components in English, mathematics, and science. All three subjects have different proportions of coursework—English has 40% (20% of which is for speaking and listening), maths has 20%, and science 25% (see Table 6.1) The three subjects also have tiered levels of entry each with restricted grade ranges—English has two tiers of entry (foundation and higher) and maths and science have three (foundation, intermediate, and higher).

The study focused on investigating the consequential and differential validity of different examination components, especially in relation to gender differences in performance and in the overall rank order of candidates. The achieved weight for each paper (by gender) was calculated (see Table 6.1). The differences between the intended and achieved weights of the examination components were also calculated. The data presented in Tables 6.1 and 6.2 are grouped into similar components as a means of establishing the extent to which any trends emerge across the three subjects.

Table 6.1
Intended and Achieved Weights for Coursework Components
for Males and Females

Subject	Paper	IW	AWm	AWf	AWm–IW	AWf–IW	p	m-f	p
English									
F Tier	P1A	20	11.03	11.48	–8.97	–8.52	**	–0.45	
	P1B	20	11.60	11.70	–8.40	–8.30	**	–0.10	
H Tier	P1A	20	12.78	13.34	–7.22	–6.66	**	–0.56	**
	P1B	20	14.95	15.24	–5.05	–4.76	**	–0.29	**
Maths A									
F Tier	P3	20	17.80	16.88	–2.20	–3.12	**	0.92	**
1 Tier	P3	20	17.30	16.18	–2.70	–3.82	**	1.12	**
H Tier	P3	20	18.29	16.22	–1.71	–3.78	**	2.07	**

Table 6.1 (continued)

Science									
Comb.									
F Tier	P7	25	18.99	19.81	−6.01	−5.19	**	−0.82	**
I Tier	P7	25	19.48	16.05	−5.52	−8.95	**	3.43	**
H Tier	P7	25	15.38	12.80	−9.62	−12.20	**	2.58	**

Notes: IW = intended weight; AW = achieved weight; m = male; f = female

** −p < = 0.01; * −p < = 0.05

$$W = \frac{SD(paper) * r \text{ (paper score and total score)}}{SD \text{ (total score)}}$$

W = weight of paper; SD = standard deviation; r = part-with-whole correlation (product moment)

ACHIEVED WEIGHTS ANALYSIS: COURSEWORK

Applying an achieved weights analysis by gender to the 1997 GCSE data highlighted some interesting results, not least that the achieved weights of components (especially coursework) actually operate differently in practice and for the male and female subgroups identified in the data. In most cases this difference is statistically significant (see Table 6.1).

The analysis of the intended versus the achieved weights of the coursework components in the three subjects shows that in almost every case, the achieved weight of the coursework component is lower than intended for males and for females (Table 6.1). This pattern is to be expected given what we know about coursework marks awarded by teachers tending to be more bunched toward the top end of the mark scale compared to the distribution of marks generated in a written examination (Cresswell 1990; Hayden et al. 1992). The fact that coursework marks are more bunched than examination marks causes, through the resultant low standard deviation, a reduced influence on the overall distributions with respect to that intended.

In relation to the coursework component having a less influential effect on the overall distribution of candidates than intended, it is possible to suggest from the figures in Table 6.1, that this component has less influence on the final grades awarded for females than for males. However, this suggestion is not straightforward for all three subjects at all tiers of entry. Coursework seems to have less influence for females in maths and modular science and in the intermediate and higher tiers of combined science, with the achieved weights in coursework for females in these particular cases being less than the achieved weights in coursework for their male counterparts. In English and the foundation tier of combined science this pattern is reversed. For example, the achieved weights of coursework for males and females across the two tiers in English show little difference between them.

These smaller differences in achieved weights between males and females in English may well reflect the nature of the coursework tasks and male and female performance on those tasks. Since 1994, a speaking and listening element has been included in the main coursework activity. Boys have been shown to outperform girls on speaking and listening activities (White 1996). The presence of a speaking and listening element in GCSE English coursework may well have balanced performance outcomes between boys and girls on this component compared to previous performance data (Stobart et al. 1992b). Indeed, there were relatively smaller differences between male and female mean marks (21.4/40 and 22.5/40 respectively) on this component than has been the case in previous studies (Stobart et al. 1992b). English has also generally promoted and sustained a culture of coursework in its assessment. Candidates know that it is an integral part of the work required to achieve success in this subject. Previous research has suggested that the large amounts of extended writing involved in coursework in English, prior to 1994, might have been putting boys at a disadvantage (Elwood 1995). The reduction in the amount of coursework and a change in the nature of the coursework requirements may be responsible for the similar achieved weights in this component for boys and girls.

In maths and science, however, where the culture of inclusion of coursework and the nature of coursework tasks are quite different, coursework tends to have less of an influence for girls than for boys. Coursework tasks in these subjects are often set by the examination board. Coursework components themselves have often been seen by teachers in these subjects as an "add-on" and not a fully integral part of the subject assessment (Nickson and Prestage 1994). Indeed, since 1994, a return to 100% examination syllabuses in maths has been very popular (SEG 1996). Table 6.1 shows that the performance of boys on coursework tasks in maths and science subjects is slightly more variable than that of girls and, therefore, has a greater influence on their overall grade distribution and hence their final grades.

ACHIEVED WEIGHTS ANALYSIS: EXAMINATION PAPERS

The analysis of the intended versus the achieved weights of examination components in the three subjects showed that in the majority of cases the examination papers have a higher achieved weight than intended (Table 6.2).

In relation to the gender differences in achieved weights illustrated in Table 6.2, 14 out of the 19 papers listed show higher achieved weights on the examination papers for females than those for males. This suggests that the examination papers play a more important role for girls than for boys in determining their final rank order; the performance of girls on the examination papers is slightly more variable than that of boys. It is interesting to note, however, that boys have higher achieved weights than girls on the second paper (P3: writing) in English that suggests that this paper has a greater influence on boys' final rank order. The better performance of females in writing tasks and papers in English is well documented (Gorman, White, Brooks, and English 1991; Stobart et al. 1992b; White 1996). In maths it is the first

Table 6.2
Intended and Achieved Weights for Examination Paper Components
for Males and Females

Subject	Tier	Paper	IW	AWm	AWf	AWm– IW	AWf– IW	p	m-f	p
English	F	P2	30	36.76	36.83	6.76	6.83	**	–0.07	
	F	P3	30	40.46	39.81	10.46	9.81	**	0.65	
	H	P2	30	34.45	34.66	4.45	4.66	**	–0.21	**
	H	P3	30	37.80	36.78	7.80	6.78	**	1.02	**
	F	P1	40	41.25	42.91	1.25	2.91	**	–1.66	**
	F	P2	40	40.94	40.16	0.94	0.16	**	0.78	**
Maths A	I	P1	40	43.73	44.51	3.73	4.51	**	–0.78	**
	I	P2	40	38.75	39.51	–1.25	–0.49	**	–0.76	**
	H	P1	40	40.96	41.64	0.96	1.64	**	–0.68	**
	H	P2	40	40.66	41.76	0.66	1.76	**	–1.10	**
	F	P1	25	28.64	28.60	3.64	3.60	**	0.04	**
	F	P2	25	25.59	26.32	0.59	1.32	**	–0.73	**
	F	P3	25	26.84	25.43	1.84	0.43	**	1.41	**
Science	I	P4	25	25.15	26.59	0.15	1.59	**	–1.44	**
Comb.	I	P5	25	28.52	30.07	3.52	5.07	**	–1.55	**
	I	P6	25	27.09	27.29	2.09	2.29	**	–0.20	**
	H	P8	25	23.34	24.02	–1.66	–0.98	**	–0.68	**
	H	P9	25	31.00	32.84	6.00	7.84	**	–1.84	**
	H	P10	25	29.81	30.13	4.81	5.13	**	–0.32	**

Notes: IW = intended weight; AW = achieved weight; F = foundation; I = intermediate; H = higher; m = male; f = female
** –p < = 0.01; * –p < = 0.05

$$W = \frac{SD\ (paper) * r\ (paper\ score\ and\ total\ score)}{SD\ (total\ score)}$$

W = weight of paper; SD = standard deviation; r = part-with-whole correlation (product moment)

papers in the foundation and intermediate tiers that have the greatest influence and more so for girls than for boys. The pattern is less consistent at the higher tier. In combined science, the biology paper (P1) in the foundation tier had the greatest influence and slightly more so for males than for females. In the intermediate and higher tiers it is the chemistry papers (P5 and P9 respectively) which have more influence and more so for girls than for boys.

CONSEQUENTIAL AND DIFFERENTIAL VALIDITY
ISSUES: DISCUSSION

A statistical test (after Delap 1994)[2] was applied to the differences between the achieved and intended weights presented in Tables 6.1 and 6.2. If the differences between the intended and achieved weights are statistically significant, then the examinations are failing to meet their published aims. This has implications for the validity of these examinations, in particular their consequential validity (Messick 1993). Thus, in Tables 6.1 and 6.2, the differences between the intended and achieved weights for all papers across all three subjects were statistically significant at the 0.01% level.

These statistical significant differences between intended and achieved weights suggest that the validity of these GCSE examinations, in relation to the extent to which they meet their published aims, is compromised. The fact that the achieved weights of the examination and coursework components rarely perform as intended must reduce the validity of these examinations. The intended (and published) weights do not operate as specified in the syllabus and thus impact on the consequential validity (Messick 1993) of these examinations. Teachers are guided by the intended weightings of examination components in preparing students for the examination. The difference between intended and achieved weights in reality may well be at odds with this preparation. At present, information regarding intended and achieved weights is not routinely fed back to teachers. A better understanding of how examinations' components operate in practice would be beneficial to teachers and students in their preparations for these examinations. It would also go some way to making the relationship between teaching, assessing, and examining more explicit.

Issues of differential validity (Gipps and Murphy 1994) also come into play if there are statistical differences between the achieved weights of different subgroups taking the examinations. Further investigations showed that there was a statistically significant difference between the achieved weights of males and females in maths and the two science syllabuses. The achieved weights for males and females in foundation tier English were not statistically significantly different but were significantly different at the higher tier (Elwood 1999). Thus, the achieved weights of examination components operate differently for girls and for boys. These findings are important, given the differential attention paid to coursework by females, and teachers' perceptions of the role that coursework plays in the final success of GCSE candidates (Elwood 1995). These findings conflict with teachers' general perceptions that coursework favors females disproportionately in the examination process. Although females are seen to benefit from coursework in curriculum terms (Elwood 1995), it is not the sole factor that explains their better overall performance in examinations in the United Kingdom (Murphy and Elwood 1998).

The example used above has focused on the subgroups of male and female pupils. The work discussed here would suggest that similar differential validity issues in relation to assessment components are of paramount concern for other pupil subgroups such as ethnic group and/or social class groupings. Further comparable research exploring the important question of differential validity issues among social class groups given the varying support offered to students in completing coursework activities outside of school would prove invaluable.

Applying the achieved weights analysis to the GCSE examinations has brought to the fore a number of interesting findings, not least that examination components do not operate in reality as intended by those who design them and that the achieved weightings of components, the coursework component in particular, operate differently for different subgroups of pupils. These shifts in validity of examination components due to the differences in achieved and intended weights are cause for concern. Previous studies have shown that teachers have a widespread perception that project work favors various pupil groups more than others (Elwood and Comber 1996; Stobart et al. 1992b). There appears to be some dissonance between the contribution that coursework makes to the overall rank order of these groups of students and its intended contribution as perceived by examiners, teachers, and students. This has major implications for the consequential validity of these examinations; the actual influence of the various examination components being quite different to their perceived influence as understood by examiners, teachers, and students. The social consequences of examination components operating differently in reality from that intended are backwash effects into the curriculum experienced by students and into their teachers' perceptions of students' potential successes.

TIERED LEVELS OF ENTRY IN EXAMINATIONS

Another common assessment technique used in examinations and tests in the United Kingdom, and which can have differential impact on the validity of examinations, is tiered levels of entry. These tiered levels of entry have been popular within the GCSE since its inception and have been adopted widely in national curriculum assessment programs in England, Wales, and Northern Ireland. Examination syllabuses are generally structured into two or three different levels, or tiers, of entry; each tier having a restricted set of grades. The two-tier model has a foundation tier (grades C–G) and a higher tier (grades A*–D). The three-tier model has a foundation tier (grades D–G), an intermediate tier (grades B–E), and a higher tier (grades A*–C). Candidates are only permitted to enter for one tier at any one sitting and any candidate not achieving the lowest restricted grades on any tier is unclassified.

Research has shown that choosing the appropriate tier of entry for pupils has proven to be problematic (Gillborn and Youdell 1998; IGRC 1992). Tiers of entry provide teachers with difficult entry decisions with regard to choosing the appropriate tier of entry that ensures a fair representation of pupils' achievements. Proponents of tiered entry schemes suggest that tiering actually increases the reliability of the assessment and has little, or no, adverse impact on validity

(Wiliam 1995). Moreover, it is a more efficient use of the assessment time as pupils are only asked those questions that are likely to tell us something useful about what pupils know and understand. However, entry decisions are based on teachers' knowledge of the pupil and it is the judgment of the teacher as well as the performance of the student that determines the range of grades available to the pupil (Wiliam, 1995).

Research (Gillborn and Youdell, 1998; Stobart et al. 1992b) has indicated that there are several aspects of tiered entry schemes in examinations that impact negatively on pupils' performance, teachers' perceptions of pupils' abilities and hence pupils' overall achievement. The research cited above has focused on tiered entry systems in examinations and their interactions with teachers' perceptions of the performance of boys and girls (Stobart et al. 1992b) and of different ethnic groups (Gillborn and Youdell 1998). The next two sections focus on these studies in some detail.

TIERED ENTRY SCHEMES AND GENDER

Stobart et al. (1992b) argued that there are several aspects of tiered entry schemes that influence differential performance between males and females. For example, in GCSE mathematics, a subject that employs the three-tier model, more boys than girls are entered for the foundation tier with its maximum grade D. Disaffection with GCSE mathematics seems to be increased by the restricted grade range at this lower tier and has been found to be greater among boys than girls. In reviewing teachers' comments from surveys and case study interviews, Stobart et al. (1992b) maintain that teachers considered boys who were placed in the lower tier to be less motivated, and as a consequence more disruptive, than girls in the same tier: "low ability girls are generally better motivated than low ability boys;" "boys tend to feel that the foundation (lower) tier is not worth it. Girls are often more content to take a lower tier" (Stobart et al. 1992b, p. 28). This greater disaffection shown by lower attaining boys influenced teachers' decisions about whether to enter them for the examination at all.

In addition more girls are entered for the intermediate tier in GCSE mathematics with its maximum grade B. Stobart et al. (1992b) suggest that the larger female entry in the intermediate tier represents an underestimation of girls' mathematical abilities by teachers who perceive girls to be less confident and more anxious of failure in maths than boys and more adversely affected by final examinations: "weaker girls feel more secure in the middle tier"; "there is a tendency (of girls) to lower expectation of self" (Stobart et al. 1992b, p. 30).

Consequently, teachers tend to place girls in the intermediate tier to protect them from such anxiety. The intermediate tier offers the key grade C while avoiding the risk of being unclassified if performance drops below this grade on the higher tier. Research has shown that schools often demand the attainment of a grade C from the *higher tier* before taking A-level mathematics; in fact grades B and A (even A*) are often the criteria (Elwood and Comber 1996).

The disproportionate number of girls who are entered for the intermediate tier are marginalized from taking their mathematics any further.

Finally, more boys than girls are entered for the higher tier and more boys obtain the top grades of A* and A (Elwood and Comber 1996). Entry for the higher tier usually provides adequate motivation for pupils. Teachers referred to pupils as competitive, expectant of good grades and hard working. However, girls' lack of confidence as opposed to boys' abundance of confidence in this tier still seems to be a factor affecting performance: "many girls do not see themselves as having the ability to get an A; at higher tier boys are more arrogant, girls more worried" (Stobart et al. 1992b, p. 30).

Boaler (1997) has shown that the underachievement of "bright" girls within the higher tier may be due to the context of the environment in top set mathematics classes. Common features of top set maths classes (which are synonymous with higher tier entry) are speed, pressure, competition and reward is given for getting answers correct rather than for the acquisition of understanding. Boaler suggests that this may cause particular conflicts for girls in the higher tier who may become more anxious in response to these environments.

TIERED ENTRY SCHEMES AND "RACE"

The research by Gillborn and Youdell (1998) suggests that tiering introduces additional barriers to equality of opportunity for pupils of differing ethnic origins, especially Black pupils. From their ethnographic study of two inner-London schools which investigated the interaction of ethnic origin and selection in GCSE English and mathematics, Gillborn and Youdell argue that the grade "ceilings" and "floors" (restricted grade ranges) in tiered entry schemes cause considerable concern for both teachers and pupils. The concern is a balance between wanting to do as well as possible but not wanting to face being unclassified if performance drops below a certain level on the day.

Gillborn and Youdell (1998) suggest that, as with gender, tiering interacts significantly with "race" in a negative way that denies equality of opportunity for Black pupils. In their study, more Black pupils were more likely to be entered for the foundation tier and less likely to be entered for the higher tier. Moreover, again paralleling the gender research, the most marked inequalities of opportunity were in those subjects with three tiers of entry with the maximum grade D in the foundation tier (in 1997 this was maths and science). Gillborn and Youdell argue that, in effect, the operation of tiered levels of entry at GCSE, means that for Black pupils, "higher grade (A*–C) passes have been rendered impossible before they [Black pupils] answer a single question on their examination papers" (p. 3).

Teachers' perspectives on tiered entry systems tended to influence them to be cautious when choosing the appropriate tier for each pupil. Teachers tended to operate more from an "exclusive view of tiers" (p. 5) that coincided with targeted grade ranges within the formal grade limits.[3] The danger of falling off the floor of the top tier is so great that teachers tend to "play safe" and thus view the higher tier in a more exclusive way. Thus, while teachers are trying to do their best for their students, their stereotypical perceptions of how students from various sub-groups perform in final examinations is interacting with the restricted practices of tiering. This inevitably leads to the underestimation of pupils abilities and hence their final achievements.

Pupils own perspectives on, and awareness of, tiering arrangements reflected their positions in these tiers. Gillborn and Youdell (1998) found that pupils in the higher tiers were most likely to display an understanding of the tiering system as a whole and to also indicate an active role in the decisions made about their tier of entry. Foundation tier pupils however, were only more likely to understand the implications of their own tiering allocation that in itself often lead to expressions of disaffection and disillusionment, more particularly among Black students. Gillborn and Youdell go on to argue that tiering has produced a situation that many pupils find "worrying often confusing and sometimes devastating" (p. 13).

Tiered entry systems continue to be used across a wide range of subjects in the secondary phase and in national tests for 11 and 14 year olds. However, there have been no investigations to date of the impact of tiered levels of entry on the expectations and achievements of students in examinations other than in the core subjects at GCSE. The research evidence cited above would suggest that the impact of differentiated entry schemes in other subjects and phases of assessing would not be wholly positive. Although supported as a valid way of assessing students that enables them to show what they know, rather than what they do not know, tiered entry tends to provide a lower status route in GCSE examinations into which many students of various subgroups—through stereotypical percep-tions of their teachers of their abilities and attainments—are unfortunately assigned, thus affecting significantly the consequential and differential validity of these tiered examination systems.

USE OF CONTEXT IN EXAMINATION ITEMS

A third common assessment technique used in assessment and examining, and with implications for the consequential and differential validity of examination components, is the use of everyday contexts in examination items. The situating of examination questions or items in "real life" scenarios can effect how pupils respond to, and perform on, examination items and thus how they perform in the actual examination. Research has shown that context affects performance by obscuring the item in dense, often irrelevant information that some pupils believe to be relevant to obtaining the answer. To enable students to access their knowl-edge and apply it they first have to see the link between what they know and its relevance to the question in hand (Murphy 1995). The use of context also intro-duces certain assumptions about similar cultural and social experiences for all groups that therefore enables all groups to understand the particular contexts used (Boaler 1994; Cooper 1996; Murphy 1995). The context then becomes inseparable from the item and integral to it.

The initial use of context in tasks and examination items focused on low attainers. However, with the introduction of the GCSE, a more widespread use of contextualization of questions in examination papers occurred. The drive to use "real life" situations, especially in the subject of mathematics, was to make the subject more relevant to students and increasingly seen as the solution to the problem of transfer, "enabling students to reflect upon the demand of real life problems and become prepared for the mathematical requirements they would face in their everyday lives" (Boaler 1994, p. 552).

Boaler (1994) outlines the reasons given for learning in context which, she describes, as falling into three broad categories. First, there is the notion that contexts provide a concrete familiar experience that makes learning more accessible for students (Donaldson 1984); second, context is perceived to motivate pupils with the use of scenarios that add life to the curriculum; and third, that the use of everyday contexts will enable transfer of learning from the classroom to pupils' outside world. Research has shown, however, that students are still not quite able to transfer their learning in school to "real world" situations as they still face problems in answering questions that are of the same demand and content but are either "abstract" or set in context (Kerslake 1986; Lave 1988, Foxman et al. 1991). Boaler (1994) asserts that students do not therefore, perceive the links between what is learned at school and problems in the "real world" just because their school textbooks present the subject content in "real life" contexts.

One of the main problems with setting examination items in context is that often the context is "made up" or not real; the situation is believable but the pupil has to suspend their common sense so as to answer the question. Wiliam (1992), in discussing the contexts used in mathematics tasks, refers to these contexts as "mathsland," a fantasy world in which common sense needs to be suspended for the pupil to get the right answer. Pupils are given a task set in a context that they then are expected to ignore to answer the question correctly. Cooper (1996) acknowledges that as a result, children often have to "negotiat[e] the boundary between esoteric [subject] knowledge and their everyday knowledge" (p. 2). He also suggests that the national curriculum paper and pencil tests, especially in mathematics, seem likely to disadvantage pupils who take seriously the injunction to relate mathematics to the "real world" (Cooper 1992). Furthermore, such tests, via the marking scheme, seem to make the "achievement of higher levels of national curriculum attainment dependent on a child's capacity and/or willingness to avoid drawing on, or referring to, everyday knowledge when responding to items" (Cooper 1996, p. 4).

Boaler (1994), Cooper (1996), and Murphy (1995) all draw attention to the fact that contexts do not offer a unique meaning for every student and that students will interpret the situations they are presented with in different ways. These interpretations will be influenced by the pupil's gender, social class, and race. This will invariably lead to different approaches in attempting the tasks and examination items, and hence results based on what the pupil believes to be relevant to the task in hand. Depending on the domain, and what is valued as achievement in this domain, pupils' socialized perceptions of what is relevant will appear either successful or unsuccessful (Murphy 1995).

If we look at pupils' responses to the contexts used in examination items we can see that assumptions about transfer and learning in context (Lave 1988) are somewhat simplistic and ignore the sociocultural influences on performance on these items. For example, in using contextual features to provide motivation, or give purpose to the assessor's task, Murphy (1995) has shown that the alternative strategies employed by some students who have engaged enthusiastically with the task can be viewed as "off-task" and irrelevant:

An APU [science] task to find out the thermal conductivity of blanket and plastic was set in the context of being stranded up a mountainside in cold, windy weather. The context was irrelevant to the understanding of the task. Many girls gave values to the contextual issues… their task involved looking at the thermal conductivity in dry and wet conditions and windy and calm conditions. This was not the task the assessor had set—indeed it was a much more difficult one. Girls' observed behaviors, such as dipping the test materials in water to judge thermal conductivity in the rain or blowing cold air through the materials to determine porosity, were considered by the teacher-assessor to be off task, This was in spite of considerable evidence of positive scientific achievement in girls' alternative strategies. (Murphy 1995, p. 265)

Similar interactions that hinder examination performance also come about for various subgroups of students when the context of the item is continually couched in the culture of one dominant group. Pupils who do not belong to the dominant culture or do not relate to the particular culture being prioritized in the context in the item will be at a disadvantage. For example, Cooper (1996) has argued that many tests and summative assessment items used in common standardized tests in schools rely on cultural understandings and experiences that inhibit working class and ethnic minority children from their true potential. The lack of understanding of the culture or social situation used in the contexts in examination items is often mistaken by teachers and examiners as lack of ability.

Cooper (1996) further argues that one of the problems of the pedagogic approach of embedding examination items in contexts is that it contributes to differential validity (Gipps and Murphy 1994) and hence introduces unfairness into tests. The combination of relatively open-ended items with "real" contexts produces a particular set of threats to valid assessment, especially if no account is to be taken of them in the assessor's view of the task and the marking of responses (Murphy 1995). These threats have been shown to operate differently for different subgroups (Cooper 1994; Murphy 1995). Cooper suggests that any attempt to address these problems of using contexts in examination items must address how "cultural knowledge mediate[s] individuals' responses to assessment in ways which alter the construct being assessed" (Gipps and Murphy 1994, p. 14).

The concerns addressed by Cooper (1996) and Murphy (1995) require difficult decisions to be made about the use of items in examinations that might, on the one hand, operate to "improve" pedagogy but, on the other, might lead to less fair and hence less valid assessment outcomes.

CONCLUSION

The selection of particular assessment and examining techniques is important in relation to providing good reliable and valid assessments. However, the selection of such techniques gives out clear messages to teachers and pupils about certain techniques being more valued than others and how achievement is ultimately defined. Yet the way in which these techniques actually operate in practice is less well known or understood. The social consequences of the choice of assessment technique must play an integral part in any evaluation of whether an assessment technique is valid and reliable.

With the shift in models that underpin the assessment and examining of students, and how we ultimately define achievement, there has emerged a parallel debate that acknowledges that examining, assessing, and indeed the examination standards by which final results are determined, are social constructs (Cresswell 1996). The measurement of pupils' performance is not an exact science, but a process that is underpinned by subjective judgments and value-laden choices, albeit made with fairness and validity in mind. What this chapter has highlighted is that those choices that are made about which assessment techniques to be used in examination components, how these techniques are evaluated, and the examination structures used in order to enhance validity, can impact negatively on different subgroups of pupils and their teachers, hence reducing the validity of the assessment for those groups of pupils.

There would seem to be a delicate balance to be had between the choice of assessment technique in looking for a better way of examining children and the effect that this choice will have on various groups of pupils' performance. It is obvious that new conceptions of validity, such as consequential and differential validity, must take precedence in guiding the process of examination development. Considerations of the consequential and differential validity of the assessment techniques chosen need to be part of the evaluation processes used in understanding the social impact of the examination systems we promote.

NOTES

1. Discrimination is used here in its technical form: "the capacity of a test to distinguish among different candidates of different levels of performance" (Good and Cresswell 1988).

2. Delap (1994) devised a statistical difference test that can be applied to the difference between the intended and achieved weights. Delap's test is based on the distribution of the achieved weights approximating to a chi-squared distribution. This enables a more

substantive interpretation to be placed on the difference between achieved and intended weights than was previously possible. See Elwood (1999) for more extensive discussion.

3. For example, even though formal grade limits on the higher tier range from A* to C, the targeted grades are A and B, that is, content covered in the papers in this tier is targeted at students of grade A and B ability.

REFERENCES

Adams, R. M., and Murphy, R. J. L. 1982. "The Achieved Weights of Examination Components." *Educational Studies* 8(1):15–22.

Airasian, P. 1988. "Measurement Driven Instruction: A Closer Look." *Educational Measurement: Issues and Practice* Winter:6–11.

Boaler, J. 1994. "When Do Girls Prefer Football to Fashion? An Analysis of Female Underachievement in Relation to 'Realistic' Mathematics Contexts." *British Educational Research Journal* 20(5): 551–564.

Boaler, J. 1997. *Experiencing School Mathematics: Teaching Styles, Sex and Setting.* Buckingham: Open University Press.

Broadfoot, P. 1996. *Education, Assessment and Society.* Buckingham: Open University Press.

Connell, R. W., Johnston, K., and White, V. 1992. *Measuring Up.* Canberra: Australian Curriculum Studies Association.

Cooper, B. 1992. "Testing National Curriculum Mathematics: Some Critical Comments on the Treatment of 'Real' Contexts for Mathematics." *The Curriculum Journal* 3(3):231–243.

Cooper, B. 1996. *Using Data from Clinical Interviews to Explore Students' Understanding of Mathematics Test Items: Relating Bernstein and Bourdieu or Culture to Questions of Fairness in Testing.* Paper presented at the American Educational Research Association Conference, New York, April.

Cresswell, M. J. 1987. "A More Generally Useful Measure of the Weight of Examination Components." *British Journal of Mathematical and Statistical Psychology* 40:61–79.

Cresswell, M. 1990. *Gender Effects in GCSE—Some Initial Analyses.* Paper presented at The Nuffield Assessment Group Seminar, Institute of Education, University of London, June.

Cresswell, M. 1996. "Defining, Setting and Maintaining Standards in Curriculum-Embedded Examinations: Judgmental and Statistical Approaches." In H. Goldstein and T. Lewis, (Eds.), *Assessment: Problems, Developments and Statistical Issues.* Chichester: John Wiley & Sons, pp. 57–84.

Delap, M. R. 1994. "The Interpretation of Achieved Weights of Examination Components." *The Statistician* 43(4):505–511.

Donaldson, M. 1984. *Children's Minds.* Glasgow: Collins.

Elwood, J. 1995. "Undermining Gender Stereotypes: Examination and Coursework Performance in the UK at 16." *Assessment in Education* 2(3):283–303.

Elwood, J. 1999. "Equity Issues in Performance Assessment: The Contribution of Teacher-Assessed Coursework to Gender-Related Differences in Examination Performance." *Educational Research and Evaluation* 5(4).

Elwood, J., and Comber, C. 1996. *Gender Differences in Examinations at 18+.* London: Institute of Education, University of London.

Foxman, D., Ruddock, G., McCallum, I., and Schagen, I. 1991. *Assessment Matters: No 3 APU Mathematics Monitoring 1984–1988 (Phase 2).* London: SEAC.

Gillborn, D., and Youdell, D. 1998. *Ethnic Origin and Selection in GCSE English and Mathematics: Final Report.* London: Institute of Education.

Gipps, C. 1994. *Beyond Testing: Towards a Theory of Educational Assessment.* London: The Falmer Press.

Gipps, C., and Murphy, P. 1994. *A Fair Test? Assessment, Achievement and Equity.* Buckingham: Open University Press.

Good, F., and Cresswell, M. J. 1988. *Grading the GCSE.* London: Schools Examination Council.

Gorman, T., White, J., Brooks, G., and English, F. 1991. *Assessment Matters: No 4 Language for Learning.* London: SEAC.

Goulding, M. 1995. *GCSE Coursework in Mathematics in 1994.* Paper presented at European Conference on Educational Research, Bath, UK, September.

Hayden, M. C. 1991. *An Investigation of the Validity and Reliability of International Baccalaureate Examinations.* Unpublished MPhil Thesis, University of Bath.

Hayden, M. C., Richards, P. N., and Thompson, J. J. 1992. *Factors Affecting the Validity and Reliability of some International Baccalaureate Examinations.* Paper presented at the 18th Annual Conference of the IAEA, Dublin, 14–18th September.

Her Majesty's Inspectorate (HMI). 1988. *The Introduction of the GCSE in Schools 1986–88* London: HMSO.

Hildebrand, G. 1996. "Redefining Achievement." In P. Murphy and C. Gipps (Eds.), *Redefining Achievement.* London/Paris: The Falmer Press/UNESCO, pp. 149–172.

Inter-Group Research Committee (IGRC). 1992. *Differentiation in GCSE Mathematics: Part B, Centres' Entry Policy.* Cambridge: UCLES for all GCSE Groups.

Kerslake, D. 1986. *Fractions: Children's Strategies and Errors.* Windsor: NFER-Nelson.

Kingdon, M., and Stobart, G. 1988. *GCSE Examined.* London: The Falmer Press.

Lave, J. 1988. *Cognition in Practice.* Cambridge: Cambridge University Press.

Macintosh, H. 1986. "The Sacred Cows of Coursework." In C. V. Gipps (Ed.), *The Sacred Cows of Coursework.* London: Institute of Education, University of London, pp. 21–29.

Madaus, G. 1988. "The Influence of Testing on the Curriculum." In J. Tanner (Ed.), *The Influence of Testing on the Curriculum.* Chicago: University of Chicago Press.

Messick, S., 1993. "Validity." In R. Linn (Ed.), *Educational Measurement* (3rd ed). Phoenix, AZ: American Council on Education/The Pryx Press, pp. 13–104.

Murphy, P. 1995. "Sources of Inequity: Understanding Students' Responses to Assessment." *Assessment in Education: Principles, Policy and Practice.* 2(3): 249–270.

Murphy, P. F., and Elwood, J. 1998. "Gendered Experiences, Choices and Achievement— Exploring the Links." *International Journal of Inclusive Education* 2(2):85–118.

Nickson, M., and Prestage, S. 1994. "England and Wales." In L. Burton (Ed.), *England and Wales.* Stoke-on-Trent: Trentham Books, pp. 41–63.

Quinlan, M. 1990. *Gender Differences in Examination Performance.* ULSEB Unpublished research paper.

Schools Curriculum and Assessment Authority (SCAA). 1995. *GCSE Regulations and Criteria.* London: SCAA.

Southern Examining Group (SEG). 1996. *Inter-Group Statistics.* Guildford: SEG.

Stobart, G., Elwood, J., and Quinlan, M. 1992a. "Gender Bias in Examinations: How Equal Are the Opportunities?" *British Journal of Educational Research* 18(3):261–276.

Stobart, G., White, J., Elwood, J., Hayden, M., and Mason, K. 1992b. *Differential Performance in Examinations at 16+: English and Mathematics.* London: Schools Examination and Assessment Council.

Sutherland, G., 1996. "Assessment: Some Historical Perspectives." In H. Goldstein and T. Lewis (Eds.), *Assessment: Problems, Developments and Statistical Issues.* Chichester: John Wiley & Sons, pp. 9–20.

Tattersall, K. 1994. "The Role and Functions of Public Examinations." *Assessment in Education* 1(3):293–305.

White, J., 1996. "Research On English and the Teaching of Girls." In P. Murphy and C. Gipps (Eds.), *Research On English and the Teaching of Girls.* London/Paris: Falmer Press/UNESCO, pp. 97–110.

Wiliam, D. 1992. *What Makes an Investigation Difficult?* Paper presented at the Secondary Mathematics Independent Learning Experience (SMILE) Conference, Nottingham, March.

Wiliam, D. 1995. "It Will All End in Tiers!" *British Journal of Curriculum and Assessment* 5(3):21–24.

Wood, R. 1990. "The Agenda for Educational Measurement." In T. Horton (Ed.), *Assessment Debates.* Buckingham/London: Open University Press/Hodder & Stoughton, pp. 48–57.

7

Professional Doctorates and Assessment Issues

David Scott and Ingrid Lunt

INTRODUCTION

The past ten years have seen considerable changes in the nature of the university in the United Kingdom, the type and numbers of participants in higher education, and the role of the university for higher professional development (Barnett 1997). The end of the binary divide, the rapid growth of student numbers and postgraduate programs, the moves toward a "learning society" and "lifelong learning," and the professions' own focus on continuing professional development have all changed the profile of the university. There has also been a change for the professions themselves; many have increased their own qualification requirements, while for some this has meant a move to a doctoral qualification. Within the professions, requirements for greater accountability and a rapidly changing environment have led to an interest in "reflective practice" (Schön 1987) and "critical reflection" within continuing professional development (Brookfield 1995). Over the past twenty years, in the United Kingdom, professional, and in some cases vocational, doctorates have been added to what was previously only an academic qualification. In addition, there have been strong moves to make the Ph.D. itself more vocational (e.g., Collinson 1998).

These factors have contributed to a widespread development of professional doctorates in the United Kingdom; this follows developments in the United States and Australia over the past twenty years, and forms part of the expansion of higher degrees for a wider range of student. The introduction of professional doctorates in the United Kingdom is relatively recent, although vocational (initial training) doctorates in fields such as psychology and psychotherapy have a longer lineage. In most professional fields, however, the doctorate provides a higher qualification for already qualified practitioners, for example, the D.Eng.

for qualified engineers, and the D.B.A. for managers, which is more akin to the longer established M.D. for medical practitioners.

The university itself is increasingly being influenced by policy-driven interventions of the state, new forms of communication, its marginalization from the center of the knowledge industry, "nonjurisdictionally bounded global discourses" (Yeatman 1990) and by crises in disciplinarity and professionalism (Brennan 1998). Moreover, the introduction of professional doctorates in the UK context signals a move by both the university and the professions to reconfigure what is considered appropriate research and practice knowledge. Yeatman (1990, p. 90) identifies three kinds of knowledge: (1) "knowledge of how to use theoretical analysis and scientifically orientated empirical research;" (2) "knowledge of how to reflect on the requirements of practice and practice setting in question;" and (3) "knowledge of how to work with 'service users' to deliver and improve the service concerned." These reflect a tension between "theory-orientated" and "practice-based" knowledges (Usher et al. 1996; Eraut 1994) and have implications for pedagogy at doctoral level, assessment of products, legitimation and more generally the relationship between higher education and the continuing development of serving professionals (Lee 1998).

This chapter will focus on professional doctorates in education that are relatively recent in the United Kingdom and have developed rapidly in response to a growing market; thus, three universities in the United Kingdom offered the degree in 1994, while it is offered in over thirty-three universities in 1999. However, the Ed.D. degrees vary considerably in their target students, approaches to curriculum, pedagogy and assessment, and their professional ethos. They are intended to provide an alternative to Ph.D. study, perhaps demonstrated in the distinction made between "professional researchers" (Ph.D.) and "researcher professionals" (Ed.D.). Educational doctorate courses comprise a number of taught courses (assessed by assignment) and a thesis of shorter length than the Ph.D. The taught courses typically include core courses on research methods, and professionalism, and subject-specific modules in fields such as management, curriculum, assessment, policy, higher education or school improvement. Educational doctorate courses may be targeted at particular professional groups (for example, the Bristol Ed.D. or Lincolnshire Ed.D. or the Lancaster Ph.D.), general (London Institute of Education Ed.D.), or taught through distance learning (Open University Ed.D.).

THE RELATIONSHIP BETWEEN ACADEMIC AND PROFESSIONAL KNOWLEDGE

A key area of concern for those universities that are developing educational doctorates is the relationship between academic and professional or practitioner knowledge. There are five possible ways of understanding this relationship, with proponents of each of them adopting a different view about how educational theory is constructed and how it relates to educational practice.

The Scientistic Approach

The first of these ways has been termed the "scientistic" approach (Habermas 1974). By this is meant that scientific description is understood as the only possible way of seeing the world and it refers to "science's belief in itself; that is, the conviction that we can no longer understand science as one form of possible knowledge, but rather must identify knowledge with science" (p. 4). All other forms of knowledge, including practitioner knowledge, are considered to be inferior or mistaken versions of it. What this also suggests is that it is possible to identify a correct method for collecting data about educational activities and if this method is properly applied, then this will inevitably lead to the construction of objective, value-free, and authoritative knowledge. Furthermore, though there are subtle differences between natural and social science knowledge, these differences are not distinctive enough to warrant the designation of two different approaches or sets of methods. There is one correct approach and one set of methods.

Educational practitioners, therefore, need to set aside their own considered and experience-based ways of conducting themselves at work because these are partial, incomplete and subjective; by contrast they need to incorporate into their practice scientific knowledge that transcends the local and the particular. Practitioner knowledge is, therefore, considered to be inferior and incomplete because it is context-dependent, problem-solving, contingent, nongeneralizable and is judged not by objective criteria but by whether it contributes to the achievement of short-term goals and problems encountered in situ.

This version of knowledge is underpinned by particular understandings of epistemology and ontology. Hacking (1981), for example, suggests that scientific knowledge conforms to the following principles:

1. Realist assumptions—There is a real world to be described that does not depend on how it is understood or articulated. Furthermore, there is a uniquely best way of describing it, which is not dependent on history or society.

2. Demarcation—Scientific theories are very different from other types of beliefs.

3. Cumulative orientation—Science works by building on previous ideas and theories; indeed, it works toward an ultimate goal, which is a proper understanding of the natural world.

4. Distinction between observation and theory—Observational statements and theoretical statements are treated as distinct.

5. Epistemological justification—Hypotheses and theories are tested deductively by observations and experiments.

6. Fixity of meaning—Linguistic terms have fixed meanings and concepts are defined precisely.

7. Distinction between judgement and procedure—The production of truthful statements is different from how they are justified.

8. Unitary method—Similar methods are appropriate to the discovery of truths about the natural and social worlds.

No single philosophy has embraced all eight points. For example, Popper (1976) rejected the distinction made between observational and theoretical statements. However, within this model, an assumption is being made that the objective knowledge that is produced about educational activities and institutions binds the practitioner in certain ways; those ways being the following of rules that can be deduced from that knowledge. Practitioner knowledge, therefore, is inferior because it is based on incorrect foundations. This has been described as the technical rationality model of the theory-practice relationship.

Technical Rationality

The second perspective conforms to this model in that it understands the relationship between theoretical and practice-based knowledge in a similar way. What is different is that the researcher constructs the original knowledge differently. Instead of conforming to the principles that underpin the scientific model described above, researchers work from different foundational principles. These may comprise a different conception of the relationship between ontology and epistemology or a different understanding of the relationship between the knower and what it is that they seek to know or a different way of conceptualizing objectivity. In short, those who adopt, even provisionally, a positivist/empiricist view of the world are going to understand their brief as researchers in a different way from those who are implicitly or explicitly located within an interpretive or hermeneutic framework. However, they share the conviction that knowledge produced by outsiders, or practitioners behaving as outsiders, is superior to the knowledge produced by practitioners working in situ.

The implications for practitioners undertaking academic study is that they should divest themselves of their prior incorrect and incomplete knowledge and adopt precepts based on the objective study of educational activities. Usher et al. (1996, p. 26) describe this model as: "the solving of technical problems through rational decision-making based on practical knowledge. It is the means to achieve ends where the assumption is that ends to which practice is directed can always be predefined and are always knowable. The condition of practice is the learning of a body of theoretical knowledge, and practice therefore becomes the application of this body of knowledge in repeated and predictable ways to achieve predefined ends." This is a view that is concerned with determining a measure of technical efficiency that will necessarily lead to the achievement of predetermined ends and these are separate from the determination of means per se.

A Multi-perspective Approach

A third way of understanding the relationship between theoretical and practice-based knowledges is a multi-method or more eclectic approach. Again, there are epistemological and ontological foundations to this view of knowledge. Researchers would deny that there is a correct way of seeing the world but would advocate a multiperspectival view. There is no one correct method, only a series of methods that groups of researchers have developed and that have greater or lesser credence depending on the way those groups are constructed and the influence they have in society. The educational texts that they produce are stories about the world, which in the process of their telling and retelling, restock, or restory the world itself. They have credence because enough practitioners see them as a useful resource for the solving of practical problems they encounter in their everyday working lives.

Whether or not the practitioner works to the prescriptive framework of the researcher, and implicit within any research text is a set of prescriptions about how the practitioner should behave, will depend on the fit between the values and frameworks held respectively by theorist and practitioner. The outside theorist can produce broadly accurate knowledge of educational settings, but the practitioner then adapts and amends them in the light of the contingencies of their own work practices. However, in all essential respects the practitioner still follows the prescriptive framework developed by the outside researcher.

Practice as the Source of Educational Theory

A fourth way of understanding the relationship between theoretical and practice-based knowledges is to see practice as the source of educational theory. Walsh (1993, p. 43) argues that the relationship that concerns us here "turns on the perception that deliberated, thoughtful, practice is not just the target, but is the major source (perhaps the specifying source) of educational theory." He goes on to suggest that "there is now a growing confidence within these new fields that their kind of theorizing, relating closely and dialectically with practice, is actually the core of educational studies and not just the endpoint of a system for adopting and delivering outside theories" (p. 43). This viewpoint takes another step away from the technical-rationality position described above. This suggests that there may not be a role at all for outside theorists, because they operate outside practice. This perspective understands practice as deliberative action concerned with the making of appropriate decisions about practical problems in situ. However, we should not conclude from this that there is no role for theory at all. What is being reconceptualized is the idea of theory itself.

Proponents of this view reject the notion of means-end implicit in the technical-rational model and argue that practitioner knowledge does not comprise the making of appropriate technical decisions about applying precepts developed by others. Practitioner knowledge is not just about the identification and application of predefined ends, it is also about the designation of ends in the light of deliberative activity about practice. As Usher et al. (1996, p. 127) suggest, practice situations are "characterized by a complexity and uncertainty which resist routinization." Such knowledge is and can never be propositional, but always involves continuous cycles of deliberation and action that cannot be transformed in the process into generalizable accounts of educational activities. This closely ties together theory and practice; informal theory central to practice is, as Usher et al. (1996) suggest, "situated theory both entering into and emerging from practice."

Practice Distinct from Theory

The fifth position that it is possible to take is an extension of this last, in that the theorist and the practitioner are actually engaged in different activities. Walsh (1993, p. 44) for instance, suggests that there are four mutually supporting but distinctive kinds of discourses: "deliberation in the strict sense of weighing alternatives and prescribing action in the concrete here and now . . . evaluation, also concrete, and at once closely related to deliberation and semi-independent of it . . . science, which has a much less direct relationship to practice . . . and utopianism, being the form of discourse in which ideal visions and abstract principles are formulated and argued over." Discourse, he defines, as "a sustained and disciplined form of enquiry, discussion and exposition that is logically unique in some way" (p. 53).

If we accept this argument, we are also accepting the idea that the practitioner and the theorist are engaged in different activities and therefore that they will operate with different criteria as to what constitutes knowledge. This creates two problems: how does one decide between these different versions of the theory-practice relationship? And how does one, therefore, conceptualize the relationship between practitioner and academic knowledge?

This is the theme of the chapter. In particular we will examine the way the three principal message systems: assessment, pedagogy, and curriculum are being constructed to configure and reconfigure the relationship referred to above. Choosing between these different accounts of the theory-practice relationship is problematic because it is not possible to derive a role for the outside theorist and a role for the practitioner from an a priori linguistic examination of the concept of education per se. In other words, how these matters are considered and what conclusions are drawn about the most appropriate relationship between theory and practice is a question of value. It involves deliberation and argument about the purposes of the educational enterprise and such deliberation is located within power structures that provide the essential contexts for action.

THE PROFESSIONAL DOCTORATE

This viewpoint creates certain problems in relation to the professional doctorate. One of these is that the accounts given by practitioners of their practice may be transformed into academic texts, indeed the practitioner may behave as an academic researcher in the context of their own practice, but the process itself may lead to poorly conceived practitioner knowledge. Indeed we should perhaps understand the process of producing a professional doctorate not as one of overcoming the tension between academic and practice-based knowledge, but of initiating the practitioner into a code of practice that more closely conforms to the production of academic knowledge; and that this itself is simply another form of practice. We are dealing here then with two competing types of practices, both of which are equally valid and credible. However, what is of interest is the way assessment and pedagogic processes constructed by the different universities act to privilege one set of practices over another.

Professional doctorates are assessed in various ways. Of the three message systems that link social identity to formal learning, assessment may be the most important (Broadfoot, 1996). She suggests that "assessment procedures are so closely bound up with the legitimation of particular educational practices, because they are overt means of communication from [educational institutions] to societies and, to a greater or lesser extent in different societies, the covert means of that society's response in the form of control." We have already identified a tension between professional and academic knowledge, and it can perhaps be surmised that the dominant influence on the type of knowledge constructed by students taking professional doctorates is the way that knowledge is assessed.

ASSESSMENT

These assessment practices, therefore, operate as control mechanisms and in the process promote one version of the theory-practice relationship over another. They comprise a number of different modalities: timing (at what stage in the course are students assessed?); the nature of that assessment (is it formative or summative?); the degree of importance attached to the assessment (does failure at this assessment hurdle mean that the student is not allowed to continue on the course or are they allowed to resit that part of the assessment framework?); the way assessment practices relate to the way the course is taught (is there a fit between the types of assessment practices being operated and the types of teaching approaches being adopted?); the way assessment practices relate to the organization of the course; and fundamentally, how assessment practices relate to the purposes of the course (e.g., in what way do the assessment practices relate to different views of the relationship between academic and practitioner knowledge?). However, these forms of control are never absolutely effective. Indeed, the process is always fragmented, allowing the possibility of resistance to the imposition of any one model. This should not detract from the powerful influence that assessment can exert on the process of producing a professional doctorate.

Assessment is understood here as more than the awarding of marks to students at different points during the course, but also as the systems set in place that structure the learning experiences of the students. A number of examples of these will be given below. The first example focuses on modularity. The taught courses may be accessed by students in a logical and progressive order or students may be required to make choices between discrete elements. The principle of modularity is that the courses are taught at a similar standard and, therefore, may be taken at any time during the taught part of the degree. They, therefore, do not relate to each other in any sequential way and tend to be organized and taught as separate stand-alone units. Frequently the modular principle is compromised by the introduction of a core set of courses that have to be taken by students usually in some logically ordered way. On the surface at least, modularity would suggest that students have a greater degree of choice about how they position themselves on the academic/practitioner continuum. Modularity would therefore suggest weak framing (Bernstein 1971). However, because modular systems are taught and assessed by a number of different teachers, the choices students make are likely to lead to a more fragmented curriculum and, therefore, to a more fragmented relationship to the student's own practice.

Another example focuses on the notion of progression within these doctorates. The taught courses may be assessed to a single standard or in terms of a progressive sequence of standards. With the former, students are expected to meet the standards of doctoral work at the beginning of the course; with the latter they are expected to reach doctoral standard at a later point in the course and some allowance is made during the earlier stages to accommodate the differential development of students' conceptual and writing skills. If a progressive element is built into the assessment design, this may be achieved by early taught units being marked to a lower standard than later ones (restricted progression), by the setting of different standards for different parts of the course (hierarchical progression), or by the completion by students of a portfolio of work at the end of the taught part of the course which meets the requirements of Ph.D. work (portfolio progression). Restricted progression requires the assignation of two different standards (logically related to each other); hierarchical progression requires a number of different standards (still logically related to each other, but at different levels of difficulty and numerous or restricted depending on the scale of the hierarchy); and portfolio progression requires one standard to be met by students at two different points in the course. These different types of progression indicate weak or strong (Bernstein 1985) boundaries between academic and practitioner knowledge; that is, if students are expected to operate at doctoral level from the beginning of the course, then the boundaries between academic and practitioner knowledge are being defined as strongly delineated, sacrosanct, not open to negotiation and impermeable. Indeed, we can go further than this, and suggest that practice knowledge is here being understood as inferior to academic knowledge and that the practitioner should, therefore, divest themselves of that knowledge and replace it with academic knowledge (see models 1 and 2 above— scientistic and technical rationality frameworks). On the other hand, if various forms of progression are built in, then weaker boundaries between academic and practitioner knowledge are being proposed. Progression comprises the ability of the student to access particular recognition and realization rules (cf. Bernstein 1985) to meet the requirements of the course; that is, students need to access these rules as they are defined by the university (though different universities will define them in different ways) and cross the divide between practitioner and academic communities of knowledge. Those rules comprise in part a recognition by the student of the standards they are expected to meet at each stage of the course and the way assessment procedures structure their learning experiences.

A third example refers to the interpretive procedures undertaken by academics, and introduces the idea that though many of these rules are visible, some are invisible to the student. Assignments are either judged by a set of general course-wide criteria that are interpreted by the markers in an holistic way or by a set of module-specific criteria agreed by the markers, and written in such a way that agreement about how they relate to the written assignments is possible. Students are expected to meet the requirements of all the criteria or some compensation is allowed. Students are usually provided with these criteria and with knowledge of the specified relationship between them and how they are to be applied, before they complete their assignments. However, what is concealed from the student is the interpretative procedures that are implicit in the assessment process. Knowledge validation both acts to control the types of knowledge that are acceptable to the academy and implicitly the designation of a proper relationship between theoretical and practitioner knowledge, and at the same time seeks to conceal the value dimensions of the procedures. This invisibility confers an authority on the procedures, regardless of the actual merits of the case being argued for.

The content and form of the assignments given to students also act as a control mechanism and seek to privilege one form of knowledge over another. If we focus on the act of writing about professional practice, the inscription of knowledge changes its nature. First, it preserves it. This allows repeated evaluations of its worth and re-evaluations by assessors of their original judgements. Second, it allows revision by the student. This may be as a result of feedback so that it conforms better to a set of written assessment criteria that are made available to the student or to a model of what an assignment should be in the mind of the assessor. The degree to which the assessment criteria or the actual assessment framework that is used is related to pedagogy and curriculum and, ultimately, to the purposes of doing the degree reflects the amount of control asserted by the assessment system over the other message systems. Third, the knowledge is codified in particular ways so that it conforms to the rules for producing an academic text.

If we take one example, we could refer to the issue of intellectual ownership. A written academic text requires the author to make reference to, and in the process acknowledge, other peoples' ideas. Spoken communication inevitably borrows from other sources without acknowledging them. The mechanism of intellectual ownership has been established to protect the rights of individuals and to encourage original writing. It also has the effect of positioning the new piece of work within the framework of previous writings on the subject, and is a way of suggesting that knowledge progresses. The new work acknowledges what has been produced before but supersedes it. The representational process—that is, the attempt to get nearer and nearer to a perfect representation of reality—is progressed. Furthermore, in relation to writing for a degree such as a professional doctorate, if the student conforms to the requirements for proper referencing, they are being inducted into a particular tradition of thought or a way of constructing knowledge.

Practice-based knowledge comprises borrowing without reference. This is not understood perjoratively in any sense for two reasons. The first is the pragmatic reason that it is impossible to police and, therefore, a line is arbitrarily drawn with regards to intellectual property rights between spoken and written texts. The second reason is more important still and this is that it is not practical to acknowledge ownership in spoken discourse, since the latter conforms to a different time scale and involves short-hand techniques. Thus, because practice-based knowledge is predominantly oral and involves meta-reflection about practice but rarely meta-reflection about the discourse itself, then it is significantly less able to be controlled and as a result is more flexible.

Other forms of control do of course have significant degrees of influence and we will come back to these later. However, the point being made is that practice-based knowledge necessarily undergoes transformation when it is reproduced as academic knowledge. Other elements of form comprise in part the degree of choice in the way the assignment can be written and in the focus of the assignment. The actual focus represents a position on a continuum, with at one end a tight focus designated by the assessor, usually with a tightly constructed connection to either the purposes of the course, its content, or its pedagogy, and at the other end, a more loosely framed focus. However, there are two caveats to this. The first is that an assignment may be loosely focused with regards to some aspect of the required knowledge but tightly focused in relation to other aspects. Second, the pedagogy may be loosely framed but the focus of the assignment and the criteria for marking may be strongly framed. In other words, the pedagogic process may allow choice and a degree of control by the student but this is not reflected in the way that they are required to complete assignments and in the way those assignments are assessed.

PEDAGOGY

In a similar fashion to the other two message systems, pedagogy is constructed weakly or strongly, with again the latter defined as the capacity of the message system to restrict or allow different meanings, interpretations, and actions. At the level of pedagogy, the focus and the frame now refer to relations between deliverers or teachers and students. A professional doctorate is likely to be delivered to the student in a number of ways. Each delivery point has a frame and a focus and these have attached to them strengths. Each pedagogic moment focuses on a particular aspect of knowledge, chosen by the deliverer. This is made visible by the act of delivery. However, there are always invisible dimensions: what is not chosen and why it was not chosen are invisible.

The pedagogic device itself is weakly or strongly framed as well. If the device is text-based with some commentary by the deliverer, the written commentary may be "readerly" or "writerly" (Barthes 1975)—that is, in the latter case, it allows the reader the opportunity to interpret or read it in a different way. Thus, the pedagogic text is both strongly/weakly framed and focused. Because it is written and thus has been subject to revision or redrafting, its message system is likely (though not necessarily) to be monolinear; that is, its focus and frame within the text is likely to be of one type. The text is not fragmented.

On the other hand, oral commentary in the form of lectures, contributions to seminars, contributions to tutorials by the deliverer operate in different ways. Again, this form of delivery is strongly/weakly framed and focused. However, there are a number of differences when compared with text-based systems. The first is alluded to above. The spoken text is likely to be multilinear—that is, because of its greater informality and flexibility (it has not been subject to revision and redrafting) it is likely to incorporate a range of different modalities: at any one moment it may be more authoritative than at another moment. It is therefore likely to be more fragmented. Fragmentation allows the student a greater degree of choice because it surfaces for the attention of the student a range of possibilities which they can then make a choice about. The boundary between what is visible and invisible is weakened.

The most common teaching device used on the Ed.D. involves student-teacher interchanges. What is significant here, depending on the degree, amount, and type of student interventions, is that the relay now necessarily becomes more fragmented. No longer can it be claimed that knowledge is passed on from deliverer to student automatically, because student interventions may actually have the effect of changing that original knowledge conception. However, the pedagogic device, even if it comprises student interventions may be strongly or weakly framed. If it is strongly framed, the teacher/student relationship may be such that the effect of the exchange is that the student is dispossessed of certain faulty, inadequate or insufficiently complex ideas, so that they know, believe, can do and have the disposition to do what was originally intended by the deliverer. Here we have a mechanical relay in which the intention is realized in practice. It may be efficiently or inefficiently achieved depending on the skill of the teacher and on other structural relations in which the teacher and student are positioned.

However, there is another possibility, which is that the deliverer does not have in mind a particular model of what the student should be able to do after the program of study, and indeed is prepared to modify their pedagogy in the light of what emerges. It is therefore weakly framed. The purpose of the exchanges is to dissolve, fragment or otherwise disrupt the models of knowledge held by the student. Here, there is no attempt made to provide a replacement, since the purpose is to provide disjuncture in the minds of students, and the responsibility for replacement is devolved to the student. Again, what is being suggested here is a relationship between theoretical and practice-based knowledge based on models 3, 4, and 5 (see above)—multiperspectival approaches, approaches in which practice is understood as the source of educational knowledge, and approaches where practice is conceived as equivalent to but different from academic knowledge.

THE CHALLENGE FOR THE PROFESSIONAL
DOCTORATE IN EDUCATION

Examples of the way pedagogic and assessment messages are constructed have been provided in relation to taught doctorates, and it has been suggested that the strengths of each relay influence the way practitioner knowledge is formed and re-formed by student/ practitioners undergoing Ed.D. study. It has further been suggested that assessment processes, tightly policed by universities, are the primary mechanism by which universities control the relative statuses given to academic and practitioner knowledge during the period of study.

As will be evident, the Ed.D. poses a real challenge in terms of a conceptualization and operationalization of the nature of the professional doctorate, the ways in which it is distinct from the Ph.D., and the forms of knowledge and expression which are considered to be valid. The degree is offered to senior and experienced professionals in education, whose practice knowledge is extensive and expert. It is equivalent to the traditional doctorate, the Ph.D., and carries similar demands in terms of originality and contribution to knowledge. Furthermore, the form its assessment and pedagogy take provides an explicit indicator of its status and power as a knowledge-producing activity. This chapter has focused on possible ways that the theory-practice relationship could be conceptualized; however, in most cases, academic knowledge has been found to have been privileged over practitioner knowledge.

REFERENCES

Barnett, R. 1997. *Realising the University: An Inaugural Lecture.* London University Institute of Education.

Barthes, R. 1975. *S/Z.* London: Jonathan Cape.

Bernstein, B. 1971. "On the Classification and Framing of Educational Knowledge." In M. Young (Ed.), *Knowledge and Control.* London: Collier-Macmillan.

Bernstein, B. 1985. "On Pedagogic Discourse." *Handbook of Theory and Research in the Sociology of Education.* Westport, CT: Greenwood Press.

Bernstein, B. 1990. *The Structuring of Pedagogic Discourse.* London: Routledge.

Brennan, M. 1998. "Education Doctorates: Reconstructing Professional Partnerships Around Research?" In A. Lee and B. Green (Eds.) *Postgraduate Studies/ Postgraduate Pedagogy.* Sydney: Centre for Language and Literacy and University Graduate School, University of Technology, Sydney.

Broadfoot, P. 1996. *Education, Assessment and Society.* Buckingham: Open University Press.

Brookfield, S. J. 1995. *Becoming a Critically Reflective Teacher.* San Francisco: Jossey-Bass.

Collinson, J. 1998. "Professionally Trained Researchers? Expectations of Competence in Social Science Doctoral Research Training." *Higher Education Review* 31(1).

Eraut, M. 1994. *Developing Professional Knowledge and Competence.* Lewes: Falmer Press.

Giddens, A. 1984. *The Constitution of Society.* Cambridge: Polity Press.

Habermas, J. 1974. "Rationalism Divided in Two." In A. Giddens (Ed.), *Positivism and Sociology.* Aldershot: Gower Publishing Company Ltd.

Habermas, J. 1987. *Knowledge and Human Interests.* Cambridge: Polity Press.

Hacking, I. 1981. "Introduction." In I. Hacking (Ed.), *Scientific Revolutions.* Oxford: Oxford University Press.

Lee, A. 1998. *Research and Knowledge in the Professional Doctorate.* Paper presented at Symposium: Professional Doctorates in New Times for the Australian University, AARE, Brisbane, December.

Popper, K. 1976. "The Logic of the Social Sciences." In T. Adorno et al. (Eds.), *The Positivist Dispute in German Sociology.* London: Heinemann.

Schon, D. 1987. *Educating the Reflective Practitioner.* San Francisco: Jossey-Bass.

Usher, R., Bryant, I., and Johnstone, R. 1996. *Adult Education and the Post-modern Challenge: Learning Beyond the Limits.* London: Routledge.

Walsh, P. 1993. *Education and Meaning: Philosophy in Practice.* London: Cassell

Yeatman, A. 1990. *Bureaucrats, Technocrats, Femocrats: Essays on the Contemporary Australian State.* Sydney: Allen and Unwin.

8

Scottish Perspectives on the Curriculum and Assessment

Wynne Harlen

BACKGROUND

Writing at a time of historic change in Scottish government adds to the uncertainty about an already fluid situation—uncertainty caused by on-going reviews of various aspects of the curriculum and assessment in Scottish education. Several matters await discussion and approval in the new Parliament, as yet only a few months old. But at least the establishment of the Scottish Parliament has had the effect of making evident to all that Scottish education is different from that in other countries of the United Kingdom. This has been so officially since 1872, and unofficially much earlier, a fact that often comes as a surprise to many outside Scotland. Indeed some differences in education across the border have their roots in earlier history, before the union between the Scottish and English parliaments in 1707. Scotland had three universities by the end of the fifteenth century and the National Education Act of 1696 (believed to be the world's first) made provision for a school in every parish. Subsequent establishment of schools, leading to a good rate of literacy in the population in the mid-nineteenth century, reflected the high status of education and respect for the teaching force that remain features of Scottish education.

THE GENERAL STRUCTURE OF EDUCATION IN SCOTLAND

Since 1936 primary education in Scotland has been defined as the seven years from age five to twelve. Within the state system all pupils transfer from primary

Figure 8.1
The Structure of the Education System in Scotland

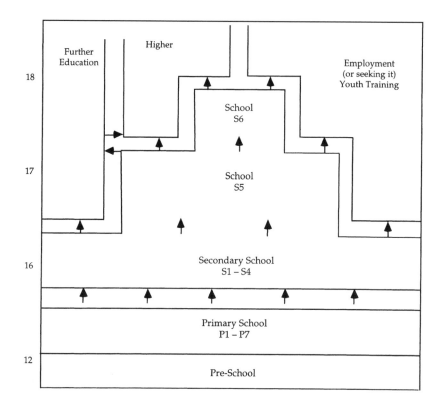

to nonselective comprehensive secondary schools after seven years of schooling (see Figure 8.1). However, it should be noted that a year group is on average six months younger than its counterpart in England because of differences in birth date admissions to school. For the first two years of secondary school, pupils follow the common 5–14 curriculum, outlined later, after which there is choice within a general framework such that at least one subject from each of eight curricular modes is chosen. Most secondary schools also offer some vocationally oriented courses from the third year of secondary school.

At the age of 16, and again at 17, pupils choose whether to stay at school, transfer to Further Education, or leave school for employment and training. Almost 90% continue in part-time or full-time education at the age of 16. Those who stay in school or college (more than three-quarters of the age group, [SOEID 1998a, b]) can, until 1999, take the Higher Grade examination of the Scottish Certificate, which is the entry requirement for university and some professional courses. This examination can be taken after one or two years of study and so students can enter university at the age of 17 or 18. However, the whole structure of education from the age of 16 is changing in 1999 and Higher Grade is being replaced by a new system of courses and qualifications, the Higher Still Program, which provides for all students and not just those following academic studies. Details of this are given later. It is also worth noting at this point that recent changes are bringing about a loosening of tight controls about what can be studied at various stages and when and how various qualifications can be obtained.

The structure of the system forms an important backcloth to the discussion of assessment, since it is at points of transition and choice that assessment is particularly relevant for pupils. Increasingly, too, points of transition are relevant for institutions, as pupil entry and exit performance data are used to estimate value-added, or evaluate the performance of the school or to set targets (SOEID 1998b).

SOME CHARACTERISTICS OF SCOTTISH SCHOOL EDUCATION

Several themes run through the discussion of curriculum and assessment in Scottish schools. One is the close association between the curriculum and assessment, despite the separation of responsibilities in two national bodies, the Scottish Qualifications Authority (SQA) and the Scottish Consultative Council on the Curriculum (Scottish CCC). A second characteristic is the preference for consensus rather than regulation. The curriculum is not governed by legislation in Scotland, as it is in the rest of the United Kingdom, and neither is national assessment imposed by law. In the absence of regulation, factors that ensure implementation of changes include a tradition of conforming with central policy, the value given to providing all pupils with educational opportunities, and wide consultation on changes. Inevitably, achieving consensus is a slow process and often means that change is evolutionary. A strong teachers' union and influential parents' bodies are also relevant in this context; indeed, changes that do not enjoy support are impossible to implement (as illustrated by the opposition to national testing in 1991, which is mentioned later).

A characteristic of assessment in Scottish education is the involvement of teachers and the use of external tests in a supplementary or confirmatory role. There is, too, a focus on using assessment formatively. The intention that assessment can serve both formative and summative purposes is inherent in the procedures at several stages and, as we shall see, can be a cause for concern. A further feature is the move to give equal status to vocational and academic qualifications, which is most obvious in the new system for 16 to 18 year olds, but that is increasingly having an influence at an earlier point in the school. Finally, as in other countries, particular attention is being given in both the curriculum and in assessment to overarching, hopefully transferable, skills, called core skills in Scotland.

A feature of Scottish education that is a significant part of the assessment landscape is the continuing operation of national surveys carried out by the Assessment of Achievement Program (AAP). The AAP, funded by the SOEID, was instituted in the early 1980s, the first surveys of English language and mathematics being conducted in the spring of 1984. Since then the AAP has conducted regular surveys in English, mathematics and science and one-off surveys in technical education, home economics, and modern foreign languages. After 1987 a three year cycle was adopted, in which one of the three subjects is tested each year. Nationally representative samples of pupils at P4, P7, and S2 are involved in each survey. Mathematics and science tests include practical activities as well as purely written tasks. The results are used to report the level of performance in various skills and areas of knowledge. The inclusion of some common tasks from one survey to the next allows reporting on changes in performance over time. Since 1996 a longitudinal element has been introduced by arranging for the same pupils who are tested at P4 to be tested again when they reach P7 and the Standard Grade achievements of the P7 and S2 pupils are also captured. Information about the preschool education of the P4 pupils is also gathered.

The close alliance of assessment and the curriculum means that it makes sense for this account to consider these together for each of the various stages of education: preschool (3–5) ; primary school (5–12); early secondary school (12–14); secondary school (14–16); and the education of 16–18 year olds in schools or further education.

THE CURRICULUM AND ASSESSMENT 3 TO 5

Preschool education is not compulsory but education authorities now provide preschool places for all four year olds whose parents wish to take advantage of it. Extra funding has been made available to extend this provision to all three year olds by 2002. With this extension in mind, the 1997 document *A Curriculum Framework for Children in their Pre-School Year* is being replaced, after consultation, by *A Curriculum Framework for 3 to 5 year olds* (Scottish CCC 1998a). The structure of the curriculum remains the same, however, based around five "key aspects" of learning:

- Emotional, personal, and social development
- Communication and language
- Knowledge and understanding of the world
- Expressive and aesthetic development
- Physical development and movement.

The framework document sets out learning outcomes for each of these aspects and provides a series of examples from practice to illustrate them and, in particular, to emphasize their interrelationship. For example, for *knowledge and understanding of the world,* some of the outcomes are that children:

- develop their powers of observation using their senses
- ask questions, experiment, and make and solve problems
- recognize patterns, shapes, and colors in the world around
- sort and categorize things into groups
- understand some properties of materials (e.g., soft/hard, smooth/rough)
- care for living things (e.g., plants, pets at home)
- understand and use mathematical processes, such as matching, sorting, grouping, counting, and measuring
- apply these processes in solving mathematical problems (SOEID 1997, p. 27).

The outcomes for *communication and language* include:

- use books to find interesting information
- recognize the link between the written and spoken word
- understand some of the language and layout of books
- experiment with symbols, letters and, in some cases, words in writing (SOEID 1997, p. 23).

The document emphasizes that the principal means for achieving these outcomes is play. Nevertheless, the identification of learning outcomes represents a considerable move from the previous position of many preschool educators who were reluctant to specify provision in terms other than desirable experiences. The link to the school curriculum is evident in many of the outcomes and is confirmed by the discussion of assessment and the explicit intention to plan for learning. Assessment is introduced in terms of the same framework as used in the assessment guidelines for the 5–14 curriculum. This takes the form of an "assessment cycle" comprising planning, staff interaction, recording, reporting, and evaluating. Planning is seen as the first step in the cycle and is aimed at "establishing clear goals for learning which are designed to match the needs and achievements of children" (SOEID 1997). Observation of children is the means for gathering information at the preschool stage and a separate publication titled *Promoting Learning: Assessing Children's Progress 3 to 5* (Scottish CCC 1998b) aims to help the preschool staff collect and use information.

CURRICULUM AND ASSESSMENT 5–14: THE PRIMARY SCHOOL

The introduction of near universal preschool education, with clear goals for children's learning brings with it an obligation to ensure continuity with learning at the start of primary education. The curriculum for the seven years of the primary school is contained within the 5–14 program that was developed and introduced gradually between 1990 and 1999. It is set out in terms of five curricular areas— language, mathematics, environmental studies, expressive arts, and religious and moral education—that are readily mapped onto the five areas of the preschool curriculum. However, in order to examine the extent of continuity and the nature and assessment of progression it is helpful to look first in more detail at the three interacting features that have an impact on teaching and learning in the primary school: the 5–14 curriculum and its assessment; national testing 5–14; and, soon to be introduced, baseline assessment.

THE 5–14 CURRICULUM AND ITS ASSESSMENT

For each of the five areas, the curriculum is expressed in terms of *attainment outcomes, strands*, and *targets. Attainment outcomes* refer to the main areas of skill, knowledge, and understanding. Each of these areas is further subdivided into *strands* that are the key aspects of learning. Each strand is set out in terms of *targets* at six levels of progression (originally five levels, a sixth was added in 1998). These levels are defined in terms of attainment of pupils. Targets in the 5–14 curriculum, then, are the equivalent of level descriptions in the National Curriculum. The levels A–F are separated by about the same two years as the levels 1–8, but are differently defined:

Level A   almost all pupils should attain this level during the first three years of primary school;

Level B   some pupils should reach this level in Primary 3 or even earlier; most by the end of Primary 4;

Level C   most pupils should reach this level in the course of Primary 4 to Primary 6;

Level D   some pupils should reach this level in Primary 5 or Primary 6 or even earlier, but certainly most should by Primary 7;

Level E   some pupils should reach this level in Primary 7 or the first year of secondary school, S1, but certainly most should in Secondary 2;

Level F   some pupils should reach this level in the course of Primary 7 or in the first or second year of secondary school.

When it is necessary to quantify "most" and "almost all," as is required for target setting (see later), these are taken to mean 75% and 90% respectively.

The draft guidance for each area was the subject of consultation for a period of about six months before being revised and issued as guidelines. There was also guidance (SOED 1993) as to the allocation of time to each area, as follows:

mathematics	15%
language	15%
environmental studies (including science, social subjects, health education, technology, and information technology)	25%
expressive arts (including physical education, art and design, music and drama)	15%
religious and moral education	10%

This leaves 20% as "optional" time for schools to use to make their own emphases or to reinforce particular areas. Research conducted in 1996–1998 suggested that primary school teachers did not recognize any time as being "optional" and that, in general, this time was being used for work in language development (McPake et al. 1999).

The development of the 5–14 program was complete in 1993 and guidelines were published on assessment, national testing, reporting, and personal and social development as well as on the five areas of the curriculum. However, implementation was spread over a decade and was accompanied by an evaluation program over six years (Harlen 1996; Malcolm and Schlapp 1997). The extended time was found to be necessary so that schools could acquire some ownership of the program and begin implementation by auditing their existing curriculum rather than sweeping this aside. When the moves toward a national curriculum and assessment began in Scotland, as in England and Wales, with the publication of a consultation document in 1987, the Scottish document noted that advice was already provided to both primary and secondary schools by the Scottish CCC, a body that had been issuing guidance to teachers since 1965 (unlike the National Curriculum Council that was set up in 1989 to implement the National Curriculum in England). The Scottish CCC had issued an important paper on the primary curriculum in 1983 that described the curriculum in terms of five areas: language arts, mathematics, environmental studies, expressive arts, and religious education. Science, health education, technology and elements of geography and history were included in environmental education and physical education in expressive arts. Thus, some continuity with existing thinking of the curriculum was to be expected and Scottish teachers were assured that there would be "a program of clarification and definition rather than of fundamental changes in teaching approaches and methods" (SED 1987).

In relation to assessment, the consultation paper promised to provide "national advice" on the assessment by teachers for each area of the curriculum. Each set of curriculum guidelines includes some advice on assessment in the areas that it covers while the overall approach is contained in specific assessment guidelines in three parts. These documents (SOED 1991 a,b), revised after a period of consultation, together communicate the message that assessment is integral to teaching and learning. Part 1 introduces the "assessment cycle," mentioned earlier in the context of preschool assessment, which is a strategy for considering assessment in five main elements of *planning, teaching, recording, reporting,* and *evaluating*. Part 2 spells out principles relating to each of these five elements, and Part 3 takes the form of a staff development pack with activities for teachers designed to help the application of the principles to their own work. Five years after the publication of these assessment guidelines the Scottish CCC published a pack of staff development activities entitled *Assessment 5–14* (Scottish CCC 1996a), which are also based around the five elements of the assessment cycle. In addition, materials to help with diagnostic assessment in mathematics, reading and writing, and science, commissioned by the SOED were developed and published by the Scottish Council for Research in Education (SCRE, 1995).

All these materials were available to support teachers in integrating assessment into teaching. It might be assumed, therefore, that assessment serves a formative purpose in teaching, as is indeed intended. Two circumstances inhibit the implementation of genuinely formative assessment, however. The first is the assumption that if teachers gather information as part of teaching then they automatically use the information in teaching. As James (1998) cogently pointed out, "any assessment is only as good as the action that arises from it" (p. 171). It is easy to underestimate the amount and nature of help that teachers need to make effective use of what they can learn about their pupils through observation during teaching. For many it requires a reorientation of their view of teaching, toward recognizing that learning depends on the active participation of learners and is progressively developed from existing ideas and skills. It also requires a clear view of goals of learning and of ways in which pupils can be helped to take steps toward these goals. While all the materials urge teachers in general terms to "match tasks to pupils" abilities and experience," only the SCRE materials provide specific ways of doing this. The others focus on obtaining, judging, and reporting information. Although there is specific help in using pupil assessment to evaluate teaching through reflection after the event, there is rather little about how to use it to improve learning in the first place.

The second circumstance constraining use of teachers' assessment for formative purposes is linked to its use for summative purposes and to the national tests. Evaluation of the implementation of the 5–14 program showed that the guidelines on assessment were taken up far more slowly than the curriculum guidelines, despite being among the first to be published in final form. A significant factor in this was the introduction of national tests. There was a strong objection to testing in the primary school from teachers and parents, which diverted attention from formative to summative assessment and overshadowed efforts to develop teacher assessment.

NATIONAL TESTS 5–14

The consultation paper of 1987 described a new system of national tests for all pupils in P4 and P7 as the core of the proposals relating to assessment. These tests would be externally set, but administered and marked by teachers. It was to be a requirement of education authorities to ensure that this testing took place.

The paper indicated that the results would be reported in terms of the objectives of the curriculum (this meant in terms of levels). Parents would receive reports on their children's tests but the results would not be used to place pupils in rank order in their class. There would be no central collection of test results or of teachers; assessments and thus no data which could be used to create "league tables" of schools on the basis of pupil assessment. As the tests had to be developed *de novo,* and would need to await the draft curriculum guidelines, it was proposed that the first testing would take place in the spring of 1991, following pilot trials in 1990.

Trial test material was developed within a new Primary Assessment Unit set up within the Scottish Examination Board (now the SQA). Despite general approval of the test materials by teachers and their unions, there was widespread objection to the principle of testing. On the occasion of the first national trial of the tests in 1991 only about one-third of pupils eligible for testing took the tests, as a result of action by teachers and parents who exercised their rights in relation to their children's education. Education authorities were urged by the government to take legal action against parents, but none did so. Certain changes were made in the test arrangements as a result of the limited national trials and, in 1992, schools were able to give the tests to their P4 and P7 pupils at times during the year chosen by themselves. Thus, the work in administering and marking tests could be spread out. However, this concession did not alter the attitude of teachers and parents and again in 1992 only about one-third of the intended tests were given. Many more fundamental changes were made after the 1992 testing, leading to the current arrangement, outlined below, and that brought about the extension of testing throughout the 5–14 stage. There was a consultation on the new arrangements and a promise to remove the regulation requiring testing if education authorities would cooperate in implementing the new arrangements and in pre-testing new test units. The regulation was subsequently removed at the end of 1992. In acknowledgment that testing was to be carried out in secondary school (beginning in 1994) the Primary Assessment Unit was renamed the Five to Fourteen Assessment Unit.

The current position, with regard to assessment of pupils in the seven years of the primary school and the first two of the secondary school, is that all pupils are assessed by their teachers across the whole curriculum against targets set out in the curriculum guidelines of the 5–14 Program. National tests are described as being an integral part of this continuous assessment in two areas of English (reading and writing) and in mathematics. The arrangements allow pupils to be tested when teachers think them ready regardless of their year level, stage, or time of year. Pupils take the tests when their teacher's own assessment indicates that they are ready to do so; thus, the tests "provide teachers with the means to check their own assessments and should ensure more consistent interpretation by teachers of what particular levels of attainment mean" (SOED 1992a).

In writing, the test consists of two units (one in imaginative or personal writing and one in functional writing). In reading, the test is also of two units (one involving narrative reading and the other reading for information). In mathematics, the test consists of four units that have to be chosen so that a wide range of attainment outcomes is included. The units are selected by the teacher from a catalog that provides a choice of contexts for each attainment outcome at each level. Thus, if a pupil does not succeed at a level expected by the teacher, there is other test material for use in testing again at that level (allowing at least twelve weeks for remedial action to be taken). Tests in reading do not have to be taken at the same time as tests in writing; similarly the mathematics tests can be taken without regard to readiness for tests in reading and writing. Pupils taught in the Gaelic language can be tested in Gaelic but from level D upward, they must also take reading and writing tests in English.

While this solution to the objection to testing serves to retain teachers' assessment at the center of the process, it also serves to emphasize the summative role of assessment. Because teachers' assessment have to be summarized in terms of whether the criteria set by the targets at each level have been met, there is an inevitable tendency to judge each observation in these terms and to use it to label rather than to develop pupils' potential. The issue here is that of using assessment information for different purposes. In the 5–14 assessment, there is indeed the opportunity to use the information gained by observation during teaching formatively, to provide feedback to pupils in terms of their own development toward their individual next steps in learning. It is possible for this to be done and for the same evidence to be collated, at appropriate times, and judged against the criteria for the various levels for summative purposes. This requires teachers and others to recognize the difference between using *evidence* for different assessment purposes and using the *results* of assessments for different purposes (Harlen and James 1997). We encounter the same ambiguity in purpose in relation to the baseline assessment, about to be introduced in Scotland and to which we now turn.

BASELINE ASSESSMENT

As in other countries of the United Kingdom, the introduction of baseline assessment explicitly serves two purposes: to enable teachers to identify the strengths and needs of individual pupils and to provide data for use in evaluating the "value-added" by the primary school. The difficulties of combining these two purposes have been well articulated in the context of baseline assessment schemes in England. The problems of comparability are complicated in England: first by the use of many different schemes, and second by the assessment being conducted in the first few weeks in the primary school. The use of baseline assessment in judging schools also raises the possibility of bias being introduced, albeit unconsciously, by underestimating the attainments of five year olds and so exaggerating the apparent value added (Goldstein 1996).

The Scottish system has avoided the first two of these pitfalls, by proposing a single scheme and proposing that assessment is not undertaken until children are well into the second term of primary school. Eight aspects of development are assessed by the teacher(s):

- personal, emotional, and social development
- physical coordination
- expressive communication
- listening and talking
- reading
- writing
- mathematics
- understanding the environment.

In each case the scheme provides a number of statements indicating "features relating to learning in that area," attainment statements and contexts in which evidence is likely to be gained, and a space for "specific comments." For example, for "understanding the environment" the features relating to learning include:

- recognizes patterns, shapes, and colors in the world around
- uses the senses to investigate and describe everyday objects and events
- sorts and categorizes things into groups
- shows care for living things and the environment.

Statements that relate to learning not expected of most children on entry to school, but that may be found in some cases include:

- recognizes patterns and relationships in nature, families, and events
- can collect systematically information on self, objects, and events
- organizes findings by sorting, matching, tally, diagram plan, and/or chart
- records findings to share with others

The first set of statements indicate learning that should occur at the preschool stage and indeed they include many similar statement to those included as outcome of preschool education quoted earlier. Teachers are provided with a brief expansion of each bulleted feature to guide interpretation and to increase uniformity. The attainment statements are the same for all aspects and teachers use a "best fit" approach in making their judgment as to whether the child displays "few," "some," "the majority," or "almost all" of the features of learning in the contexts identified. Assessments are based on observation during normal classroom activities and are intended to be unobtrusive to the children.

LINKING THE PRESCHOOL TO THE 5–14 CURRICULUM

Having looked at the preschool curriculum and its assessment, at the 5–14 program and at baseline assessment, it is useful to examine how these link together at the transition from preschool to school. The SOEID sees this relationship as in Figure 8.2, taken from SOEID's information for staff involved in pilot trials, where the aspects of learning recorded for baseline assessment are in the boxes overlapping the two curricula.

Figure 8.2
Relationship Between Preschool and the 5–14 Curriculum in the Primary School (SOEID 1998c)

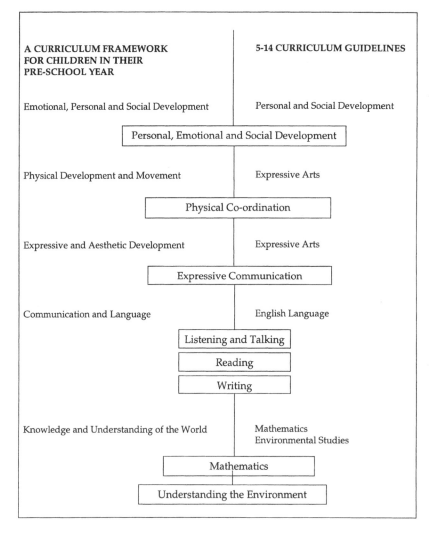

THE CURRICULUM AND ASSESSMENT 12–14

The 5–14 program crosses the primary/secondary boundary with the intention of preserving breadth, balance, coherence, continuity, and progression (the principles explicitly underpinning the 5–14 program) across the transition. At the same time, the secondary curriculum for S1 to S6 as a whole is the subject of guidance issued under the title: *Curriculum Design for the Secondary Stages: Guidelines for Schools.* These guidelines are revised from time to time, involving extensive consultation with all schools and others with a stake in secondary education. They present an overall philosophy for secondary education and propose areas of the curriculum, which should be represented in every pupil's program, and the proportion of time to be allocated to them, at various stages. A recent revision of the guidelines has been carried out to take account of the introduction of the 5–14 program in the early secondary years and of the Higher Still, in the later secondary years. The curriculum for S1 and S2 lies somewhat awkwardly both within the 5–14 program and subject to the secondary curriculum guidelines. This awkwardness was manifested in the slowness to implement the 5–14 guidelines and reluctance to introduce national testing in S1 and S2. Small changes in the titles of two areas of the 5–14 program have been introduced in acknowledgment of the reality of the subject-based nature of secondary school programs. For S1 and S2 the areas and the time to be allocated to them are as follows:

Language	20%
Mathematics	10%
Science, Technology and Society	30%
Expressive Arts and Physical Education	15%
Religious and Moral Education	5%

These advised time allocations apply over the two year period, so that there is room for blocking times for different areas if schools so wish. The remaining 20% is for other activities, including essential events such as registration.

Despite the description of the S1 and S2 curriculum in terms of "areas," and that for S3 and S4 in terms of "modes," in reality most schools have a subject-based program. This has attracted criticism for being "conceived of, designed, implemented and taught in terms of fragmented pieces with no obligation, moral or managerial, to make connections among the fragments" (Barr 1999). The guidelines call for a "holistic view of the curriculum" and emphasize the need for pupils to be able to make connections across subjects and across curriculum areas. However, in practice this would appear to require change on the scale that can only take place over the long term, given the essentially conservative approach to innovation in the Scottish system.

Assessment in S1 and S2 follows the same pattern as in the primary years, with teachers' assessments in reading, writing, and mathematics being confirmed by national tests. In other subjects, as in the primary school, teachers report pupils' achievements at the end of each year in terms of level A to F, without the confirmation of external tests.

THE CURRICULUM AND ASSESSMENT FOR S3 AND S4

After the first two years of secondary school, pupils begin to make choices from a range of subjects in preparation for taking the Standard Grade examination of the Scottish Certificate of Education at the age of 16. Subjects are grouped into eight modes and pupils are required to study at least one subject from each mode. These modes articulate at one end with the curriculum areas of the 5–14 program and at the other with the post-16 curriculum as shown in Figure 8.3.

Figure 8.3
Curriculum Links Across the Secondary Stages

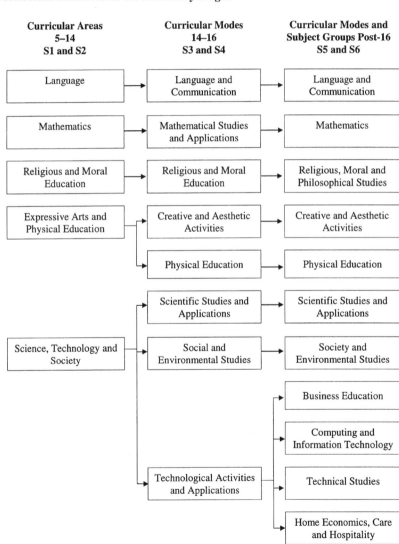

The Standard Grade examination, introduced gradually between 1984 and 1992, caters for pupils across the full range of achievement. In general, Standard Grade examinations can be taken at three levels: credit, for the top end of the ability range; general, for the middle band; and foundation, for the lower end of the range. Pupils generally take up to 8 Standard Grade courses, for each of which an overall grade will be given as well as a profile of grade assessments for separate elements within some courses.

There are nationally agreed criteria that set out for each level descriptions of performance against which pupils' achievements are measured and that require all essential aspects of the subject to be covered to some degree. These criteria are given in both summary form (broad descriptions of performance) and in extended form (more detailed descriptions used by examiners). The Scottish Qualifications Authority (SQA), which both awards and accredits the certificates, also issues statements of learning outcomes at the three levels and of learning activities that support the outcomes. In some areas of the curriculum (e.g., mathematics), pupils follow courses at the three levels, while in others there is differentiation within a single course. For most courses there are separate examinations that lead to a grade 1 to 7, awarded according to level and performance at that level as follows:

Credit level	Grades 1 and 2
General level	Grades 3 and 4
Foundation level	Grades 5 and 6
Course completed	Grade 7

While there is an external component in most Standard Grade examinations, for the majority of courses there is a considerable component of teacher-based examination. For some courses a folio of work completed during the course is sent to the SQA. In all cases, teachers' estimates of pupils' performance are submitted and these may be used to improve grades where external and internal assessment disagree. Thus, a system for moderation, or quality assurance, operates to facilitate what is seen as an essentially teacher-based examination.

Quality assurance takes the form of central moderation where the product is written. Each year a random sample of schools is required to send a sample of work of 12 candidates to the SQA. The sample is selected according to instructions from SQA and the work is graded by moderators against the same criteria as used by the teachers. A report is sent to the school, which may be required to regrade the work of other candidates if systematic bias has been detected. A school where application of criteria does not seem to be up to standard is included in the sample for the following year. Where the assessment is of performance or of products that are not easily transportable, moderators visit the school, where they may carry out a professional development function in respect of interpretation of criteria as well as checking teachers' assessments. These quality assurance procedures ensure confidence in a system which can claim to be criterion-referenced and based on teachers' assessment confirmed by external examinations or moderation.

CURRICULUM AND ASSESSMENT 16 +

The curriculum and assessment for 16–18 year olds has been going through a period of extensive review since 1990 and as a result, courses in schools and colleges will undergo radical change from August 1999. Up to that time, the majority of pupils remaining at school after taking S grade in S4 were studying one or more of three kinds of courses: the Higher Grade of the Scottish Certificate of Education, popularly known as Highers; the Certificate of Sixth Year Studies; and National Certificate Modules.

Higher Grade has a long and "distinguished history since its introduction in 1888" (SOED, 1992b). Highers are individual subject examinations which, until revision between 1987 and 1992, were entirely external. They can be taken after one year of study, in S5, or in S6 and those aiming for university entrance will take up to five subjects. The results are graded in four bands. Students who stay on in S6 can study for the Certificate of Sixth Year Studies (CSYS) in those subjects where they have already obtained a Higher. The CSYS is broadly equivalent to A level in standard but is qualitatively different since it depends to a considerable extent on independent study. Assessment is based on project work as well as on written examinations and results are graded in five bands.

Both Higher Grade and CSYS courses were revised between 1987 and 1992 to provide better articulation with Standard Grade on the one hand and with changing requirements of further and higher education on the other hand. An element of teacher assessment was introduced for those aspects that are not readily and validly assessed externally but the externally assessed aspects generally constitute at least two-thirds of the final result. The teacher assessment is moderated by each school (or each examination center) being required to send a sample of students' work to the SQA. Despite these changes, however, a growing discontent with the Higher/CSYS led to the introduction of the *Higher Still* program, which is being phased in from 1999.

The National Certificate was introduced in the late 1980s to unify awards for nonadvanced vocational education and training. It comprises a system of modular courses of 40 hours study that are entirely internally teacher-assessed, as pass or fail with no grading. It required changes not only in assessment procedures and course structure, but also in methods of teaching and learning. Teachers were encouraged to rely less on "didactic" styles of teaching and to place greater emphasis on student-centered approaches. "Pair and group work, discussion, practical work, case studies, projects and simulations were encouraged and teachers were asked to increase students' involvement in their own learning, to focus on their individual needs and to use assessment 'diagnostically' to help them to learn" (Black, Hall, and Martin 1991).

National Certificate modules have been taken by pupils in school as well as by students of all ages in further education colleges, either in full-time study or part-time or day-release from employment. Although these modules initially had the image of being for the less able, those who have taken them enjoyed the experience, liking the practical element, the active approach to teaching, and learning and preferring continuous assessment to an end of course examination. Gradually more use was made of modules in schools to provide the optional element in the S3/S4 curriculum and in S5 and S6 as an alternative to, or as a supplement to, Highers or CSYS.

Scottish Vocational Qualifications (SVQs) were introduced in 1989 to provide occupationally specific awards that can be gained at various levels (usually three levels). Criteria for achievement at the various levels are determined by Lead Bodies that have been given the responsibility for setting standards of competence in a particular occupation. This link gives industry responsibility for setting standards of competence, thus strengthening the voice of industry in vocational qualifications, always present but not dominant. General Scottish Vocational Qualifications (GSVQs) were introduced in 1991 as more broadly based qualifications not linked to specific occupations. Each GSVQ includes the assessment of core skills such as communication, numeracy, information technology, problem-solving, and interpersonal skills.

The new system of courses and qualifications being introduced from August 1999 makes provision for all students studying beyond Standard Grade. It will gradually replace Highers, CSYS, GSVQs, National Certificate Modules, various group awards, and Lifestart and Workstart (schemes for the least able). Work-based SVQs and advanced vocational awards remain outside the program. The new system is based on proposals outlined in *Higher Still: Opportunity for All* (SOEID 1994) and has become known as Higher Still. It provides courses and qualifications (National Qualifications) at five levels:

1. Advanced higher (roughly the equivalent of the level of CSYS)
2. Higher (equivalent to existing Higher)
3. Intermediate 2 (roughly equivalent of credit level at Standard Grade)
4. Intermediate 1 (roughly equivalent of general level at Standard Grade)
5. Access (which has three levels, the highest being equivalent of Foundation level at Standard Grade, the next for those with moderate learning difficulties and the lowest for those with more severe learning difficulties).

The courses are modular and comprise combinations of units of 40 hours' study. Most students will follow courses, at one of the five levels, of 160 hours of study made up of three units plus an additional 40 hours to provide coherence and prepare for external assessment. Group Awards constitute groups of courses that make up a coherent program; they replace GSVQs.

The assessment of units and courses is criterion-referenced. Units, whether they are free-standing or components of courses or group awards, are assessed internally.

They have specified learning outcomes and performance criteria that include reference to relevant core skills. It is intended that the criteria are applied by teachers and lecturers holistically to give pass/fail judgments. As most units will be being studied as components of a course, the unit assessment is seen as providing targets for students and as serving a formative purpose as well as contributing to the summative assessment of the course. The difficulties that this dual purpose is likely to present to teachers has been noted and action taken in the form of the development of a bank of assessment tasks. Teachers can draw on materials from this National Assessment Bank for assessing units. The use of this bank also serves to ensure that national standards are applied in unit assessments. All outcomes of a unit have to be passed but they do not have to be assessed at the same time. Those who do not succeed at first can undertake additional work and be reassessed.

To pass a *course assessment* students have to have achieved success in all the course units and in addition have undertaken an external assessment, set by the SQA. This includes written examination papers, project work, or practical performance, depending on the subject. Course passes are graded A, B, and C.

The development of Core Skills is a central part of the Higher Still program. The core skills and their components are:

- Communication (components: oral communication; written communication)
- Numeracy (components: using graphical information; using numbers)
- Problem-solving (components: critical thinking; planning and organizing; reviewing and evaluating)
- Information technology
- Working with others

The SQA has approved national standards for core skills and a structure for certificating their achievement at the various levels. Recognition of achievement of core skills is particularly important for those seeking a Group Award, where it is necessary to have achieved all core skills at the level, or the level below, at which the Group Award is sought. In some cases, the achievement of a core skill is part of the achievement of a course (e.g., numeracy will be automatically achieved in mathematics courses). All units and courses have been reviewed for their contribution to core skills or components of core skills. Where core skills have not been achieved in this way, there are special core skills units and related assessment up to Higher level for each of the five core skills which can be added to students' programs. Group awards will be awarded (at pass, merit, or distinction grades) for combinations of courses, units and core skills as indicated in Figure 8.4 (from Scottish CCC 1996c).

Figure 8.4
Group Awards in the Higher Still Program

Level	Group award assessment	Core skills attainment
Advanced Higher	Two Advanced Higher courses two Higher courses and four Higher units, or equivalent	Communication and personal effectiveness and problem solving at Higher level; numeracy and IT at Intermediate 2
Higher	Three Higher courses and eight units at Intermediate 2, or equivalent	All core skills at intermediate 2
Intermediate 2	Two Intermediate 2 courses and eight units at Intermediate 1, or equivalent	All core skills at intermediate 1
Intermediate 1	Two Intermediate 1 courses and eight units at Access Band 3, or equivalent	All core skills at Access Band 3
Access	Six units at Access Band 3 and six units at Access Band 2	Communication, numeracy and personal effectiveness and problem solving at Access band 2 level

USING ASSESSMENT TO INFLUENCE TEACHING: TARGET SETTING

There has long been resistance in Scotland to the notion of using pupil assessment to label schools. League tables for primary schools have been successfully resisted and "naming and shaming" of schools is not part of the strategy for raising standards. Using pupil assessment to place schools in rank order, as a way of forcing change in the curriculum or in teaching methods, is recognized as being unfair unless some measure of value-added by the school is used. Even then, ranking may alienate those at the bottom and fail to motivate those at the top of the order; it does not support the message that all schools can improve. Giving schools individual targets is a way of ensuring that all schools are expected to contribute to raising standards.

The use of assessment data for target setting at the institution level has been presented in Scotland as a further step in the general effort toward school improvement (SOEID 1998d, e). Since 1996, schools have been using qualitative performance indicators in school audit, self-evaluation, and development planning. Guidelines for these qualitative procedures were published under the title

How Good is Our School (SOEID 1996a) that included performance indicators for the "quality of pupils' learning." From 1998, however, there has been an emphasis on using pupil attainment as indicators of school effectiveness. A document, under the title *Raising Standards—Setting Targets,* stated that "[w]hat we can now expect is a sharpening of focus so that the attainment dimension becomes explicit and success becomes measurable" (SOEID 1998d). Rather more persuasively, the document claims that:

Setting targets would not work if self-evaluation were not already accepted as the way we do things in Scotland. We have known for a long time that the most effective way of improving the quality of education for individual pupils is for teachers in schools to evaluate what they are doing and to make the necessary changes. Targets are the logical next step. (SOEID 1998e, p. 2)

Target setting in Scotland is concerned with the attainment in numeracy and literacy (reading and writing). At all stages school targets are set in terms of numbers of pupils reaching certain levels, by comparing current performance with the performance of schools with "similar characteristics." These characteristics are represented by the proportion of pupils entitled to free school meals, since "research indicates that, while many characteristics of schools may be relevant to successful performance, of data currently available nationally, entitlement to free school meals consistently has the highest correlation to performance" (SOEID 1998e). Targets are set on 5–14 levels, Standard Grade and Higher Grade performance. In each case, national records are used to identify for a school its "scope for improvement," by comparing the school's performance averaged over the most recent three years with the average performance of the ten schools above and the ten schools below it when schools are ranked by their free school meals entitlement. The "scope for improvement" for a school already performing above the benchmark defined in this way will be the average level of improvement across all schools over the past three years. Targets are agreed between schools and their education authorities, taking into account their starting level, scope for improvement, and guidelines as to the lower and upper values of targets. The Audit Unit of the Scottish Office has provided packs of materials for primary and secondary schools to guide implementation and to indicate adaptations of the procedures necessary for small schools (SOEID 1998d).

DISCUSSION: THE INTERACTION OF CURRICULUM AND ASSESSMENT

This chapter has given an account of the curriculum and assessment in Scottish schools in terms of its history, present practice, and future intentions. Behind the detail, certain underlying themes can be discerned in the development of these two aspects of education. This final section summarizes these themes and looks at the interaction between the curriculum and assessment.

In relation to the curriculum, the main themes are that, in Scotland, the curriculum:

- is nonstatutory and implemented by consent
- requires a lengthy change process
- is arrived at by consultation and represents, as far as possible, consensus
- caters for the full range of abilities within a single program at each stage
- is set out in terms of outcomes
- aims to provide for breadth, balance, coherence, continuity, and progression in pupils' education.

In relation to assessment, the main goals and characteristics are that:

- it is criterion-referenced in intention and in application, although the criteria are identified by reference to norms
- it has a strong dependence on teacher assessment at all levels, using external tests at some stages to confirm these and to assure uniform interpretation of criteria
- it aims to ensure that all intended learning outcomes are assessed
- it is designed to make use of the same assessment formatively and summatively
- it uses pupil performance for setting individual school targets for raising standards of achievement.

It is now widely accepted that a strong interaction between the curriculum and assessment cannot be avoided. If this interaction is to have a positive supportive effect, helping to promote a broad and balanced curriculum, it is important that, as far as possible, the full range of intended learning is assessed. The insertion of "as far as possible" signals that this is not a straightforward matter. Ensuring that assessment supports learning of all kinds is often in conflict with the requirement to have reliable data for purposes of reporting the outcomes of learning at the individual, institution, or national level. Assessment in Scottish education attempts to avoid this conflict by using teachers to assess across all intended outcomes and using external tests to confirm the reliability of the judgment. This approach can be effective in opposing any narrowing of the curriculum to those outcomes that are tested, just as long as teachers' assessment are considered trustworthy and external tests do not dominate.

In other respects, too, assessment in Scotland is designed to support breadth in the curriculum. The continued existence of the AAP provides a means of monitoring national performance by providing a much more detailed picture of achievement than is possible by central collection of national test data, as in England. Using a range of assessment procedures at Standard Grade helps to preserve breadth within subjects and the absence of league tables of primary schools avoids competition based only on national tests. The danger of assessment narrowing the curriculum comes not from these procedures but from other directions.

Two related developments need to be monitored carefully for their effect on the breadth and balance of the curriculum. One is the current focus on numeracy and literacy, which in Scotland has been presented in the context of spending more time on "direct teaching" in English and mathematics and grouping pupils by attainment (SOEID 1996b). In the context of primary education this is in itself worrying, since other subjects have, by implication and time-tabling, been given the status of "second class" parts of the curriculum. Even more worrying is the second development, of target setting for schools in terms of pupil performance in English and mathematics. This focuses attention on the aspects of these two subjects that are assessed in the external tests at the 5–14 levels and the Standard Grade examination. While these are important they must not be allowed to over-shadow the aims of the curriculum that concern creativity, problem-solving, understanding of the world, and so on, which are outcomes of education widely agreed to be essential for future generations.

There is also anecdotal evidence that the pressure on teachers imposed by target setting is being passed on to pupils; anxiety about achievement in terms of outcomes measured by tests is being transmitted and transferred from teachers to learners. Involving pupils in their own assessment and helping them to identify short-term goals is fine in the context of enabling them to know what they should be aiming for. But it can acquire a negative rather than a positive influence on motivation and learning if pupils perceive pressure to meet expectations imposed by others and are constantly being measured against these expectations. This exposes a fine line between involving pupils in assessment and taking responsibility for their learning and blaming them for not attaining the teacher's goals. It is important that both teachers and pupils recognize the value of learning for reasons other than passing tests. It would be a matter for great regret if Scottish education allowed this approach to raising standards to devalue the broad ranging curriculum that has been established over the years through painstaking consultation and consensus.

REFERENCES

Barr, I. 1999. *Making the Connections: A Consideration of the Secondary Curriculum in Terms of Systemic Thinking.* Paper presented at the SCRE Forum on Educational Research I Scotland, Dunfermline, May.

Black, H., Hall, J., and Martin, S. 1991. *Modules: Teaching, Learning and Assessment.* Edinburgh: Scottish Council for Research in Education

DES/WO. 1987. *The National Curriculum 5–16: A Consultation Document.* DES/WO July.

Goldstein, H. 1996. *Times Educational Supplement,* June 14.

Harlen, W. 1996. *Four Years of Change in Education 5–14.* Edinburgh: SCRE.

Harlen, W., and James, M. 1997. "Assessment and Learning: Differences and Relationships Between Formative and Summative Assessment." *Assessment in Education* 4 (3):365–380.

James, M. 1998. *Using Assessment for School Improvement.* Oxford: Heinemann.

Malcolm, H., and Schlapp, U. 1997. *5–14 in the Primary School: A Continuing Challenge.* Edinburgh: SCRE.

McPake, J., Harlen, W., Powney, J., and Davidson, J. 1999. *Teachers' and Pupils' Days in the Primary Classroom.* Edinburgh: Scottish Council for Research in Education.

Scottish CCC. 1996a. *Assessment 5–14: Staff Development Activities.* Dundee: Scottish CCC.

Scottish CCC. 1996b. *Assessment.* Edinburgh: Scottish CCC Higher Still Development Unit.

Scottish CCC. 1996c. *Scottish Group Awards.* Edinburgh: Scottish CCC Higher Still Development Unit.

Scottish CCC. 1996d. *Assessment in Scottish Group Awards.* Edinburgh: Scottish CCC Higher Still Development Unit.

Scottish CCC. 1998a. *A Curriculum Framework for Children 3 to 5: Consultation Draft.* Dundee: Scottish CCC.

Scottish CCC. 1998b. *Promoting Learning: Assessing Children's Progress 3 to 5.* Dundee: Scottish CCC.

SCRE. 1995. *Taking a Closer Look Series: Introductory Booklet; English Language Package; Mathematics Package; Science.* Edinburgh: Scottish Council for Research in Education.

SED. 1987. *Curriculum and Assessment in Scotland. A Policy for the 90s.* Edinburgh: SED.

SOED. 1991a. *The Framework for National Testing in Session 1991-2.* Edinburgh: SOED.

SOED. 1991b. *Assessment 5–14 Part 3 Staff Development Pack.* Edinburgh: SOED, Scottish Office, October.

SOED. 1992a. *Arrangements for National Testing.* Edinburgh: SOED, Circular 12/92, November.

SOED. 1992b. *Upper Secondary Education in Scotland* (the Howie report). Edinburgh: HMSO.

SOED. 1993. *The Structure and Balance of the Curriculum 5–14.* Edinburgh: SOED.

SOEID. 1994. *Higher Still: Opportunity for All.* Edinburgh: Scottish Office.

SOEID. 1996a. *How Good is Our School?* Edinburgh: Audit Unit, SOEID.

SOEID. 1996b. *Achievement for All.* Edinburgh: SOEID.

SOEID. 1997. *A Curriculum Framework for Children in their Pre-School Year.* Edinburgh: Scottish Office.

SOEID. 1998a. *Statistical Bulletin,* Edn/C3/1998/11, December 1998. Edinburgh: Scottish Office.

SOEID. 1998b. *Scottish Education Statistics Annual Review 3 1998 Edition.* Edinburgh: SOEID.

SOEID. 1998c. *Baseline Assessment in Scotland Pilot Procedures. Information for Staff.* Edinburgh: SOEID. draft.

SOEID. 1998d. *Raising Standards—Setting Targets. Primary Schools Support Pack.* Edinburgh: Audit Unit, SOEID.

SOEID. 1998e. *Setting Targets—Raising Standards in Schools.* Edinburgh: Audit Unit, SOEID.

9

Conceptual Frameworks to Accommodate the Validation of Rapidly Changing Requirements for Assessments

Anthony J. Nitko

Changes in society, economics, and technology impact on our ideas about the appropriate outcomes of schooling. New ideas about school outcomes and accompanying rapid technological change, in turn, change the way we view appropriate educational testing and evaluation. There is an increasing emphasis on criterion-referenced and standards-based assessment, a greater focus on requiring candidates to demonstrate their learning in ways that are creative, authentic, and related to real-world problem-solving, an increased focus on the development of expertise, and a slow but accelerating global movement toward computer-assisted testing.

Innovative schooling proposals and new assessment concepts challenge our traditional thinking about examinations and testing. How should we view these challenges to those traditional assessment frameworks? What conceptual tools do we have at our disposal to help us both to evaluate the quality of proposals put before us and to develop high quality assessments of our own? These are some of the questions that are addressed in this chapter.

Five frameworks are briefly considered. Two of these frameworks refer to those agencies that develop assessments. One framework challenges us to reexamine how agencies organize themselves to monitor assessment quality. Another asks us to view the organization's activities as one part of a broader assessment system for a nation or a region. The third and fourth frameworks focus on how we describe assessment quality at the technical level—here we need to reexamine traditional validity and reliability concepts. The fifth framework examines the development of problem-solving skills and the challenge they present when we craft assessments.

These frameworks were selected because they seem to be: (1) useful for evaluating both traditional as well as the newer proposals for assessment; (2) durable enough to sustain us both for our immediate needs as well as for our long-term needs; and (3) practical both for low resource and for high resource assessment agencies. These frameworks present us with ways of thinking about how to review existing assessment policies, how to evaluate proposed new assessment technologies and formats, and how to prepare assessment validation strategies.

THE FIRST FRAMEWORK: ORGANIZATIONAL MATURITY

Let us turn first to the organizations and agencies that produce assessments. The first question that needs to be answered is whether our organization's capability to produce assessments has matured. A test development agency is considered mature if it has the following two characteristics: first, that it is capable of publicly stating the processes everyone in the organization consistently uses to guarantee that the assessments it produces are of the highest possible quality; second, that everyone in the agency works daily to improve production processes leading to higher quality assessments.

The conceptual framework for thinking about this is called the *Capability Maturity Model* (CMM). It was originally formulated to evaluate an organization's capacity to engineer quality computer software (Paulk, Weber, Garcia, Chrissis, and Busch 1993). It is used here as a framework for evaluating how we craft high quality tests, examinations, and other assessments. The framework may be used to conduct either formative or summative evaluations of an organization's maturity.

In the Capacity Maturity Model framework, a test development agency is considered mature when it has four characteristics. First, it must *officially implement and monitor a set of standard procedures* that all persons who are responsible for developing assessments in that agency are required to follow for each assessment they develop. These standard procedures should aim to guarantee that every assessment product developed by the agency is of the highest possible quality. Second, a mature test development agency must *officially define the quality standards* every assessment product must meet before being released. Third, the agency must *measure the quality of its own development processes and its own products,* and use these measures to monitor and guarantee assessment production quality. Fourth, the agency must *create a culture of quality improvement.* In such a culture, all persons in the organization, from the lowest to the highest, continually invent and implement ways to improve the assessments and the assessment development process.

A testing agency's progress in reaching the highest level of maturity is described below. Level 1 is the lowest level and is characterized by a lack of virtually all four of the maturity characteristics described previously. The intermediate levels of maturity shown describe how an agency may partially meet some or all of the four characteristics. Level 5 is the highest maturity level. At this level all four maturity characteristics are accounted for.

A CAPABILITY MATURITY MODEL FOR DEVELOPING ASSESSMENTS

Level 1: The Initial Level

At this level, the organization does not provide a stable development environment. The benefits of good assessment practices are undermined by poor planning and reaction-driven procedures. The capability of the organization to produce assessments is unpredictable, processes constantly change as work progresses, and success depends primarily on the capability of the individual(s) (often one) who happen(s) to be employed at the moment.

Level 2: The Repeatable Level

At this level, the organization establishes and implements policies for managing assessment development. The goal at this level is to institutionalize procedures for managing assessment development, including tracking development costs, schedules, and validation procedures; the integrity of each assessment product is controlled. Quality standards for assessments are defined, and the organization ensures they are monitored and met. The assessment development process is under the control of the management system and follows realistic plans based on previous assessment development projects.

Level 3: The Defined Level

At this level, the organization adopts and implements a standard assessment development process, including both management and technical development procedures. The standard process may be improved or changed over time as a result of experience and new technical development. A specific group is responsible for the organization's assessment development process activities. Training and staff development programs are instituted to ensure staff and managers have the knowledge and skills needed to produce high quality assessment tools. Since assessments of different formats in different curricular areas have somewhat different development characteristics, the standard process may need to be tailored to each unique type of assessment product, but the tailored process still fits within the framework of the organization's standard process. The tailored process is well-defined, meaning that the production process articulates elements such as necessary inputs, standards, and procedures for doing work; verification procedures (such as, peer review, tryout data analyses); outputs; and completion criteria. Management has a good grasp and understanding of the technical progress of the assessment development in each curricular area.

Level 4: The Managed Level

At this level, the organization sets quantitative goals for the assessments and the development process. The organization measures quality for all development activities across all assessment products. Assessment products' qualities are measured in an institution-wide attempt to improve or maintain quality. The organization's assessment products are of a predictable quality because quality tolerances and quality control measures are instituted. The organization takes corrective action when the assessments fall outside of the organization's quality tolerances.

Level 5: The Optimizing Level

At this level, the entire organization focuses on continuously improving the assessment development process. The organization has the ability and means to work actively to strengthen the assessment development process and to prevent the development of poor quality assessment products. New procedures and technology are evaluated and implemented throughout the organization if they can be shown to improve assessment quality. Assessment development processes are analyzed to identify faulty procedures, and the lessons learned are disseminated to all assessment development projects. (Capacity maturity ideas are adapted from Paulk et al. [1993].)

A detailed discussion of this first framework is beyond the scope of this chapter. However, a few simple examples of specifying assessment quality standards and measuring them may be helpful to understanding the model at this point. These examples are shown in Figure 9.1. Extensive discussions of quality standards are found in several sources such as the forthcoming revised *Standards for Educational and Psychological Testing* (Joint Committee 1999) and *Enhancing Quality in Assessment* (Harlen 1994).

Figure 9.1
Translating Broad Quality Goals to Specific Performance Goals for Examination Items: Simple Examples

Quality Purpose	Conceptual Performance	Measurement	Performance Goal
Accuracy	Accuracy of the items' content	Content experts' rating of each item (0–4)	Each item has average rating of 3.5 or higher
	Correspondence of the items to thinking skills	Content experts' rating of each item (0–4)	Each item has average rating of 3.5 or higher
Relevance	Relevance and importance of the task posed to the candidate	Content experts' rating of each item (0–4)	Each item has average rating of 3.5 or higher

Highest Technical Merit	Flawlessly written	Review of item by professional item-writer	Zero item writing flaws for each item
	Appropriate vocabulary	All words in an item are from the officially designated list(s) of appropriate vocabulary	Each item contains only those words on the list(s)
	Appropriate difficulty	Item p-value, or facility value from an appropriate sample of examinees	$.05 < p < .95$
	Appropriate discrimination[a]	Item discrimination index from an appropriate sample	$r > .2$
	Avoidance of ethnic and gender stereotypes	Judgments of representatives of affected groups	No item is judged to contain a stereotype
	Avoidance of bias	Judgments of representatives of affected groups	No item is judged to contain bias

Note: [a]Examples are for multiple-choice items. Open-response and performance items might use other statistical indices. If item response theory models are used, indices consistent with this approach should be specified.

THE SECOND FRAMEWORK: PROCESS MODELING

The second framework to consider is that of *process modeling.* In order for an organization to evaluate its maturity in producing consistently high quality assessments, it is first necessary for the organization to identify the development steps it requires everyone to follow in order to craft quality assessments. An organization's capability maturity rests on how well it can define, implement, and manage an appropriate model on a standard process for assessment development. There is no universally acceptable standard process because each agency crafts a unique set of assessment products. However, each mature organization should develop a standard model for its own use.

In some national assessment organizations the problem might be considered from a systems perspective. That is, an organization may view itself as included in and contributing toward a national or regional assessment system rather than only as an independent assessment product producer. An *assessment system* is a set of processes for producing as well as using highly valid educational assessments. It describes procedures for the day-to-day production and uses of assessment products and procedures that fit a wide range of assessment needs in the region's or nation's educational system.

The alignment of assessments with national curricula is a special case for those countries that have a requirement to implement a centrally-devised curriculum. A *curriculum-based assessment system* must adhere to the following principles:

1. All processes used to develop assessment tasks must begin and end with the curriculum.

2. The overall process model assures that every step in assessment development is systematically and carefully linked to the curriculum.

3. The process must produce assessments that are seamless with both curriculum and teaching. *Seamless assessment* means that each assessment product is easily recognized by school officials, teachers, students, parents, and the public as requiring the same types of knowledge and abilities that are not only desirable but that, in fact, have been taught in the school over a long period of time. In this way, teaching and assessment become aligned and integrated.

Figure 9.2 shows one process model for developing curriculum-based assessments. Discussion of the details of this model is presented elsewhere (Nitko 1994, 1998). For our purposes here, it is important to note that the model shows only the major stages of assessment development and those outcomes that are expected at each stage. The stages begin with the lower left box and move to the right, thus showing how curriculum needs drive the process. Before implementing this model, an assessment-crafting organization will need to flesh out the details of each step of the process. An example of this is given in Nitko (1994).

The models that an organization adopts must become the conceptual frameworks for *all* persons in the organization. Quality can not be sustained unless all persons in the organization agree that these models are the way this organization chooses to operate. The process models adopted become part of the "quality culture" of the organization. They contribute to the organization's capacity maturity.

THE THIRD FRAMEWORK: ARGUMENT-BASED VALIDATION

The next framework focuses on validating assessments. Thus far in our discussion, we have constantly referred to the quality of assessments. Assessment quality is described using the technical concept of validity. *Validity* refers to the soundness of the interpretations and uses of assessment results, rather than to the assessment instrument itself.

Traditionally, we have used a tripartite model of validities:

Figure 9.2
Process Model for Curriculum-Driven Assessment Development

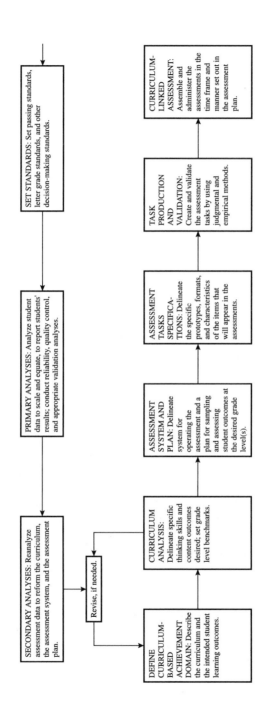

Source: Nitko (1995, p. 8)

1. *Content validity,* which describes how well the tasks sample a defined content domain.
2. *Construct validity,* which describes how well results can be interpreted as assessing the test's focal construct.
3. *Criterion-related validity,* which describes how well results correlate or predict criterion measures that are external to the focal assessment.

As useful as these three ideas have been in the past, it is now generally recognized that we are better served if validation is viewed as one entity rather than as three separate entities. The framework we may consider as we look forward to validating both traditional and new assessments is the framework of argument-based validation (Kane 1992).

The *argument-based validation* framework asks us to describe clearly three criteria for each assessment used. First, we describe the interpretations we propose to make of the assessment results. Second, we describe the reasons why this interpretation is relevant to the major use(s) we plan to make of the results. Third, we explain how the evidence we have collected supports our proposed interpretation in the context of the use(s) we plan to make of the results.

There are many different types of evidence that can be brought to bear on the validity argument. The evidence may be a combination of types. It may be empirical and statistical, it may be based on theory and literature review, or it may consist of the results of logical analyses. The mix of particular evidence needed depends on the particular interpretation and use(s) we propose. For example, suppose a mathematics test is administered as part of a computer-assisted university entrance examination. Suppose further that the test is intended to assess a candidate's readiness for university level work requiring certain prerequisite mathematics achievements. The validity argument for such an interpretation and use must supply evidence to support the following kinds of propositions or claims about the test:

1. The mathematics content and skills assessed by the examination are in fact necessary for the university level work.
2. The examination tasks were crafted by representatively sampling the appropriate domains of prerequisite mathematics skills and knowledge.
3. The way the tasks are chosen and presented by the computer are faithful to the mathematics constructs that are the target of assessment and instruction.
4. The examination scores are consistent and generalizable across different representative sets of items from the domain.
5. The computerized interface, mode of testing, the candidates' familiarity with computers, and the candidates' test and computer anxiety do not seriously affect the examination scores.
6. If the test is expected to predict success at the university level, the work of candidates who are at the university level can be assessed well.
7. Those students with higher levels of success with the university work have attained the higher scores on the computer-assisted test and vice versa.

Table 9.1
Summary of the Different Types of Validity Evidence for Educational Assessments

Type of Evidence	Examples of questions needing to be answered	Techniques often used to obtain answers
1. Content representativeness and relevance (called *content evidence*)	a. How well do the assessment tasks represent the domain of important content? b. How well do the assessment tasks represent the curriculum as you define it? c. How well do the assessment tasks reflect current thinking about what should be taught and assessed? d. Are the assessment tasks worthy of being learned?	A description of the curriculum and content to be learned is obtained. Each assessment task is checked to see if it matches important content and learning outcomes. Each assessment task is rated for its relevance, importance, accuracy and meaningfulness. The assessment procedure is viewed as a whole and judgments are made about representativeness and relevance of the entire collection of tasks.
2. Types of thinking skills and processes required (called *substantive evidence*).	a. How much do the assessment tasks require students to use important thinking skills and processes? b. How well do the assessment tasks represent the types of thinking skills espoused as important curriculum outcomes? c. Are the thinking skills and processes that students actually use to complete the assessment procedure the same ones claimed to be assessed?	The assessment procedure is analyzed to reveal the types of cognitions required to perform the tasks successfully. The relationship between the strategies students are taught to use and those they are required to use during the assessment are determined. Students may be asked to "think aloud" while performing the assessment tasks and the resultant protocols analyzed to identify cognitions the students used. Judgments are made about the assessment procedure as a whole to decide whether desirable, representative, and relevant thinking skills and processes are being assessed.

Table 9.1 (continued)

3. Relationships among the assessment tasks or parts of the assessment (called *internal structure evidence*)	a. Do all the assessment tasks "work together" so that each task contributes positively toward assessing the quality of interest? b. If the different parts of the assessment procedure are supposed to provide unique information, do the results support this uniqueness? c. If the different parts of the assessment procedure are supposed to provide the same or similar information, do the results support this? d. Are the students' scored in a way that is consistent with the constructs and theory on which the assessment is based?	a. If student's performance on each task is quantified, correlations of tasks scores with total scores, from the assessment are studied to decide whether all tasks contribute positively. b. Each part of the assessment may be scored separately and these part scores intercorrelated to see whether the desired pattern of relationships emerges. c. Logic, substantive knowledge, and experience are used to generate explanations for high and low performance on the assessment. Not all hypotheses should be consistent with the intended interpretations of how the parts function. d. Empirical studies, both experimental and correlational, are conducted to support or refute the hypotheses generated in (c) above.
4. Relationships of assessment results to the results of other variables (called *external structure evidence*)	a. Are the results of this assessment consistent with the results of other similar assessments for these students? b. How well does performance on this assessment procedure reflect the quality or trait that is measured by other tests? c. How well does performance on this assessment procedure predict current or future performance on other valued tasks or measures (criteria)? d. How well can the assessment results be used to select persons for jobs, schools, etc? What is the magnitude of error? e. How well can the assessment results be used to assign pupils to different types of instruction? Is learning better when pupils are assigned this way?	a. The criterion tasks are identified and analyzed. Assessment of their important characteristics are created. b. Scores from the assessment are compared to scores on the criterion to be predicted. c. Studies of various classification and prediction errors are made. d. Studies show whether the results from this assessment converge with or diverge from results from other assessments in the way expected when the proposed interpretation of the students' performance is used. (Called *convergent and discriminant evidence*.)

5. Reliability, over time, assessors, and content domain (called *reliability evidence*)	a. Will the same students obtain nearly the same results if the assessment procedure was applied on another occasion? What is the margin of error expected? b. If different persons administered, graded, or scored the assessment results, would the students' outcomes be the same? What is the margin of error? c. If a second, alternate form of the assessment procedure were to be developed with similar content, would the students' results be very similar? What is the margin of error?	Studies are conducted focusing on the consistency (reliability) of the assessment results.
6. Generalizability over different types of people, under different conditions, or with special instruction/ intervention (called *generalizability evidence*).	a. Does the assessment procedure give significantly different results when it is used with students from different socio-economic and ethnic backgrounds, but of the same ability? If so, is this fair or unbiased? b. Will students' results from the assessment procedure be altered drastically if they are given special incentives or motives? If so should this change how the assessment results are interpreted? c. Will special intervention, changes in instructions, or special coaching significantly alter the results students obtain on the assessment? If so, should this change how the assessment results are interpreted?	a. Logic, substantive knowledge, and experience are used to generate explanations (hypotheses) about how the interpretation of the assessment results might change when the procedure is applied to different types of people, under different conditions, or with special instruction (*intervention*). b. Empirical studies, both experimental and correlational, are conducted to support or refute the hypotheses generated in (a) above.

153

7. Value of the intended and/or unintended consequences (called *consequential evidence*).	a. What do we expect from the students if we interpret and use the assessment results in this particular way? To what degree do these expected consequences happen, and is that good? b. What side effects do we anticipate happening to the students if we interpret and use the assessment results in this particular way? To what degree are these anticipated side effects occurring, and are they positive or negative? c. What unanticipated negative side effects happened to the students for whom we interpreted and used the assessment results in this particular way? Can these negative side effects be avoided by using other assessment procedures/techniques or by altering our interpretations?	a. Studies are conducted to describe the intended outcomes of using the given assessment procedure and to determine the degree to which these outcomes are realized for all students. b. Studies are conducted to determine whether anticipated or unanticipated side effects have resulted from interpreting and using the given assessment procedure in a certain way. c. Logical analyses, substantive knowledge and value analyses are used to evaluate whether the existing assessment procedure should be continued or replaced by an alternative.
8 Cost, efficiency, practicality, instructional features (called *practicality evidence*)	a. Can the assessment procedure accommodate typical numbers of students? b. Is the assessment procedure easy for teachers to use? c. Can the assessment procedure give quick results to guide instruction? d. Do teachers agree that the theoretical concepts behind the assessment procedure reflect the key understandings they are teaching? e. Do the assessment results meaningfully explain individual differences? f. Do the assessment results identify misunderstandings that need to be corrected? g. Would an alternative assessment procedure be more efficient?	Logical analyses, cost analyses, reviews by teachers, and field trial data are used to come to decisions about the factors of cost, efficiency practicality and usefulness of instructional features.

Note: These types of validity evidence have been suggested by Messick (1989; 1994b) and Linn, Baker, and Dunbar (1991).

Source: Nitko (1996, pp. 44–45).

The categories or classes of evidence that need to be collected to support a validity argument are not unlimited (Messick 1989). Basically there are eight types of evidence (Nitko 1996); these are shown in Table 9.1. A complete discussion of each type is beyond the scope of this chapter, but can be found in *Revised Standards for Educational and Psychological Testing* (Joint Committee 1999).

FOURTH FRAMEWORK: GENERALIZABILITY THEORY

Reliability is a psychometric framework that refers to the way we describe the consistency of examinees' assessment results. Traditionally, we have asked whether content sampling, occasions (time) sampling, or marker sampling seriously affect the scores examinees attain. With the broadening of assessments to include mixtures of performance assessments and response-choice items, or new assessment formats such as computer-assisted testing, we may need to choose a somewhat broader framework to study reliability.

Traditionally, we have viewed reliability as a limiting factor for validity. That is, we have held that test scores cannot be valid unless they are reliable. New assessment methods have challenged this conventional wisdom. In some educational assessment systems, both the content of the assessment and the administrative conditions have become less standardized and more flexible. School-based projects, experiments, portfolios, and investigations have allowed students to choose the topics, to vary the time for completion, and to decide whether to work individually or cooperatively in groups. A social studies project, for example, may require students to identify local environmental issues for which a survey of community members is administered, the data collected, conclusions drawn, and oral and written reports prepared. Such wide-ranging assessment tasks provide serious challenges for both defining and evaluating the impact of measurement error.

It can be argued that less standardized and more flexible tasks such as performance assessments and projects are more valid because they increase the breadth of coverage and, therefore, assess more construct-relevant variance. Wide-ranging and less standardized tasks also may be less reliable. If it can be demonstrated that the loss of reliability that is most likely to result when using these assessments also reduces construct-irrelevant variances and increases construct-relevant variances, then validity is likely to increase. Thus, the conventional wisdom, that reducing reliability automatically reduces validity, may need to be modified or at least seriously qualified (Feldt 1997).

Sources of measurement error can be roughly organized into two groups: those stemming from the person being assessed and those stemming from conditions external to the person. When a person's attention fluctuates, or motivation wanes, or anxiety temporarily increases, these are factors internal to the examinee. When conditions vary from one examination site to the next, when the themes of essays vary from one assessment to the next, or when markers fluctuate in their scoring, these are factors external to the examinee. In different assessment situations some factors are more of concern than in other situations.

In classical measurement theory, however, error of measurement is discussed as a single entity, even though it may arise from several sources. When assessment contexts become more flexible or when new assessment technologies are used, it is more important to separately evaluate the impact of different sources of error, rather than to treat measurement error as a single entity. If so, then the generalizability theory framework is a better way in which to discuss reliability. (See, for example, Cronbach, Gleser, Nanda, and Rajaratnam [1972]; Brennan [1983]; Feldt and Brennan [1989].)

A *generalizability theory framework* allows for study of each source of error. It also permits the evaluation of the interaction among sources of errors. The framework uses analysis of variance methodology to estimate the magnitude of the variance components attributed to each source (and possibly their interactions). This permits us to estimate the relative contribution of each source to the variance in the overall scores. Once the contributions are identified, we can modify our assessment procedures in ways to reduce the influence of undesirable sources of error. Thus, generalizability theory is a better framework than classical reliability theory when we wish to improve the quality of the assessments we craft.

As an example, consider the generalizability study of mathematics performance assessments conducted by Lane, Liu, Ankenmann, and Stone (1996). They investigated the relationships among examinees, raters of examinee responses, and performance tasks within the same subject (junior secondary mathematics). The variances due to raters, examinee × rater interaction, and rater × task interaction were very small. In their assessment situation, they had controlled these sources of error by using well-developed scoring rubrics and highly-trained raters. Notice how the generalizability study has pinpointed those aspects of assessment that were done well.

However, the examinee × task interaction variance was quite large, accounting for the largest proportion of the total variance. This finding is important to the assessment developers since it tells them that the particular task to which a particular examinee responded had a very large impact on the examinee's results. The impact of the overall difficulty or ease of a particular task (as contrasted with a task being difficult for one person but not another) was small. Thus, it was not task difficulty per se that was the source of measurement error, but how individuals interacted with specific tasks that created the error. This finding has implication for designing the assessments.

Figure 9.3 shows a graph of how reliability (called "generalizability coefficient" in the graph) increases in relation to both the number of raters and the number of tasks. Adding more well-trained raters who use well-developed rubrics does not improve reliability very much. The graph shows that instead of increasing raters, assessment crafters need to increase the number of tasks to be more certain that they have reasonable levels of score reliability. This projection

Figure 9.3
Change in Reliability as the Number of Tasks and the Number of Raters

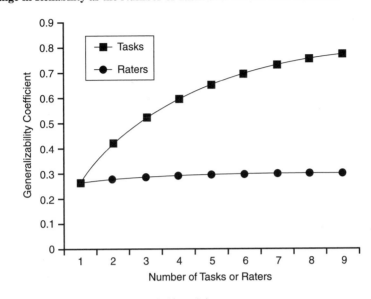

Source: Lane et al. (1996, p. 82, Figure 1). Reprinted with permission.

is a direct result of the large examinee × task interaction variance discovered through generalizability theory analysis.

THE FIFTH FRAMEWORK: DEVELOPMENT OF PROBLEM-SOLVING

The final framework that we need to consider focuses on assessing problem-solving abilities. Unlike the four frameworks described previously, this important area of assessment is less well developed and less well validated. However, we should consider how our traditional and our newer assessment systems might improve on the current state of affairs.

Before presenting the framework, we need to adopt a definition of what constitutes a *problem* for a person. A person incurs a problem when he or she wants to reach a specific outcome or goal but does not automatically recognize the proper path or solution to use to reach it. By contrast, if the procedure to reach a goal is so well known to a person that the person can complete the task without having to reason, the person does not have to use problem-solving abilities. The teenagers' slang for the latter class of tasks is "no-brainers." They recognize that if you do not have to think about a proper solution to achieve the desired outcome, it is a "no-brainer," or, in other words, there is no problem to solve.

Unfortunately, many problems in textbooks and in some examinations are only a few notches above "no-brainers." They present tasks that are clearly laid out. All of the information a student needs is given, and there is usually one correct answer that students can give by applying a procedure taught in class. These are known as well-structured problems (Frederiksen 1984). Well-structured problems are not like the real-life or authentic problems students will eventually have to face. Most authentic problems are poorly structured (Simon 1973). When a problem is poorly structured, it is not clear exactly what the problem is. For poorly structured problems, persons have to: (1) organize the information presented in order to understand it; (2) clarify the problem itself; (3) obtain all the information needed (which may not be immediately available); and (4) recognize that there may be more than one equally correct answer.

We should recognize the dilemma that teachers face when presenting students with problem-solving tasks. The point of much instruction is to show students efficient strategies to solve common tasks. Teachers wish students to learn a wide repertoire of strategies that can be used to find solutions to very specific tasks which they may encounter. In fact, for experts many tasks that novices would classify as genuine problems are, perhaps, "no brainers" because experts have encountered such tasks many times and can easily solve them. Asking students to solve poorly structured problems, problems without a single solution, or problems for which incomplete information is given, goes against the grain of many teachers' thinking, who wish to help students find answers rather than put obstacles in their way. This is an area for curriculum discussion about what are the proper goals of instruction and assessment in a subject area.

In general, we may approach the assessment of a person's problem-solving ability from two perspectives. According to one perspective, we could adopt a model for the process persons tend to use to solve problems and then assess whether examinees have the skills associated with each step in the problem-solving process. Another perspective is more developmental. According to this perspective we identify the characteristics of expert problem solvers in a particular subject area and then assess how well examinees are developing or progressing along a growth continuum for these characteristics.

The framework that has the best chance of meeting these criteria is the *developmental problem-solving perspective* proposed by Glaser, Lesgold, and Lajoie (1985). They view problem-solving as a set of complex skills that persons develop as they master a field of study. Based on research about the differences between experts and novices, they have developed a set of dimensions along which cognitive problem-solving ability grows. These dimensions are listed in Table 9.2, and each dimension is briefly described below.

Table 9.2
Glaser, Lesgold, and Lajoie's Dimensions of Problem-Solving Skill Development

Knowledge organization and structure

Depth of problem representation

Quality of mental models

Efficiency of procedures

Automaticity of performance

Metacognitive skills for learning

Knowledge Organization and Structure

Experts' Schemata—Experts in an area use their extensive knowledge to solve problems that arise in their area of expertise. However, beyond their very extensive knowledge, experts' knowledge is well-organized and a great many facts, concepts, principles, and ideas are conceptually related to each other. Novices, on the other hand, have less well-organized knowledge—they often see concepts and procedures in an area as separate pieces of knowledge that are not connected.

Assessment Implications—To assess a person's growth in this dimension, we need to gather information about how each person organizes and connects the concepts in order to solve the problems in a subject area. Assessment should focus on discovering whether a person sees different parts of a subject domain as distinct or separate. For example, does a student see the arithmetic operations of addition, subtraction, multiplication, and division as isolated, separate, or unrelated? How well integrated are the concepts in a subject? Currently, our methodology has not allowed us to proceed with assessing this dimension in large-scale assessments. Progress has been made in assessing this dimension with individuals, however. Computers with graphical interfaces have also proved useful for rudimentary assessment of individual's knowledge organization (e.g., Ju 1989; Fisher 1990; Young 1993; Zhu 1997).

Depth of Problem Representation

Experts' Representations—Experts and novices tend to represent the problem to themselves at different levels. Experts represent or characterize problems according to the principles of the discipline that underlie the problems' solutions. Novices, on the other hand, tend to represent problems according to the problem's surface features. By using a deeper, principle-based way of representing problems, experts are more likely than novices to activate an appropriate scheme for solving a problem.

Assessing Representation—Currently we do have a useful way of assessing how well a student represents problems in terms of their deeper features. In research studies, giving persons a set of diverse problems and asking them to sort the problems into groups is used sometimes to assess this dimension. After sorting, persons are interviewed to discuss why they grouped the problems that way. The interviewer tries to discover whether the person is using deeper principles or surface features to organize the problem.

Quality of Mental Models

Experts' Models—The quality of experts' mental models are intricate. They can show how things work in an area, how they are related and how they form systems. Experts can create mental images of how systems in a knowledge domain operate and are organized. Novices' models, on the other hand, are vague, and concepts and systems are unrelated. Students who do not have a mental model of proportional reasoning, for example, may see division, fractions, and decimals as separate arithmetic systems, rather than linked into a single system. As a result, when faced with a complex problem that requires using all three concepts, they represent the problem in a limited way.

Assessment of Mental Models—This dimension also presents an assessment challenge. One approach is to have a person diagram, sketch, or draw to communicate his or her understanding or model. This has limited usefulness and requires some skill in communicating via spatial or graphical modes.

Efficiency of Procedures

Experts' Efficiency—Experts are more efficient when they solve problems. They use fewer, and eliminate, unnecessary steps. Novices may follow a step-by-step procedure that reaches a correct solution, but many of the steps may not be necessary. They do not know the "short-cuts" and "quick tricks" that experts use to reach solutions quickly. Efficiency is a sign that a person is becoming a better problem solver.

Assessing Efficiency—This dimension provides an assessment challenge also. On an individual level, one can observe how persons solve both well-structured and poorly-structured problems. It is possible to ask persons to show the process they used to solve a problem or to show their intermediate work. They are then interviewed about how they go about solving a problem.

Automaticity of Performance

Experts' Automaticity—Experts solve problems more automatically and smoothly than novices. Experts, however, tend to spend more "up-front" time thinking about a complex problem and planning its solution than do novices.

Novices often begin to solve a problem without thinking through their approach. Once experts begin, they proceed quickly toward a solution.

Assessing Automaticity—When automaticity is considered as a developmental strand for problem-solving, one must focus on assessing the smoothness and speed with which the person solves a problem, writes a paper, or completes an experiment. Novices tend to ponder each step or follow a set of algorithms slavishly. These observations of persons can be done reasonably well at the individual level, but we have not reached the point of using them in large-scale assessment programs.

Metacognitive Skills

Experts' Metacognition—Experts' cognitions are often characterized by planning and monitoring. Experts plan their approach to solving problems. They monitor how well they are progressing in solving a problem. They are quick to modify or change their approach if their monitoring indicates that they are not progressing well. Novices do not plan well. Once they start down a path, they may ignore signs that they are not proceeding in a correct direction.

Assessing Metacognitions—Assessing this dimension is difficult because planning, monitoring, and thinking are internal. Two assessment strategies have been tried. One strategy is to interview students or ask persons to think aloud as they solve problems. One may focus the interview on how the person plans the problem solution and what the person does to monitor progress. Another strategy is to use a questionnaire to assess a person's awareness of their use of metacognitions. While these strategies appear to have promise for classroom assessment, at present assessment is a real challenge for large scale assessment programs.

SUMMARY

This chapter has attempted to challenge individuals and organizations to better meet new and emerging assessment needs. First, it challenged the testing agency to organize itself for continual improvement of the quality of its assessment products. The Capacity Maturity Model was presented as one possible framework for evaluating how well one has accomplished that goal. Second, it challenged the testing agency to view itself as part of a broad system of local or national assessment—a system that included assessment at all levels of the educational enterprise. An example of a process model for curriculum-based assessment was presented to illustrate one approach. Next it turned to a closer examination of what quality assessment means. It discussed the validity argument framework as a way to support the quality of interpretations and uses of assessment results. In addition, it challenged assessment developers to use a generalizability theory framework to identify and study the impact of multiple sources of measurement error. The use of generalizability theory was shown to point to assessment design factors that should be the focus of development. Finally, it looked at assessing problem-solving ability. A developmental framework was discussed which looked at six dimensions of problem-solving ability along which experts and novices differ. At present these dimensions have not been well-assessed. They present a challenge for future assessment methods and technologies.

REFERENCES

Brennan, R. L. 1983. *Elements of Generalizability Theory.* Iowa City, IA: American College Testing Program.

Cronbach, L. J., Gleser, G. C., Nanda, H., and Rajaratnam, N. 1972. *The Dependability of Behavioral Measurements: Theory of Generalizability for Scores and Profiles.* New York: John Wiley and Sons.

Feldt, L. S. 1997. "Can Validity Rise When Reliability Declines?" *Applied Measurement in Education* 10:377–387.

Feldt, L. S., and Brennan, R. L. 1989. "Reliability." In R. L. Linn (Ed.), *Educational Measurement* (3rd ed.). Phoenix, AZ: Oryx Press, pp. 105–146.

Fisher, K. 1990. "Semantic Networking: The New Kid on the Block." *Journal of Research in Science Teaching* 27:1001–1018.

Frederiksen, N. 1984. "Implications of Cognitive Theory for Instruction in Problem-solving." *Review of Educational Research* 54:363–407.

Glaser, R., Lesgold, A., and Lajoie, S. 1985. "Toward a Cognitive Theory for the Measurement of Achievement." In R. Ronnug, J. Gloveer, J. Conoley and J. Witts (Eds.), *The Influence of Cognitive Psychology on Testing and Measurement.* Hillsdale, NJ: Erlbaum, pp. 41–85.

Harlen, W. (Ed.). 1994. *Enhancing Quality in Assessment.* London: Paul Chapman Publishing.

Joint Committee. 1999. *Final Draft of the Revision of the Standards for Educational and Psychological Testing.* Available on the World Wide Web at www.apa.org/science/standards.html.

Ju, T-P. 1989. *The Development of a Microcomputer-Assisted Measurement Tool to Display a Person's Knowledge Structure.* Pittsburgh, PA: University of Pittsburgh, unpublished doctoral dissertation.

Kane, M. 1992. "An Argument-Based Approach to Validity." *Psychological Bulletin* 112:527–535.

Lane, S., Liu, M., Ankenmann, R., and Stone, C. 1996. "Generalisability and Validity of a Mathematics Performance Assessment." *Journal of Educational Mathematics* 33:71–92.

Linn, R. L., Baker, E. L., and Dunbar, S. B. 1991. "Complex, Performance-Based Assessment: Expectations and Validation Criteria." *Educational Researcher* 20(8):5–21.

Messick, S. 1989. "Validity." In R. L. Linn (Ed.), *Educational Measurement* (3rd ed.), Phoenix, AZ: Oryx Press, pp. 13–103.

Nitko, A. J. 1994. "A Model for Curriculum-Driven Criterion-Referenced and Norm-Referenced National Examinations for Certification and Selection of Students." *Journal of Educational Evaluation: Special Conference Edition,* pp. 39–55.

Nitko, A. J. 1995. "Is the Curriculum a Reasonable Basis for Assessment Reform?" *Educational Measurement: Issues and Practice* 14(3):5–17, 35. (Errata in 14(4):iii).

Nitko, A. J. 1996. *Educational Assessment of Students* (2nd ed.). Englewood Cliffs, NJ: Prentice-Hall/Merrill Education.

Nitko, A. J. 1998. "Model egzaminow panstwowych opartych na programmie nauczania, sprawdzajacych I ronicujcych, przeznaczonych do dyplomowania I selekeji uczniow," B. Niemierko trans. In B. Niermierko and E. Kowalik (Eds.). *Perspecktywy Diagnostyki Edukacyjnej: System Dydaktyczny.* Gdansk: Wydawictwo Universytetu GdaÕskiego, pp. 83–95.

Paulk, M.C., Weber, C.V., Garcia, S.M., Chrissis, M., and Bush, M. 1993. *Key Practices of the Capability Maturity Model,* Version 1.1 (CMU/SEI 93-TR-25, ESC-TR-93-178), Pittsburgh, PA: Carnegie Mellon University, Software Engineering Institute.

Simon, H. A. 1973. "The Structure of Ill-Structured Problems." *Artificial Intelligence,* 4:181–201.

Young, M. J. 1993. *Quantitative Measures for the Assessment of Declarative Knowledge Structure Characteristics.* Pittsburgh, PA: University of Pittsburgh, unpublished doctoral dissertation.

Zhu, Y. 1997. *Validity and Reliability of Selected Knowledge Structure Assessment Methods.* Pittsburgh, PA: University of Pittsburgh, unpublished doctoral dissertation.

10

An Overview of the Relationship Between Assessment and the Curriculum

Dylan Wiliam

INTRODUCTION

For most of this century, and in most countries, the most common method for certifying achievement in schools, whether for purposes of social accountability, or for providing information to aid decisions on the futures of individuals, has been by the administration of an assessment instrument that is devised, and is scored, externally. These external assessments, typically written examinations and standardized tests, can assess only a small part of the learning of which they are claimed to be a synopsis. In the past, this has been defended on the grounds that the test is a random sample from the domain of interest, and that, therefore, the techniques of statistical inference can be used to place confidence intervals on the estimates of the proportion of the domain that a candidate has achieved, and indeed, the correlation between standardized test scores and other, broader measures of achievement are often quite high.

However, it has become increasingly clear over the past twenty years that the contents of standardized tests and examinations are not a random sample from the domain of interests. In particular, these timed written assessments can assess only limited forms of competence, and teachers are quite able to predict which aspects of competence will be assessed. Especially in "high-stakes" assessments, therefore, there is an incentive for teachers and students to concentrate on only those aspects of competence that are likely to be assessed. Put crudely, we start out with the intention of making the important measurable, and end up making the measurable important. The effect of this has been to weaken the correlation between standardized test scores and the wider domains for which they are claimed to be an adequate proxy.

This is one of the major reasons underlying the shift in interest toward "authentic" or "performance" assessment (Resnick and Resnick 1992)—assessments that measure valued performance like writing essays, undertaking scientific experiments, solving complex mathematical problems and so on, directly, rather than through the use of proxies like multiple-choice or short-answer tests.

In high-stakes settings, performance on standardized tests can not be relied upon to be generalizable to more authentic tasks. If we want students to be able to apply their knowledge and skills in new situations, to be able to investigate relatively unstructured problems, and to evaluate their work, tasks that embody these attributes must form part of the formal assessment of learning—a test is valid to the extent that one is happy for teachers to teach toward the test (Wiliam 1996a).

However, if authentic tasks are to feature in formal "high-stakes" assessments, then users of the results of these assessments will want to be assured that the results are sufficiently reliable. The work of Linn and others (see, e.g., Linn and Baker 1996) has shown that in the assessment of individual authentic tasks, the variability of tasks is a significant issue. In other words, the score that a student gets on a specific task depends partly on how good the student is, but also on whether that particular task suited the student's strengths and weaknesses. If we use only a small number of tasks, then the overall score achieved by students will depend to a significant extent on whether the particular tasks they were asked to do suited them—in other words, we are assessing how lucky they are as much as how competent they are in the domain being assessed. Using authentic tasks improves validity, in that they tell us about students' performance on important aspects of the domain that are generally neglected in multiple-choice and short-answer tests, but reliability is generally weakened, in that the results of authentic tasks taking the same amount of time as multiple-choice tests are generally less reliable.

This can be illustrated by drawing an analogy with stage lighting. For a given power of illumination, we can either focus this as a spotlight or as a floodlight. The spotlight brings real clarity to a small part of the stage, but the rest of the stage is in darkness. This is analogous to a highly-reliable multiple-choice test, in which the scores on the actual matter tested are highly reliable, but we know nothing about the other aspects of the domain that were not tested. A floodlight, on the other hand, illuminates the whole stage. We may not be able to make quite such accurate distinctions in the small part of the domain assessed by the multiple-choice test, but what we can say about the other areas will be *more* accurate.

The work of Shavelson, Baxter, and Pine (1992) shows that we don't get adequately reliable results even in subjects like mathematics and science unless we use at least six tasks, and in other subjects, where students' liking of the task may be more important, we may need ten or more. Since it is hard to envisage many worthwhile authentic tasks that could be completed in less than an hour or two, the amount of assessment time that is needed for the reliable assessment of authentic tasks is considerably greater than can reasonably be made available in formal external assessment. The only way, therefore, that we can avoid the narrowing of the curriculum that has resulted from the use of timed written examinations and tests is to conduct the vast majority of even high-stakes assessments in the classroom.

One objection to this is, of course, that such extended assessments take time away from learning. There are two responses to this argument. The first is that authentic tasks are not just assessment tasks, but also learning tasks; students learn in the course of undertaking such tasks and we are, therefore, assessing students' achievement not at the start of the assessment (as is the case with traditional tests) but at the end—the learning that takes place during the task is recognized. This also has the effect of integrating learning and assessment, which is taken up in more detail below. The other response is that the reliance on traditional assessments has so distorted the educational process leading up to the assessment that we are, in a very real sense, "spoiling the ship for a half-pennyworth of tar." The ten years of learning that students in most developed countries undertake during the period of compulsory schooling is completely distorted by the assessments at the end. Taking (say) twelve hours to assess students' achievement in order not to distort the previous *thousand* hours of learning in (say) mathematics seems like a reasonable compromise.

Another objection that is often raised is the cost of marking such authentic tasks. The conventional wisdom in many countries is that, in high-stakes settings, the marking of the work must be conducted by more than one rater. However, the work of Linn cited earlier shows that rater variability is a much less significant source of unreliability than task variability. In other words, if we have a limited amount of time (or, what amounts to the same thing, money) for marking work, results would be more reliable if we had six tasks marked by a single rater than three tasks each marked by two raters. The question that remains, then, is who should do the marking?

The answer to this question appears to depend as much on cultural factors as on any empirical evidence. In some countries (e.g., England, and increasingly over recent years, the United States) the distrust of teachers by politicians is so great that involving teachers in the formal assessment of their own students is unthinkable. And yet, in many other countries (e.g., Norway, Sweden) teachers are responsible not just for determination of their students' results in school leaving examinations, but also for university entrance. Given the range of ephemeral evidence that is likely to be generated by authentic tasks, and the limitations of even authentic tasks to capture all the learning achievements of students, the arguments for involving teachers in the summative assessment of their students seem compelling. As one German commentator once remarked: "Why rely on an out-of-focus snapshot taken by a total stranger?"

The arguments outlined above suggest that high-quality educational provision *requires* that teachers are involved in the summative assessment of their students. However, it is also clear that high quality educational provision requires effective formative assessment as well (see Black, this volume). Are the formative and summative functions of assessment compatible? Some authors (e.g., Torrance, 1993) have argued that formative and summative assessment are so different that the same assessment system cannot fulfill both functions. Maintaining dual assessment systems would appear to be quite simply beyond the capabilities of the majority of teachers, with the formative assessment system being driven out by that for summative assessment. If this is true in practice (whether or not it is logically necessary), then there are only three possibilities:

- teachers are not involved in the summative assessment of their students
- teachers are not involved in the formative assessment of their students
- we find ways of ameliorating the tension between summative and formative functions of assessment.

In view of the foregoing arguments, I consider the consequences of the first two of these possibilities to be unacceptable, and, therefore, I would argue that if we are to try to create high-quality educational provision, ways must be found of mitigating the tension between formative and summative functions of assessment.

Of course, this is a vast undertaking, and well beyond the scope of this, or any other single article. The remainder of this chapter is, therefore, intended simply to suggest some theoretical foundations that would allow the exploration of possibilities for mitigating, if not completely reconciling, the tension between formative and summative assessment.

SUMMATIVE ASSESSMENT

If a teacher asks a class of students to learn twenty number bonds, and later tests the class on these bonds, then we have what Hanson (1993) calls a "literal" test. The inferences that the teacher can justifiably draw from the results are limited to exactly those items that were actually tested. The students knew which twenty bonds they were going to be tested on, and so the teacher could not with any justification conclude that those who scored well on this test would score well on a test of different number bonds.

However, such kinds of assessment are rare. Generally, an assessment is "a representational technique" (Hanson 1993, p. 19) rather than a literal one. Someone conducting an educational assessment is generally interested in the ability of the result of the assessment to stand as a proxy for some wider domain. This is, of course, an issue of validity—the extent to which particular inferences (and, according to some authors, actions) based on assessment results are warranted.

In the predominant view of educational assessment it is assumed that the individual to be assessed has a well-defined amount of knowledge, expertise or ability, and the purpose of the assessment task is to elicit evidence regarding the amount or level of knowledge, expertise or ability (Wiley and Haertel 1996). This evidence must then be interpreted so that inferences about the underlying knowledge, expertise or ability can be made. The crucial relationship is, therefore, between the task outcome (typically the observed behavior) and the inferences that are made on the basis of the task outcome. Validity is, therefore, not a property of tests, nor even of test outcomes, but a property of the inferences made on the basis of these outcomes. As Cronbach and Meehl noted over forty years ago, "One does not validate a test, but only a principle for making inferences" (Cronbach and Meehl 1955, p. 297).

More recently, it has become more generally accepted that it is also important to consider the *consequences* of the use of assessments as well as the validity of inferences based on assessment outcomes. Some authors have argued that a concern with consequences, while important, go beyond the concerns of validity— George Madaus for example uses the term *impact* (Madaus 1988). Others, notably Samuel Messick, have argued that consideration of the consequences of the use of assessment results is central to validity argument. In his view "Test validation is a process of inquiry into the adequacy and appropriateness of interpretations and actions based on test scores" (Messick 1989, p. 31).

Messick argues that this complex view of validity argument can be regarded as the result of crossing the basis of the assessment (evidential versus consequential) with the function of the assessment (interpretation versus use), as shown in Figure 10.1.

Figure 10.1
Messick's Framework for the Validation of Assessments

	Result Interpretation	Result Use
Evidential basis	Construct validity A	Construct validity and Relevance/utility B
Consequential basis	Value implications C	Social consequences D

The upper row of Messick's table relates to traditional conceptions of validity, while the lower row relates to the *consequences* of assessment interpretation and use. One of the most important consequences of the interpretations made of assessment outcomes is that those aspects of the domain that are assessed come to be seen as more important than those not assessed, resulting in implications for the values associated with the domain. The assessments do not just represent the values associated with the domain, but actually serve to define them—what gets assessed tells us what the subject is "really" about, and teachers and students act accordingly.

The use of Messick's framework can be illustrated by considering whether a student's competence in speaking and listening in the mother tongue should be assessed in an assessment of their overall competence in the language. Each of the following sets of arguments relates to one of the cells in Figure 10.1.

A. Many authors have argued that an assessment of English that ignores speaking and listening skills does not adequately represent the domain of "English." This is an argument about the evidential basis of result interpretation (such an assessment would be said to underrepresent the construct of "English").

B. There might also be empirical evidence that omitting speaking and listening from an assessment of English reduces the correlation with other accepted assessments of the same domain (concurrent validity) or with some predicted outcome, such as advanced study (predictive validity). Either of these would be arguments about the evidential basis of result use.

C. It could certainly be argued that leaving out speaking and listening would send the message that such aspects of English are less important, thus distorting the values associated with the domain (consequential basis of result interpretation).

D. Finally, it could be argued that unless such aspects of speaking and listening were incorporated into the assessment, then teachers would not teach, or would place less emphasis on, these aspects (consequential basis of result use).

Messick's model presents a useful framework for the structuring of validity arguments, but it provides little guidance about how (and perhaps more importantly, with respect to what?) the validation should be conducted. That is an issue of the referent of the assessment.

REFERENTS IN ASSESSMENT

For most of the history of educational assessment, the primary method of interpreting the results of assessment has been to compare the results of a specific individual with a well-defined group of other individuals (often called the "norm" group), the best known of which is probably the group of college-bound students (primarily from the northeastern United States) who in 1941 formed the norm group for the Scholastic Aptitude Test.

Norm-referenced assessments have been subjected to a great deal of criticism over the past thirty years, although much of this criticism has generally overstated the amount of norm-referencing actually used in standard setting, and has frequently confused norm-referenced assessment with *cohort*-referenced assessment (Wiliam 1996b).

However, the real problem with norm-referenced assessments is that, as Hill and Parry (1994) have noted in the context of reading tests, it is very easy to place candidates in rank order, without having any clear idea of what they are being put in rank order *of*. It was this desire for greater clarity about the relationship between the assessment and what it represented that led, in the early 1960s, to the development of criterion-referenced assessments.

CRITERION-REFERENCED ASSESSMENTS

The essence of criterion-referenced assessment is that the domain to which inferences are to be made is specified with great precision (Popham 1980). In particular, it was hoped that performance domains could be specified so precisely that items for assessing the domain could be generated automatically and uncontroversially (Popham 1980).

However, as Angoff (1974) pointed out, any criterion-referenced assessment is underpinned by a set of norm-referenced assumptions, because the assessments are used in social settings and for social purposes. In measurement terms, the criterion "can high jump two metres" is no more interesting than "can high jump ten metres" or "can high jump one metre." It is only by reference to a particular population (in this case human beings), that the first has some interest, while the latter two have little or none. Furthermore, no matter how precisely the criteria are drawn, it is clear that some judgment must be used—even in mathematics— in deciding whether a particular item or task performance does yield evidence that the criterion has been satisfied (Wiliam 1993).

Even if it were possible to define performance domains unambiguously, it is by no means clear that this would be desirable (Mabry 1999). Greater and greater specification of assessment objectives results in a system in which students and teachers are able to predict quite accurately what is to be assessed, and creates considerable incentives to narrow the curriculum down onto only those aspects of the curriculum to be assessed (Smith 1991). The alternative to "criterion-referenced hyperspecification" (Popham 1994) is to resort to much more general assessment descriptors which, because of their generality, are less likely to be interpreted in the same way by different assessors, thus re-creating many of the difficulties inherent in norm-referenced assessment. Thus, neither criterion-referenced assessment nor norm-referenced assessment provides an adequate theoretical underpinning for authentic assessment of performance. Put crudely, the more precisely we specify what we want, the more likely we are to get it, but the less likely it is to mean anything.

The ritual contrasting of norm-referenced and criterion-referenced assessments, together with more or less fruitless arguments about which is better, has tended to reinforce the notion that these are the only two kinds of inferences that can be drawn from assessment results. However the oppositionality between norms and criteria is only a theoretical model, which, admittedly, works well for certain kinds of assessments. But like any model, it has its limitations and it seems likely that the contrast between norm and criterion-referenced assessment represents the concerns of, and the kinds of assessments developed by, specialists in educational and psychological measurement. Beyond these narrow concerns there are a range of assessment events and assessment practices that are typified by the traditions of school examinations in European countries, and by the day-to-day practices of teachers all over the world. These practices rely on authentic rather than indirect assessment of performance, and are routinely interpreted in ways that are not faithfully or usefully described by the contrast between norm and criterion-referenced assessment.

Such authentic assessments have only recently received the kind of research attention that has for many years been devoted to standardized tests for selection and placement, and, indeed, much of the investigation that has been done into authentic assessment of performance has been based on a "deficit" model, by establishing how far, say, the assessment of portfolios of students' work, falls short of the standards of reliability expected of standardized multiple-choice tests. An alternative approach is, instead of building theoretical models and then trying to apply them to assessment practices, we try to theorize what is actually being done. After all, however illegitimate these authentic assessments are believed to be, there is still a need to account for their widespread use. Why is it that the forms of assessment traditionally used in Europe have developed the way they have, and how is it that, despite concerns about their "reliability," their usage persists?

What follows is a different perspective on the interpretation of assessment outcomes—one that has developed not from an a priori theoretical model but one that has emerged from observation of the practice of assessment within the European tradition.

CONSTRUCT-REFERENCED ASSESSMENT

The model of the interpretation of assessment results that I wish to propose is illustrated by the practices of teachers who have been involved in "high-stakes" assessment of English Language for the national school-leaving examination in England and Wales (the General Certificate of Secondary Education or GCSE). Until the government's recent change in national examinations, which required all GCSEs to have an externally-assessed component, the GCSE grade for the vast majority of students in England and Wales was determined not by performance on an examination, but entirely on the basis of a portfolio of work, prepared by the student, and assessed by her or his teacher. In order to safeguard standards, teachers were trained to use the appropriate standards for marking by the use of "agreement trials." Typically, a teacher is given a piece of work to assess and when she has made an assessment, feedback is given by an "expert" as to whether the assessment agrees with the expert assessment. The process of marking different pieces of work continues until the teacher demonstrates that she has converged on the correct marking standard, at which point she is "accredited" as a marker for some fixed period of time.

The innovative feature of such assessment is that no attempt is made to prescribe learning outcomes. In that it is defined at all, it is defined simply as the consensus of the teachers making the assessments. The assessment is not objective, in the sense that there are no objective criteria for a student to satisfy, but the experience in England is that it can be made reliable. To put it crudely, it is not necessary for the raters (or anybody else) to know what they are doing, only that they do it right. Because the assessment system relies on the existence of a construct (of what it means to be competent in a particular domain) being shared among a community of practitioners (Lave and Wenger 1991), I have proposed elsewhere that such assessments are best described as "construct-referenced" (Wiliam 1994). Another example of such a construct-referenced assessment is the educational assessment with perhaps the highest stakes of all—the Ph.D.

In most countries, the Ph.D. is awarded as a result of an examination of a thesis, usually involving an oral examination. As an example, the regulations of the University of London regulate what some people might regard as a "criterion" for the award. In order to be successful the thesis must make "a contribution to original knowledge, either by the discovery of new facts or by the exercise of critical power." The problem is what is to count as a new fact? The number of times the letter "e" occurs in this book is, currently, I am sure, not known to anyone, so simply counting occurrences of the letter "e" in this book would generate a new fact, but there is surely not a university in the world that would consider it worthy of a Ph.D.

The "criterion" given creates the impression that the assessment is a criterion-referenced one, but in fact, the criterion does not admit of an unambiguous meaning. To the extent that the examiners agree (and of course this is a moot point), they agree not because they derive similar meanings from the regulation, but because they already have in their minds a notion of the required standard. The consistency of such assessments depends on what Polanyi (1958) called *connoisseurship,* but perhaps might be more useful regarded as the membership of a community of practice (Lave and Wenger 1991).

The touchstone for distinguishing between criterion- and construct-referenced assessment is the relationship between the written descriptions (if they exist at all) and the domains. Where written statements collectively *define* the level of performance required (or more precisely where they define the justifiable inferences), then the assessment is criterion-referenced. However, where such statements merely *exemplify* the kinds of inferences that are warranted, then the assessment is, to an extent at least, construct-referenced.

HOW TO DO THINGS WITH ASSESSMENTS: ILLOCUTIONARY SPEECH ACTS AND COMMUNITIES OF PRACTICE

In the 1955 William James lectures, J. L. Austin, discussed two different kinds of "speech acts"—illocutionary and perlocutionary (Austin 1962). Illocutionary speech acts are *performative*—by their mere utterance they actually do what they say. In contrast, perlocutionary speech acts are speech acts *about* what has, is or will be. For example, the verdict of a jury in a trial is an illocutionary speech act—it does what it says, since the defendant becomes innocent or guilty simply by virtue of the announcement of the verdict. Once a jury has declared someone guilty, they *are* guilty, whether or not they really committed the act of which they are accused, until that verdict is set aside by another (illocutionary) speech act.

Another example of an illocutionary speech act is the wedding ceremony, where the speech act of one person (the person conducting the ceremony saying "I now pronounce you husband and wife") actually does what it says, creating what John Searle calls "social facts" (Searle 1995). Searle himself illustrates the idea of social facts by an interview between a baseball umpire and a journalist who was trying to establish whether the umpire believed his calls to be subjective or objective:

Interviewer: Did you call them the way you saw them, or did you call them the way they were?

Umpire: The way I called them *was* the way they were.

The umpire's calls bring into being social facts because the umpire is authorized (in the sense of having both the power, and that use of power being regarded as legitimate) to do so. The extent to which these judgments are seen as warranted ultimately resides in the degree of trust placed by those who use the results of the assessments (for whatever purpose) in the community of practice making the decision about membership (Wiliam 1996b).

In my view a great deal of the confusion that currently surrounds educational assessments—particularly those in the European tradition—arises from the confusion of these two kinds of speech acts. Put simply, most summative assessments are treated as if they were perlocutionary speech acts, whereas they are perhaps more usefully regarded as illocutionary speech acts.

These difficulties are inevitable as long as the assessments are required to perform a perlocutionary function, making warrantable statements about the student's previous performance, current state, or future capabilities. Attempts to "reverse engineer" assessment results in order to make claims about what the individual can do have always failed, because of the effects of compensation between different aspects of the domain being assessed. However, many of the difficulties raised above diminish considerably if the assessments are regarded as serving an *illocutionary* function. To see how this works, it is instructive to consider the assessment of the Ph.D. discussed above

Although technically, the award is made by an institution, the decision to award a Ph.D. is made on the recommendation of examiners. In some countries, this can be the judgment of a single examiner, while in others it will be the majority recommendation of a panel of as many as six. The important point for our purposes is that the degree is awarded as the result of a speech act of a single person (i.e., the examiner where there is just one, or the chair of the panel where there are more than one). The perlocutionary content of this speech act is negligible, because, if we are told that someone has a Ph.D., there are very few inferences that are warranted. In other words, when we ask "What is it that we know about what this person has/can/will do now that we know they have a Ph.D.?" the answer is "Almost nothing" simply because Ph.D. theses are so varied. Instead, the award of a Ph.D. is better thought of not as an assessment of aptitude or achievement, or even as a predictor of future capabilities, but rather as an illocutionary speech act that *inaugurates an individual's entry into a community of practice.*

This goes a long way towards explaining the lack of concern about measurement error within the European tradition of examining. When a jury makes a decision the person is either guilty or not guilty, irrespective of whether they actually committed the crime—there is no "measurement error" in the verdict. The speech act of the jury in announcing its verdict creates the social fact of someone's guilt until that social fact is revoked by a subsequent appeal, creating a new social fact. In the European tradition of assessment, duly authorized bodies create social facts by declaring the results of the candidates, provided that the community of users of assessment results accepts the authority of the examining body to create social facts. Until recently, the same was true of the award of a high-school diploma in the United States.

Now the *existence* of a community of practice is no evidence of its legitimacy. There is an inevitable tendency for such communities of practice to reproduce themselves by admitting only "people like us." But the *authority* of such communities of practice (as opposed to *power*) will depend on the trust that individuals beyond that community are prepared to place in its judgments. In order to maintain this trust, communities will have to show that their procedures for making judgments are fair, appropriate and defensible (i.e., that they are *valid*), even if they cannot be made totally transparent, and the paper by Anthony Nitko (this volume) provides a framework within which this can be accomplished.

The foregoing theoretical analysis creates, I believe, a framework for the validation of teachers' summative assessments of their students. Such assessments are construct-referenced assessments, validated by the extent to which the community of practice agrees that the student's work has reached a particular implicit standard. Achievement of this standard should not be interpreted in terms of a range of competences that the student had, has, or is likely to achieve at some point in the future, but instead is a statement that the performance is adequate to inaugurate the student into a community of practice. The advantage of such a system of summative assessment is that the evidence-base for the assessment is grounded in the learning environment, so that it can also support formative assessment.

FORMATIVE ASSESSMENT

Strictly speaking, there is no such thing as a formative assessment. The formative-summative distinction applies not to the assessment itself, but to the use to which the information arising from the assessment is put. The same assessment can serve both formative and summative functions, although in general, the assessment will have been designed so as to emphasize one of the functions.

As noted by Black (this volume), formative assessment can be thought of "as encompassing all those activities undertaken by teachers and/or by their students which provide information to be used as feedback to modify the teaching and learning activities in which they are engaged" (Black and Wiliam 1998a). Although perhaps somewhat simplistic, it is useful to break this general idea into three (reasonably distinct) phases: the elicitation of evidence regarding achievement, the interpretation of that evidence, followed by appropriate action.

The evidence of achievement provides an indication of the actual level of performance, which is then interpreted relative to some desired or "reference" level of performance. Some action is then taken to reduce the gap between the actual and the "reference" level. The important thing here—indeed some would argue the defining feature of formative assessment—is that the information arising from the comparison between the actual and desired levels *must* be used in closing the gap. If, for example, the teacher gives feedback to the student indicating what needs to be done next, this will not be formative unless the learner can understand *and act* on that information. An essential prerequisite for assessment to serve a formative function is, therefore, that the learner comes to understand the goals toward which she is aiming (Sadler 1989). If the teacher tells the student that she needs to "be more systematic" in her mathematical investigations, that is not feedback unless the learner understands what "being systematic" means—otherwise this is no more helpful than telling an unsuccessful comedian to "be funnier." The difficulty with this is that if the learner understood what "being systematic" meant, she would probably have been able to be more systematic in the first place. The teacher believes the advice she is giving is helpful, but that is because the teacher already knows what it means to be systematic. This is exactly the same issue we encountered in the discussion of criterion-referenced assessment above, and why I believe, in contrast to Klenowski (1995), that learning goals can never be made explicit. The words used—whether as criteria or for feedback—do not carry an unambiguous meaning, and require the application of implicit knowledge (Claxton 1995).

Now this should not be taken to mean that "guidelines" or "criteria" should not be used in helping learners come to understand the goals the teacher has in mind. These criteria can be extraordinarily helpful in helping learners begin to understand what is required of them. But it is a fundamental error to assume that these statements, however carefully worded, have the same meaning for learners as they do for teachers. Such statements can provide a basis for negotiating the meaning, but ultimately, the learners will only come to understand the statements by seeing them exemplified in the form of actual pieces of students' work.

This notion of "understanding the standard" is the theme that unifies summative and formative functions of assessment. Summative assessment requires that teachers become members of a community of practice, while formative assessment requires that the learners themselves become members of the same community of practice. As the paper by Broadfoot et al. (this volume) makes clear, as well as understanding the cognitive aims of the community of practice, becoming a full participant also requires understanding how the classroom "works," with the students "given a central role in the management of their own learning, but are also given the knowledge and skills to discharge their responsibilities" (Simpson this volume).

This process of becoming *attuned* to the *constraints* and *affordances* (Gibson 1979) of the classroom is an essential part of being an effective learner. Whether success in one particular classroom is effective beyond that classroom depends on the extent to which the constraints and affordances of that classroom are available in other settings. Boaler (1997) provides a stark example of students who were highly successful in one particular community of practice, but because the constraint and affordances to which they had become attuned were not present in their examinations, their performance was considerably weakened.

For the teacher's part, however, as both Black (this volume) and Simpson (this volume) point out, it is not enough just to "understand the standard." Where a learner understands the standard, and is able to assess her or his own performance, they can become aware of the "gap" between current and desired achievement. What they lack, however, is any clear idea of how to go about closing the gap. They know *that* they need to improve, but they are unlikely to have any clear idea of *how* to improve (for if they did, they would be able to reach the desired level). An essential role for the teacher in formative assessment is, therefore, to *analyze* the gap between present and desired performance, and be able to break this down into small, comprehensible steps that can be communicated to the learner (recall the teacher quoted by Simpson who realized that he had, in the past been telling his pupils that they "must work harder at problem-solving"). Put crudely, summative assessment requires teachers to understand the standard, while formative assessment requires learners to understand the standard, and for teachers to understand the standard and the "gap."

The summative and formative functions of assessment are further distinguished by how they are validated. With summative assessments any unfortunate consequences tend to be justified by the need to establish consistency of meanings of the results across different contexts and assessors. With formative assessment, any lack of shared meanings across different contexts is irrelevant—all that matters is that they lead to successful action in support of learning. In a very real sense, therefore, summative assessments are validated by their meanings and formative assessments by their consequences.

The foregoing theoretical analysis provides a basis for distinguishing between formative and summative functions of assessment, but does not address the issue raised earlier in this paper and by Val Klenowski (this volume) of the tension between the formative and summative functions of assessment. As Klenowski shows, in the context of portfolio assessment, the requirements of the summative function for a portfolio to contain particular elements results in a situation in which the formative function is weakened.

Of course, the formative and summative functions of assessment will always be in tension, but the identification of three phases of the assessment cycle above (elicitation, interpretation, action) suggests some ways in which the tension can be mitigated somewhat (for a fuller version of this argument, see Wiliam 1999). When evidence is being elicited, the basis of the assessment must be broad, and must, as far as possible, not be predictable (at least not to the extent that those being assessed can ignore certain parts of the domain because they know that they will not be assessed). Consideration should also be given to changing the focus of the assessment from a quality control orientation, where the emphasis is on the external assessment as the measurement of quality, to a quality assurance orientation, where the emphasis is on the evaluation of internal systems of self-assessment, self-appraisal or self-review. In the case of Klenowski's example of teacher training, we might insist that the portfolio includes statements about the procedures used by the student in evaluating their own practice rather than insisting on actual examples of the evaluations.

Once evidence is elicited, it must be interpreted differently for different purposes, and it is important to note that once the data has been interpreted for one purpose, it cannot easily serve another. For formative purposes, the focus will be on learning. Some items are much more important than others, since they have a greater propensity to disclose evidence of learning needs. In particular, the results on some sorts of very difficult assignments can be especially significant, because they can point clearly to learning needs that were not previously clear. However, the results of these difficult assignments should not count against the learner for summative purposes—what goes into the portfolio, for example, must be only a selection from all possible work, and may even be redrafted or reworked before it is included. The relationship between the summative and the formative assessment is not the aggregation of the latter into the former, but rather the result of a reassessment, for a different purpose, of the original evidence.

Finally, summative assessments are best thought of as retrospective. The vast majority of summative assessments in education are assessments of what the individual has learned, knows, understands, or can do. Even where the assessments are used to predict future performance, this is done on the basis of *present* capabilities, and assessments are validated by the consistency of their meanings. In contrast formative assessments can be thought of as being *prospective*. They must contain within themselves a recipe for future action, whose validity rests in their capability to cause learning to take place.

There is no doubt that, for most of the school year, the formative function should predominate:

We shouldn't want [a shift to formative assessment] because research shows how it improves learning (we don't need to be told that—it has to be true). We should want it because schools are places where learners should be learning more often than they are being selected, screened or tested in order to check up on their teachers. The latter are important; the former are why schools exist. (Peter Silcock, Personal communication, March 1998)

As part of their day-to-day work, teachers will be collecting evidence about their students, and, for most of the year, this will be interpreted with a view to gauging the future learning needs of the students, and helping the students to understand what it would mean to be a member of the community of practice. In such a system "assessment is seen as continuous, concerned with the creation of a flow of contemporary information on pupil progress which will genuinely inform the teaching and learning processes" (Simpson this volume).

However, at intervals (perhaps only as often as once each year) the original evidence of attainment can be revisited and reinterpreted holistically, to provide a construct-referenced assessment that is synoptic of each student's achievement—an indication of the extent to which they have become full members of the community of practice.

REFERENCES

Angoff, W. H. 1974. "Criterion-Referencing, Norm-Referencing and the SAT." *College Board Review* 92(Summer):2–5, 21.

Austin, J. L. 1962. *How to Do Things with Words.* Oxford and New York: Oxford University Press.

Black, P. J., and Wiliam, D. 1998a. "Assessment and Classroom Learning." *Assessment in Education: Principles Policy and Practice* 5(1):7–73.

Black, P. J., and Wiliam, D. 1998b. *Inside the Black Box: Raising Standards through Classroom Assessment.* London: King's College London School of Education.

Boaler, J. 1997. *Experiencing School Mathematics: Teaching Styles, Sex and Setting.* Buckingham: Open University Press.

Claxton, G. 1995. "What Kind of Learning Does Self-Assessment Drive? Developing a "Nose" for Quality; Comments on Klenowski." *Assessment in Education* 2(3): 339–343.

Cronbach, L. J., and Meehl, P. E. 1955. "Construct Validity in Psychological Tests." *Psychological Bulletin* 52(4):281–302.

Gibson, J. J. 1979. *The Ecological Approach to Visual Perception.* London: Houghton Mifflin.

Hanson, F. A. 1993. *Testing Testing: Social Consequences of the Examined Life.* Berkeley: University of California Press.

Hill, C., and Parry, K. 1994. "Models of Literacy: The Nature of Reading Tests." In C. Hill and K. Parry (Eds.), *From testing to assessment: English as an international language.* Harlow: Longman, pp. 7–34.

Klenowski, V. 1995. "Student Self-Evaluation Processes in Student-Centred Teaching and Learning Contexts of Australia and England." *Assessment in Education* 2(2):145–163.

Lave, J., and Wenger, E. 1991. *Situated Learning: Legitimate Peripheral Participation.* Cambridge: Cambridge University Press.

Linn, R. L., and Baker, E. L. 1996. "Can Performance-Based Student Assessment be Psychometrically Sound?" In J. B. Baron and D. P. Wolf (Eds.), *Performance-Based Assessment—Challenges and Possibilities: 95th Yearbook of the National Society for the Study of Education Part 1*. Chicago: National Society for the Study of Education, pp. 84–103.

Mabry, L. 1999. "Writing to the Rubric: Lingering Effects of Traditional Standardized Testing on Direct Writing Assessment." *Phi Delta Kappan* 80(9):673–679.

Madaus, G. F. 1988. "The Influence of Testing on the Curriculum." In L. N. Tanner (Ed.), *Critical Issues in Curriculum: The 87th Yearbook of the National Society for the Study of Education,* Part 1. Chicago, IL: University of Chicago Press, pp. 83–121.

Messick, S. 1989. "Validity." In R. L. Linn (Ed.), *Educational Measurement.* Washington, DC: American Council on Education/Macmillan, pp. 13–103.

Polanyi, M. 1958. *Personal Knowledge.* Chicago: University of Chicago Press.

Popham, W. J. 1980. "Domain Specification Strategies." In R. A. Berk (Ed.), *Criterion-Referenced Measurement: The State of the Art.* Baltimore: Johns Hopkins University Press, pp. 15–31.

Popham, W. J. 1994. *The Stultifying Effects of Criterion-Referenced Hyperspecification: A Postcursive Quality Control Remedy.* Paper presented at Symposium on Criterion-referenced clarity at the annual meeting of the American Educational Research Association held at New Orleans, April. Los Angeles: University of California Los Angeles.

Resnick, L. B., and Resnick, D. P. 1992. "Assessing the Thinking Curriculum: New Tools for Educational Reform." In B. R. Gifford and M. C. O'Connor (Eds.), *Changing Assessments: Alternative Views of Aptitude, Achievement and Instruction.* Boston: Kluwer Academic Publishers, pp. 37–75.

Sadler, D. R. 1989. "Formative Assessment and The Design of Instructional Systems." *Instructional Science* 18:145–165.

Searle, J. R. 1995. *The Construction of Social Reality.* London: Allen Lane, The Penguin Press.

Shavelson, R. J., Baxter, G. P., and Pine, J. 1992. "Performance Assessments: Political Rhetoric and Measurement Reality." *Educational Researcher* 21(4):22–27.

Smith, M. L. 1991. "Meanings of Test Preparation." *American Educational Research Journal* 28(3):521–542.

Torrance, H. 1993. "Formative Assessment: Some Theoretical Problems and Empirical Questions." *Cambridge Journal of Education* 23(3):333–343.

Wiley, D. E., and Haertel, E. H. 1996. "Extended Assessment Tasks: Purposes, Definitions, Scoring and Accuracy." In M. B. Kane and R. Mitchell (Eds.), *Implementing Performance Assessment: Promises, Problems and Challenges.* Mahwah, NJ: Lawrence Erlbaum Associates, pp. 61–89.

Wiliam, D. 1993. "Validity, Dependability and Reliability in National Curriculum Assessment." *The Curriculum Journal* 4(3):335–350.

Wiliam, D. 1994. "Assessing Authentic Tasks: Alternatives to Mark-Schemes." *Nordic Studies in Mathematics Education* 2(1):48–68.

Wiliam, D. 1996a. "National Curriculum Assessments and Programmes of Study: Validity and Impact." *British Educational Research Journal* 22(1):129–141.

Wiliam, D. 1996b. "Standards in Examinations: A Matter of Trust?" *The Curriculum Journal* 7(3):293–306.

Wiliam, D. 1999. *"There is no Alternative:" Mitigating the Tension Between Formative and Summative Functions of Assessment.* Paper presented at the 8th biennial meeting of the European Association for Research on Learning and Instruction held at Gothenburg, Sweden. London: King's College London School of Education, August.

Index

About the Editor and Contributors

Paul Black is Professor Emeritus of King's College London, United Kingdom. He has been involved in numerous research and development projects in both curriculum and assessment. He has contributed to several of the curriculum projects sponsored by the Nuffield Foundation, and has also worked in international projects, notably with the OECD. He was co-director of the national science surveys in the United Kingdom Assessment of Performance Unit from 1978 to 1987 and in 1987–1988 he was chair of the government Task Group on Assessment and Testing, which advised on the new United Kingdom policy for national assessment. He is currently a member of the Board on Testing and Assessment of the USA National Academy of Sciences.

Patricia Broadfoot is currently Professor of Education in the Graduate School of Education at the University of Bristol, United Kingdom and was Head of School between 1993 and 1997. She directed the School's Centre for Assessment Studies for ten years from 1987 to 1997. She is the author of a number of books and articles in the fields of assessment and comparative education. She is the editor of both *Assessment in Education* and *Comparative Education*. She was co-director on two recently-completed ESRC-funded research projects: *Primary Assessment Curriculum and Experience* (PACE) from 1989–1997 and *Quality in Experiences of Schooling Transnationally* (QUEST) from 1995–1997 and is currently co-directing a new ESRC-funded comparative study of pupil learning and identity in secondary schools in England, France, and Denmark. She is the current president of the *British Association of International and Comparative Education*.

Jannette Elwood is Professor of Education at the Graduate School of Education, Queen's University of Belfast, United Kingdom. She has worked in educational research, teaching and policy in a variety of organizations. She has a background in examinations and assessment research and has led nationally funded research projects into gender differences in United Kingdom examinations at 16+ and 18+. Her work into the impact of assessment construction on sub-group performance is internationally recognized. She has advised United Kingdom policy makers and awarding bodies on the impact of assessment and testing systems on boys' and girls' performance and has worked with educational practitioners at all levels in the area of gender and performance.

Wynne Harlen was director of the Scottish Council for Research in Education until May 1999 and before that was Professor of Science Education at the University of Liverpool, United Kingdom. She is now visiting Professor at the University of Bristol, although still based in Edinburgh. She has spent many years engaged in curriculum research, development and assessment and has published widely in these fields and in science education. She was President of BERA in 1994–1995 and is an Executive Editor of *Assessment in Education*.

Val Klenowski is a Senior Lecturer in the Curriculum Studies Academic Group, Institute of Education, University of London, United Kingdom. Her research interests are in the areas of curriculum development, evaluation, assessment for learning and teacher education. She has also worked as a Senior Lecturer in the Curriculum and Instruction Department of the Hong Kong Institute of Education and has worked for the Education Department of Western Australia as a curriculum writer and senior policy officer.

Ingrid Lunt is a Reader in the Culture, Communications and Society Academic Group, Institute of Education, University of London, United Kingdom. She is a former President of the British Educational Psychological Association. She has published widely in the field of Special Needs in Education. She has an interest in and responsibility for doctoral students at the Institute of Education.

Anthony J. Nitko is Adjunct Professor, Department of Educational Psychology, University of Arizona, and Professor Emeritus and former Chairperson of the Department of Psychology in Education at the University of Pittsburgh. He has published widely in the field of educational assessment. He has been editor of *Educational Measurement: Issues and Practice* and of *d'News*, the AERA, Division D Newsletter. In addition, he was elected as Fellow to the American Psychological Association, Secretary of AERA Division D and President of the National Council on Measurement in Education. He has served as consultant to various government and private agencies in Bangladesh, Barbados, Botswana, Indonesia, Jamaica, Namibia, Singapore, and the United States.

Marilyn Osborn is Senior Research Fellow in Education in the Graduate School of Education at the University of Bristol, United Kingdom. She is co-director of the *Centre for International and Comparative Studies in Education* and coordinator of the research methods line of study within the M.Ed program and of Ed.D qualitative research methods units in both Bristol and Hong Kong. She is also qualitative research support adviser to staff and research students. Her publications include a number of books and articles on teachers' work and professional perspectives, on pupil perspectives and on comparative education. She was co-director of two recently completed ESRC funded projects: *Systems, Teachers, and Educational Policy* (STEP) and *Quality in Experiences of Schooling Trans-Nationally* (QUEST). She is currently directing a new ESRC funded study: *Education and National Culture: A Comparative Study of Attitudes to Secondary Schooling* (ENCOMPASS) and a study funded by QCA comparing primary school children's learning strategies in England and France.

Claire Planel is a Research Associate in the School of Education, University of Bristol, United Kingdom. She is bilingual and bicultural in English and French with an academic background in Social Anthropology and Linguistics. She has trained in primary education and has taught social science and French in England (at different levels and to different ages) as well as having taught English in French primary schools. She took up comparative research in English and French education at the School of Education in 1993.

David Scott is a Senior Lecturer in the Centre for Curriculum and Teaching Studies at the Open University in the United Kingdom. He has previously worked at the Universities of Warwick, Southampton, and London. He has published widely in the fields of curriculum, assessment and research methodology. His most recent books include *Reading Educational Research and Literacy, Realism and Educational Research: New Perspectives and Possibilities* and (with Robin Usher) *Researching Education: Data, Methods and Theory in Educational Enquiry.* He is the current editor of *The Curriculum Journal.*

Keith Sharpe has worked with Patricia Broadfoot, Marilyn Osborn and Claire Planel on a number of projects at the University of Bristol, United Kingdom, and has published with them in the fields of assessment and comparative education.

Mary Simpson has recently been appointed to the Chair of Classroom Learning at Edinburgh University, United Kingdom. She has been engaged in research in the field of classroom learning and the development of the curriculum in Scotland for the past twenty years. The main focus of her work has been pupil learning difficulties in curriculum areas, particularly in science, the development of assessment as a tool to support learning and teaching, strategies for differentiation and, more recently, the use of ICT in classrooms. She is currently co-director of *The Evaluation of the Impact in Scottish Classrooms of the Scottish*

Executive's Funding Initiatives in ICT. In addition to academic publications she has communicated research findings in articles accessible to teachers, and has explored with the profession the implications of research for practice through regular inservice and teachers' conferences.

Dylan Wiliam is Head of the School of Education and Professor of Educational Assessment at King's College London, United Kingdom. His teachings on Masters and Doctorate programs includes courses on educational assessment, research methods, and the use of information technology in academic research. He divides his research time between mathematics education and research in educational assessment and evaluation, where his main interests are the interplay between meanings and consequences in conceptualizations of validity and formative assessment.